This book provides an insightful analy[...] erful grip that OPEC has over a very[...] ural resource, explaining how there is no shortage [...] oil and why oil prices should be much lower. It also provides all the necessary rationale for standing up and defeating this economic evil.

> —Henry Kaufman, president of Henry
> Kaufman & Company, author of *On
> Money and Markets*

Learsy's indictment of OPEC reads like a twelve-step recovery program for ending America's addiction to Middle East oil. He shatters the economic myths that perpetuate our dependence, exposes how the oil curse undermines Arab stability and American security, and shows how the United States can kick the habit.

> —Stanley A. Weiss, chairman of Business
> Executives for National Security

Learsy makes a powerful argument that OPEC's traditional charade of shortage is aided and abetted by the oil industry, its lobbyists, and oil-producing states themselves. By trying to exempt oil from the laws of supply and demand, vested interests are pulling oil-soaked wool over the eyes of the public.

> —Steven J. Gilbert, chairman of Gilbert
> Global Equity Partners

It is a rare phenomenon that a book on a major issue of public policy appears at a crucial moment in history and is well written, free of jargon, and to the point. Our security and prosperity depend on our willingness to respond to Learsy's eloquent challenge.

—Leon Botstein, president of Bard College, author of *Jefferson's Children*

About every ten years the United States has an oil shock. In 2005, it is in the form of very high prices. Again, we wring our hands, but we still have no national energy policy. Mr. Learsy's *Over a Barrel* is a provocative analysis of the cause of our problem, complete with suggestions for the solution. A great read.

—Gerald Greenwald, chairman emeritus of United Airlines, former vice chairman of the Chrysler Corporation

He gets it right in four dimensions—politics, geology, engineering, and economics—and explains it all in a fashion a non-expert can understand.

—Gordon M. Kaufman, Morris A. Adelman Professor of Management, MIT Sloan School

Over a Barrel

BREAKING OIL'S GRIP ON OUR FUTURE

Raymond J. Learsy

ENCOUNTER BOOKS
NEW YORK · LONDON

Published by Encounter Books, an activity of Encounter for Culture and Education, Inc., a nonprofit tax exempt corporation.

Encounter Books website address: www.encounterbooks.com

Manufactured in the United States and printed on acid-free paper.

The paper used in this publication meets the minimum requirements of ANSI/NISO Z39.48-1992 (R 1997) (Permanence of Paper).

Library of Congress Cataloging-in-Publication Data

Learsy, Raymond J.
 Over a barrel : breaking oil's grip on our future / Raymond J. Learsy.
 p. cm.
 Revised and updated ed. of: Over a barrel : breaking the Middle East oil cartel. Nashville, Tenn. : Nelson Current, c2005.
 Includes bibliographical references and index.
 ISBN-13: 978-1-59403-203-5 (pbk. : alk. paper)
 ISBN-10: 1-59403-203-3 (pbk. : alk. paper) 1. Organization of Petroleum Exporting Countries. 2. Petroleum industry and trade—Political aspects—Middle East. 3. Petroleum reserves. 4. Petroleum products—Prices. I. Title.
 HD9578.M52L43 2007
 382'.42282—dc22   2007030277

10 9 8 7 6 5 4 3 2 1

Contents

Introduction

In the harsh old days of Britain's Royal Navy, a sailor caught stealing rum was trussed over the barrel of a cannon and left to broil in the sun, waiting to be flogged. Figuratively speaking, you and I and everyone else in the oil-consuming world are already caught in just such a predicament. Instead of a cannon, though, ours is a barrel of oil. And the people who put us there are the members of the OPEC oil cartel, profiteers who have been flogging us for years with no end in sight.

There is a mystique surrounding oil. It is a deliberate one, trumped up to make everyone thankfully accept a manipulated market with hugely inflated prices. These market machinations rob the world's consumers of literally hundreds of billions of dollars every year, both in higher energy prices and in artificially inflated costs for just about every other kind of good. Over the past three decades, according to one U.S. government estimate, the tab has totaled a staggering $7 trillion.

These costs land disproportionately on those least equipped to bear them, the people in the developing world. Already treading a precarious path of existence, Third World countries lack the money and technology to introduce energy-efficient techniques and processes, and typically have little or no access to energy sources that can be substituted for oil. With nothing to shield them from the full brunt of rising prices, the world's poorest people are thus forced

1

to spend more of their meager resources on food, fuel, and transport. The hole they are in just gets deeper.

For this thievery from all the world's citizens, we can blame OPEC, the Organization of the Petroleum Exporting Countries. Though OPEC's twelve member states (Algeria, Angola, Indonesia, Iran, Iraq, Kuwait, Libya, Nigeria, Qatar, Saudi Arabia, the United Arab Emirates, and Venezuela) account for an estimated 40 percent of world oil production, their brazen market manipulations largely determine the price for all the rest.

Blame must also go to OPEC's co-conspirators in what I call the *oiligopoly*—nonmember countries like Mexico and Russia; the Western oil companies and their minions who collude with the cartel; and Western governments (including, at key junctures, the United States) that actively support the conspiracy. And the guilt is shared by the media, with its willingness to swallow and regurgitate OPEC's propaganda, and by all the rest of us who have stood by and passively watched this disaster unfold.

Don't get me wrong. Yes, I think oil—and everything made from it—is too expensive, and I want to bring the price down. But this doesn't mean I want to keep using oil to run the world until the world runs out of oil. I believe that global warming is a disaster and is mainly caused by burning fossil fuels; and I want us all to switch to alternative energy sources as fast as possible. But in reality, that transition will take at least a generation. While it's going on, the less we spend on oil and oil products, the more we'll have available for research and investment in renewable energy, fuel cells, nuclear power, hydrogen, and any other power we can find that won't ruin the planet. Step one is to get the oiligopoly off the world's back.

Astonishingly enough, President George W. Bush has admitted the U.S. government's complicity in the conspiracy. Speaking of our dealings with Middle Eastern countries during a press conference in early 2005 at NATO headquarters in Brussels, the president said: "The policy in the past used to be, 'Let's just accept tyranny for the sake of "cheap" oil or whatever it might be,' and just hope everything would be okay." He added that the events of September 11, 2001, changed all that when pent-up Arab hatred exploded on U.S. shores. But where the president went wrong in his Brussels remarks was that OPEC oil has not been "cheap" for quite some time, at least not in the way free-market advocates understand that term.

OPEC is a cartel of suppliers, and all cartels are inherently suspect. They earn that suspicion by joining in schemes to control production, allocate markets, and fix prices to balloon their profits. Price fixing is illegal in this country, and the Justice Department has prosecuted any number of antitrust cases over the years (most notably, perhaps, John D. Rockefeller and Standard Oil). But U.S. courts have decided that the "foreign sovereign immunity doctrine" precludes the Justice Department from suing OPEC. Various senators have sought to override the doctrine with legislation that would subject government-owned commercial ventures, such as the state-controlled and state-owned oil companies of the OPEC members, to antitrust laws. These efforts have been derailed by a Senate provision that allows senators from oil-producing states to put the legislation on indefinite "hold," thus guaranteeing that it will never make it to a floor vote and never threaten the conspiracy.

The damage wrought by the oiligopoly is not only economic. America's security is also at risk. As I will detail later in this book, President Bush's father made a Faustian bargain with OPEC in 1986, selling our soul for a steady supply of oil and giving Washington's blessing to the steep escalation of oil's price. And ever since, the United States has squandered a great national resource: the independence that would be secured by moderating, or more intelligently providing for, our own energy needs. We have placed our security in the hands of an extortionist cartel, just to keep our industrial heart beating. Worse, the world's addiction to Middle Eastern oil means that hundreds of billions of dollars are being pumped into a region where people despise us and where too many preach and pray for our destruction.

In fact, prominent members of OPEC openly work to undermine democratic ideals in the United States and other Western countries. Millions of dollars of Saudi Arabian and Kuwaiti money go to finance schools, mosques, and supposedly charitable organizations that actively promote the virulently anti-Western Wahhabi strain of Islam and encourage Muslim citizens of Western nations to reject the principles upon which their governments were founded.

Ironies abound, not least that we supply the money that buys the textbooks and prayer books stuffed with venomous words designed to bury us. American citizens' gas money is used to pay the salaries of imams and school officials who propagate the poison. But it isn't only hate-filled teaching and preaching that we support. The sheer volume of this torrent of funds practically guarantees that some of our dollars will wind up in the hands of people—both stateless terrorists and recognized leaders of rogue nations—who are capable of acquiring biological, chemical, or nuclear weapons, and eager to use them against us. Indeed, at this very moment, Iran's Islamic regime is putting its oil money to work acquiring long-range ballistic missile capability. It is also producing enriched uranium that could be used to make nuclear weapons. Iranian leaders deny that their intentions are malignant, of course, but the CIA isn't convinced.

Meanwhile, Osama bin Laden and his terrorist networks continue to plot new attacks on the United States. Since 9/11, we have been lucky; an unknown number of planned assaults have been exposed or disrupted, and none have hit American soil as yet—though our friends in Britain, India, Indonesia, Malaysia, Russia, Spain, and Turkey have suffered. But we remain terrifyingly vulnerable; our seaports, our cities, our chemical industry, to name just a few weak points, cry out for better protection. The nation's intelligence officials warn grimly that the odds are against them, and sooner or later another attack is likely to succeed.

When it does, we will have paid for that, too. Petrodollars will buy the dirty bombs, explosives, or chemical or biological weapons and smuggle them into the country; they will help procure fake visas and passports for the terrorists and guarantee safe passage through Canada or Mexico and into the United States. In countries where life is touched by fanaticism and virtually everything is for sale, the combination of limitless wealth, seething hatred, and weapons of mass destruction is more than frightening. It is a threat to our very existence.

There is one more peril that we can blame on the oiligopoly, and it is only slightly less imminent than the terrorist threat: the global warming that threatens us with environmental destruction and economic ruin. Many oilmen and their coal-mining colleagues like to pretend that there's no proof that manmade greenhouse gases are to blame, but the overwhelming scientific consensus has now concluded that the burning of fossil fuels is directly responsible for the fastest rise of global temperatures in the history of the earth. The results promise catastrophe, from drowned seacoasts and spreading deserts to the extinction of species, disrupted economies, and widespread famine and starvation. And we Americans use more fossil fuels than anyone else in the world—billions of tons of coal, trillions of cubic feet of natural gas, an ocean of oil. We buy 10,000 gallons of gasoline *every second.*

Obviously, we must drastically curtail consumption of fossil fuels. Achieving that would require conservation and the development of alternative energy sources. Clearly, we should be getting better mileage from our cars and trucks; producing more hybrid vehicles; pushing to develop better electric cars; building more nuclear power plants to replace coal-fired generators; and speeding up research on alternative power sources including hydrogen fuel cells, biofuels, and ways to store wind and solar power.

Each of those actions, of course, would be a thumb in the eye for OPEC and its collaborators. And although President Bush has correctly called America's use of oil an "addiction," neither he nor oil's reliable friends in Congress show any inclination to take real steps to cure it. Oklahoma's Senator James Inhofe, formerly the Republican chairman of the Senate Environment and Public Works Committee, has called global warming "the greatest hoax ever perpetrated on the American people." Perhaps, with the Democrats now in control of Congress, there will be more willingness to face reality. But I predict that the industry's money will continue to talk, and the foot-dragging will go on until the voters make it clear that they have had enough and insist on reforms.

This book aims to awaken us all to the dangers posed by the great oil conspiracy, to explain how it evolved and what it could do to the world, and to suggest ways we can escape our shameful dependence on OPEC oil and break OPEC's extraordinary grip on the world's economy. So great are the perils that we can no longer permit the unfettered consumption of oil. Our national honor, our security, and the health of our planet all depend on it.

But before I go any further, let me answer the inevitable questions: Who am I? How do I know what I am talking about? And why am I writing this book now?

For openers, I am not an oilman. (By the time you finish reading this book, I think that fact will enhance my credibility, not erode it.) I have spent more than twenty-five years of my professional life trading in commodities—and that's just what oil is, no more and no less than a simple commodity. Despite all the hyped-up rhetoric about its being uniquely political, strategic, scarce, and rapidly depleting, oil is merely one of the unglamorous raw materials of civilization, no different from any other. Its mystique is a manufactured justification for its outrageous price.

OPEC, as I said, is a cartel, but not just any cartel; it is the world's most egregious combine and its most damaging. It blatantly violates the spirit of free trade, as well as the rules of the World Trade Organization (WTO), while being meekly thanked by its holdup victims. And the longer it prevails, the stronger it grows. OPEC uses the fictional shortage of oil to extort not just money but diplomatic favors from dependent buyers as diverse as China and the United States. As the Council on Foreign Relations has warned, America's dependency on imported oil has greatly weakened our foreign policy influence in the world—and it increasingly threatens our national security.

I am writing this book because OPEC and its machinations make me very angry. OPEC's dealings offend my sense of fairness and justice. Like most traders I know, I take pride in playing by the rules on a level playing field. In the markets I worked in, traders who tried to take unfair advantage soon found themselves frozen out. But there is a whole industry, led by OPEC, that is permitted to hoodwink the world, while governments collude in the robbery and hardly a protest gets registered. Just imagine the firestorm of indignation that would erupt if the public found out that the world's big grain exporters (say, the United States, Canada, Brazil, Argentina, and Australia) were conspiring to triple or quadruple the price of such basic commodities as soybeans, corn, and wheat. If growers conspired as OPEC does, the prices of grain and products made from it would balloon, and the plotters would be seen as preying on humanity's basic needs. Yet oil is just as basic, just as essential, and the damage done by the OPEC oil cartel and its friends is every bit as costly to the world as a grain conspiracy would be.

This shakedown also alarms me because of the danger it poses not only to my country but to the world. I served in the U.S. Navy as a district security officer and was given a sound but frightening education in all the basic elements of chemical, biological, and nuclear warfare. (Ironically, part of my service was spent in the federal building at 90 Church Street in lower Manhattan, a building that was destined to become the northern demarcation line of the hallowed quadrant that was once the World Trade Center.) I know what I'm talking about—more sometimes than I want to know. I know how easy it is, especially for those who are determined and willing to sacrifice themselves, to buy or steal these weapons or their equivalents, move them around the world, and use them to destroy vulnerable targets and kill as many of us as they can. We are in imminent deadly peril, and every dollar we ship off to the Middle East for oil increases the danger.

I have also been to China and seen the future, in the form of the massive shroud of pollution that fouls the air and spreads all the way to California. That's just the visible marker of the unseen carbon dioxide, methane, and other greenhouse gases that are inexorably changing the face of the earth and threatening our way of life, if not life itself.

The cartel must be broken, as must our addiction to fossil fuels, and the United States must lead the fight. Our government alone carries the clout to stand up to OPEC and the oil interests, their powerful friends and well-entrenched allies, and the accumulated billions of dollars that bankroll their activities. The time has come for our leaders to honor their commitment to this nation by coming down squarely on the side of its people; they must defend us against the greed and destructiveness of OPEC and its minions in the oil and related industries. Anything else would be a dereliction of duty.

I have nothing to gain from OPEC's demise. If the cartel were broken tomorrow, I would receive no more than one man's share of the resulting rise in global prosperity.

Commodity trading has been good to me. I can indulge my fondness for travel and my passion for art, a love that began when I was a young man hanging around the Cedar Bar in Greenwich Village, listening to arguments among such esteemed artists as Franz Kline, Jackson Pollock, and Willem de Kooning. My interest continued, and I was privileged to be appointed by President Ronald Reagan to serve on the National Council on the Arts (part of the National Endowment for the Arts), as well as serving on the boards of museums and other arts organizations.

I found my way to commodity trading by a natural route: I originally came from Luxembourg, the son of a leather goods wholesaler with clients all over Europe. My family immigrated to the United States at the outset of World War II. I attended the Wharton School of Finance and Commerce at the University of Pennsylvania, majoring in what was then quaintly called "international commerce." Two years of my life were spent in the Navy, after which I landed an apprenticeship in commodity trading with a large trading company. From there, I started operating on my own.

Most people never give commodity trading a thought, but it is a fascinating, complex business that keeps the world running. To be a trader, you have to know a lot—what's needed where, what it's worth there, and where you can find it at what cost. You negotiate for the purchase and sale, arrange financing and letters of credit, take possession of the goods, move them to a port, charter ships or planes for the long haul, arrange to move the material from the port of arrival to the final destination, and buy insurance to cover any conceivable loss along the way. Even so, you worry until the goods are safely delivered and the check is in the bank.

Forty years ago, the commodities business was less formal than it is now. We got along on our character, our connections, and what we knew. We didn't need vast amounts of capital to get financing, or flow sheets detailing every move in every part of each transaction. We calculated our deals on the back of an envelope and made our bets. And sometimes we lost. A partner and I once loaded two tons of fresh strawberries in California, flew them to New York, and transferred them to a flight to London, where we had an eager buyer. But the plane's cargo refrigerator wasn't up to the job, so the plane landed in London with two tons of strawberry jam. Still, we survived.

I got an education in those years, and part of it came when I encountered my first cartel. In hindsight, that taught me everything I needed to know about OPEC. It was in the mid-1960s, and this cartel controlled the world market in sulfur, most of which was then extracted from huge underground domes in the southern United States. Forming a joint export association under the Webb-Pomerene Act would allow the three companies dominating the business to operate legally as an export cartel. So they formed the Sulfur Export Corporation, or Sulexco, which in effect had a world monopoly. Sulexco set the price and controlled the supply, and it kept the market so tight that some buyers couldn't get sulfur at all.

Few people realize how essential sulfur is, to both industry and agriculture. You can't make steel or industrial explosives without sulfuric acid; the entire "green revolution" in agriculture would have been impossible without the sulfuric acid that converts phosphate rock into phosphate-based fertilizer. In the mid-1960s, Sulexco was saying there wasn't enough of it to meet demand—a claim that was almost surely untrue. The sulfur domes were virtually limitless, and all the producers had to do was pump in heated water to dissolve the sulfur, pump it back out, and then separate the mineral from the water. In classic cartel fashion, Sulexco probably decided that rather than increase production, it could make money with less effort by fabricating a shortage and raising the price. This manufactured shortage ensured that those lucky enough to get their hands on some sulfur were grateful to Sulexco, rather than resentful over the egregiously high price.

But the shortage, though artificially induced, still meant that some people couldn't find the sulfur they needed, and they became fairly desperate to get it. In South Africa, for example, the mining industry was about to come to a halt for lack of explosives, which would have dealt a mortal blow to the country's economy. Meanwhile, a French company was producing sulfur as a byproduct of a new process to remove hydrogen sulfide from "sour" natural gas. A rumor spread in the commodity business that the South African government, worried about its mining industry, had offered to equip its air force with French-made Mystère jet fighters if the French would sell sulfur to South Africa's explosives producer, African Explosives & Chemical Industries (AECI). But the negotiations seemed to stall.

AECI was partly owned by Britain's then-monolithic Imperial Chemical Industries (ICI), so Pretoria also put pressure on ICI to deliver the needed sulfur by threatening to nationalize AECI if it didn't. Sulexco still held the upper hand, though. Based on its claim that there wasn't enough to go around, it would sell ICI only what it needed for its own use, not for AECI's. ICI was almost frantic to find another source of sulfur to prevent the loss of its AECI investment.

That source turned out to be me. I was operating at the time in western Canada, where some oil companies were experimenting with the same process the French were using to sweeten sour natural gas by removing its foul-smelling and dangerous hydrogen sulfide. So I went to a number of these companies and offered them a reasonable price for their sulfur byproduct. I put together small parcels until I had commitments for 20,000 to 30,000 tons, a major portion of what South Africa needed. Then I offered it to ICI.

It was a heady scene. There I was, twenty-eight years old, a small trader based in Canada, having a boardroom luncheon in ICI's grand London Millbank headquarters with a lot of starchy British executives in Savile Row suits. I told them I would supply AECI with sulfur, but they would have to support me in purchasing other commodities particular to the chemical fertilizer industry, including nitrogen products, phosphates, and potash. We struck the bargain, and I set up my trading business with that deal. I called my company Brimstone Export Ltd., using the biblical term for sulfur.

After that, more and more companies began using the new process to separate sulfur from natural gas, and the so-called shortage eased considerably. It soon became clear that Sulexco was going to lose its market control, because the huge amount of sulfur coming from gas was a lot less expensive than the sulfur pumped from underground domes.

This brings me to the real parallel with OPEC: For years, Sulexco put out propaganda to persuade its customers that sulfur was still in short supply and that anyone who didn't buy at full price from Sulexco was in danger of running out. It used all the tactics practiced by OPEC—writing articles, hiring "experts" to parrot the message, and feeding the cartel's line to the press. The aim was to persuade the world that sulfur was strategic, that it was a fast-depleting finite resource, that its sale and movement were politically sensitive, and that high prices were beneficial because they would help Sulexco ration the precious element and make sure it was wisely used. In time, Sulexco's fiction collapsed of its own weight, but until it did, the cartel reaped enormous profits.

I never forgot that. Years later, after the 1973 Arab oil embargo enabled OPEC to gain a stranglehold on the world, I began to sense that something similar to the Sulexco fraud was being perpetrated on oil consumers throughout the world. I wrote a letter that the *New York Times* graciously published, arguing that oil was no more scarce or strategic than the commodities that make agriculture possible. By then, however, the alleged shortage of oil had already been accepted as received wisdom, reinforced by the environmental movement and various reports from so-called experts.

For a while, the 1973 embargo seemed to backfire on the cartel. There was an active push to find new reservoirs of oil and alternative sources of energy. Oil prices drifted lower. But late in the 1980s, it became clear that OPEC and the world's major oil companies had joined forces to push up the price of oil, and that the U.S. government was helping them. After the Persian Gulf War in 1991, OPEC became a major force in world markets, influencing both the supply and the price of oil with its machinations. And not surprisingly, I found myself reading the same kind of propaganda from OPEC that Sulexco had foisted on its consumers years before.

In March 1991, shortly after the end of the first Gulf War, I wrote an op-ed article for the *Times* asking, "Did we fight the war to save OPEC?" It argued that OPEC was restraining global trade and imposing an unfair tax on the world economy. I suggested that since we had saved Kuwait and protected Saudi Arabia from Saddam Hussein, the least those countries could do in return was to leave OPEC and trade their oil on a free-market basis.

That didn't happen, of course. Instead, OPEC continued to spread its propaganda and hardly anyone spoke up in protest, least of all the cartel's friends in Washington and other world capitals.

A decade later, the United States again went to war with Iraq. The uncertainty and fears of an oil supply crisis pushed prices to unimagined heights. OPEC happily fed the panic.

In September 2003, the cartel's chief propagandist, Omar Farouk Ibrahim, wrote a letter to the *International Herald Tribune* that reached a new level of hubris. He said the cartel was ensuring the steady flow of "a finite resource ... at a price that is fair and reasonable," and thus doing nothing less than "fulfilling our obligations to humanity." Ibrahim went on to claim that the Western nations were "the biggest beneficiaries of high oil prices," since the oil companies were headquartered in these countries, and OPEC spent its oil riches on Western goods and investments. His brazen claim that OPEC was good for all humanity prodded me to write another piece. "OPEC Follies: Breaking Point" was published by *National Review Online* in December 2003, after which I began writing this book.

It is heartening to consider that Sulexco no longer exists and few people even remember it. My goal in publishing this book, now updated and expanded in this new edition—and also in my regular columns for the *Huffington Post*—is to send OPEC along the same track to oblivion, by exposing its deceptions and corruptions, its extortionist tactics, and the pathetic complicity of its victims.

This is no easy task. The conventional wisdom foisted on us by the conspirators is deeply ingrained; when I tell people that oil is no scarcer than other commodities, they simply can't believe it. When this book was first published, it was discouraging to see how many reviewers had swallowed the oiligopoly's line and dismissed my argument without even debating it. But I don't intend to shut up until the message is heard. The issue is too important. Our safety and prosperity, our nation's honor, and the fate of our only planet are all at stake.

My own thinking about the energy future has evolved since this book was first published, and this edition has been updated and revised to reflect, among other topics, the urgency of the global warming crisis. I hope to drive home the vital need for a rapid end to the use of all fossil fuels and a transition to a world economy powered by clean alternatives. Breaking the power of the oiligopoly will liberate us to achieve that, and the money the world will save on oil during the transition will finance the research to make it possible.

Clearly, it is no fun for any of us to be over a barrel. But there is another way to look at it. The phrase "over the barrel" was also used to describe a sailor's way to resuscitate someone from drowning. Victims were placed not over the barrel of a cannon, but on a wooden barrel, and then rocked back and forth until they expelled the water from their lungs and gasped for life-giving air. Maybe if we rock our oil barrel long enough and hard enough, we can expel the strangling forces of OPEC and become self-reliant once again.

PART ONE

The Barrel We're Over

1

The Scarcity Myth

Nothing lasts: not fame, fortune, beauty, love, power, youth, or life itself. Scarcity rules. Accordingly, scarcity—or more accurately, the perception of scarcity—spells opportunity for manipulators.

This is precisely the approach pursued by the Organization of the Petroleum Exporting Countries (OPEC), the biggest and most relentless manipulator ever foisted on the oil-addicted economies of the world. It has become a vicious cycle of boom and bust, carrot and stick, lies and deceptions. The best—perhaps the only—way to stop this devastating cycle is to rise up and thunder a simple truth: Oil is not scarce. We only fear that it is.

If this idea comes as a surprise to you and seems to deny accepted truth, you're in good company. The fear of scarcity has been carefully cultivated, and it makes oil unique among commodities. No one loses sleep over shortages of bauxite or phosphate or molybdenum. But an anxiety approaching panic grips us at the mere thought of an oil-bereft future. Visions of dying industries, freezing houses, stalled cars, and grounded airplanes send a shiver up our collective spine. There is surely no doubt that much of the developed world would go to war—and perhaps already has, in Iraq—to prevent such a future.

But worries about petroleum shortages are needless. If a shortage of anything exists, it's of truth and candor and market transparency. The fact is, the oil shortage we are warned about is a fiction.

The *alleged* oil shortage, well, that's directly tied to the ability of a scheming group of oil producers to deceive consumers across the globe.

Oil Runs Out—Over and Over and Over

From the beginning, the story of oil has been a continuing cycle of discovery, followed by fear of scarcity, followed by more discovery and more fear. In 1855, when people were making patent medicine from crude oil that bubbled up to the surface of the Pennsylvania earth (and touting it as a cure for everything from diarrhea and rheumatism to cancer and deafness), an advertisement for Samuel Kier's Rock Oil instructed buyers: "Hurry, before this wonderful product is depleted from Nature's laboratory!"

Soon after, when the area's first drilled well hit pay dirt just sixty-nine feet below the surface, alarmists began predicting dry wells ahead. In 1874, the state geologist of Pennsylvania, then the nation's leading oil producer, estimated that the United States had only enough oil to keep kerosene lamps burning for another four years. As chronicled by Daniel Yergin in *The Prize: The Epic Quest for Oil, Money, and Power,* his Pulitzer Prize–winning history of the oil industry, a Standard Oil executive named John Archbold began selling his company shares in the 1880s because engineers told him the country was nearing the end of its petroleum supply. When other experts informed him about signs of oil in Oklahoma, Archbold was incredulous, famously replying, "Why, I'll drink every gallon produced west of the Mississippi!"

In 1885, California was tagged by the U.S. Geological Survey as having "little or no chance" of finding oil. In 1914, the Federal Bureau of Mines assessed the U.S. oil supply as adequate for only ten more years, and two years later the bureau amplified its rhetoric to predict "a national crisis of the first magnitude," with "no assured source of domestic supply in sight." In 1940, sixteen years beyond the designated day of doom, and apparently unfazed by its history of misreckoning, the bureau predicted that reserves would now be exhausted in fourteen years. Clearly, the oil industry was on its way to compiling a record of failed prognostications perhaps unmatched by any other industry, past or present.

The dire prophecies continued, as did the dearth of supporting evidence. In 1972, for example, the Club of Rome, an international consortium of prestigious worrywarts, predicted a global energy shortage that would stunt economic growth and force the world into a new pastoral age. They estimated that only 500 billion barrels of oil remained to be tapped, and warned that the world would run out of crude by 1990. Once again, however, the doomsayers were wrong—this time because they ignored the effects of technological advances like computer-assisted imaging that raised the odds of finding new pools of oil.

The journalists Amy Myers Jaffe and Robert A. Manning pointed up the utterly incorrect analyses of the "sky-is-falling" crowd of oil forecasters. In the January/February 2000 issue of *Foreign Affairs,* they noted that two decades' worth of pundits' predictions for a decline of 3.6 million barrels a day in non-OPEC production had been given the lie by an outright *increase* of more than 4 million barrels a day. None of this is to mention that the world in those two decades used up 600 billion barrels of oil—more than the Club of Rome thought even existed back in 1972. By the millennium, proved reserves exceeded a trillion barrels.

Though buried deep in the consumer psyche, the fear of shortages never quite disappeared. For instance, a widely used 1981 textbook on economic geology, *Economic Mineral Deposits,* again warned of an "energy gap." The authors, Mead L. Jensen and A. M. Bateman, predicted a 125-year-long calamity that would pinch hardest shortly after the year 2000. But, lo and behold, by 1986 a soft economy, cheating on OPEC production quotas, and increased output from non-OPEC rivals had combined to produce an oil glut that drove prices below $10 a barrel.

Nevertheless, the voices of doom persisted, even in the face of contrary facts and low prices. In 1989, one expert warned that world oil production would peak that same year and the ensuing catastrophic crash in output would drive the price to $50 a barrel. At least this fellow got the price right—until the manipulators pushed it even higher.

So it went, and so it goes. Similar predictions of imminent calamity appeared in 1995, 1998, and 1999, relayed in somber tones by such prestigious journals as *Nature, Science,* and *Scientific American.* No matter that in the real world, oil production and, more important, proved oil reserves continued to rise all through the 1990s, as prices hovered between $20 and $30 a barrel. As a result, the life index of existing world oil reserves, measured by the ratio between proved reserves and current production, has risen from twenty years in 1948 to about forty-three years by the end of 2003.

Yet the Chicken Littles continue to scratch and tremble, sometimes to the point of absurdity. In 1997, for example, the widely quoted British oil analyst Colin Campbell wrote in *The Coming Oil Crisis* that peak world production was just around the corner (again). Plunging supplies, he speculated, could bring "war, starvation, economic recession, possibly even the extinction of *Homo sapiens.*" So far, no one has trumped Campbell's ace—though it is hard to imagine a prediction much bleaker than the end of humanity. But neither has his prediction come true, and I don't believe it ever will—at least not for lack of oil.

Why the persistent predictions of calamity? In plain words, they suit the purposes of the people who make them. A little background will make this clear.

After World War II, an abundance of oil made possible widespread electrification, mass transportation by automobile and airplane, and the production of an array of new materials ranging from synthetic rubber to artificial fibers and plastics, fertilizers, pesticides, and detergents. Each of these dramatically changed life in the developed world. Accordingly, the use of oil exploded. Increased oil consumption became not just the driver of economic growth, but, ironically, a consequence of it as well.

Seizing on this remarkable global transformation and keen to push up the price of its key ingredient, OPEC began training consumers—indeed, most governments around the world—to believe that oil is a much more finite resource than it really is. OPEC perpetuates the phony theory of scarcity and successfully manipulates the price of oil with the help of Mexico, Russia, and other non-OPEC producers, as well as the oil industry in general. Even the environmentalists chime in with the scarcity chorus, hoping that warnings of the imminent exhaustion of oil will discourage use of fossil fuels and hasten the rise of alternative energy sources.

Running on Full

It would seem to be just common sense that the world's supply of oil is finite and must run out someday. But the same is true of any commodity, including water and oxygen. Contrary to what the casual observer may believe, there is no identified fixed supply of world oil that dwindles with each passing year of growing consumption. Instead, the oil business is built on a series of gambles that more fields will be found and that the development of any given field will pay a big enough reward to justify the cost of coping with the industry's negative conditions and obstacles. A gamble is, by definition, no sure thing, and oil well drilling is often deferred to await the lower costs, better technology, or higher prices that might increase the odds of success. The point is, even if we knew exactly how much total oil the earth holds, the number would be tangential to the issue that matters: How much oil is accessible for drilling at a profit right now?

Over the long term, despite heavy production and dire predictions of oil depletion, all data show a net gain over time in the worldwide pool of extractable oil. Take California's Kern River field, for example. Discovered in 1899, it was declared largely depleted after forty-three years of production, with remaining reserves thought to total 44 million barrels. Instead, over the next forty-four years it produced more than twelve times that much, pouring out another 736 million barrels. And that isn't all: Further geological examination has turned up yet another 970 million barrels of profitably recoverable oil at Kern River.

Or how about the more recently discovered Kashagan field in Kazakhstan? One of the largest finds in the last thirty years, it was thought to contain 2 billion to 4 billion barrels when test drilling was begun in the latter half of the 1990s. By February 2004, the official estimates had climbed all the way to 13 billion barrels.

Pessimists say flatly that there are no more giant oil fields remaining to be discovered. But the big oil companies, which call such fields "elephants," have been on an elephant hunt in the deepwater Gulf of Mexico in recent years, drilling at previously impossible depths through two miles of water and another four miles of rock and salt deposits. BP was the first to find oil in 2001—an estimated 1 billion barrels in its Thunder Horse field. After a dozen similar finds, Chevron and two partners announced in August 2006 that they had bagged an elephant in the oil field known as Jack, with deposits of 3 billion to 15 billion barrels. At the high end, that would be enough to double the nation's proved reserves. First estimates are almost always conservative, with later drilling finding more, and what has been found so far has oilmen predicting that the deepwater Gulf now holds some 40 billion barrels in undiscovered reserves.

The Kern River, Kashagan, and Gulf of Mexico experiences have been repeated many times the world over. During a fifteen-year span ending in 1996, for example, no new giant fields were discovered. (There is, however, a steady flow of lesser discoveries that tend to be buried in the back pages of business sections: 140 million barrels in Egypt late in 2006, a new find in Papua New Guinea a few weeks later, and so it goes.) But despite the lack of new giant deposits, the estimated reserves of 186 known huge oil fields around the globe jumped from 617 billion to 777 billion barrels, even though they were constantly producing oil during those fifteen years.

Did all these fields grow more oil? Not likely. What grew was know-how and the tools to drill deeper, wider, and more efficiently. So rather than shortages, the real story of the oil industry over the past century—and most especially the past fifty years—has been one of discovery enormously enhanced by technological improvements that have lowered the cost of bringing oil out of the ground.

Those deepwater Gulf of Mexico fields, for example, were located using advanced seismographic technology that provides detailed three-dimensional views of rock formations six miles below the surface. This has made drilling far more predictable than ever before. Even though it may cost up to $100 million to drill a single deepwater well, two out of three exploratory wells now strike oil. Just twenty-five years ago, only one well in six came in.

As at Kern River, technology is also giving new life to fields once thought exhausted. The new seismology locates new deposits in old oil fields, and they can be tapped by wells slanting down from existing platforms or heading sideways from old holes. Oil can be forced from the ground by pumping in steam or carbon dioxide, and advanced recovery methods use enzymes or bacteria to winkle out oil molecules trapped in rock. Indeed, the recovery rate of existing oil fields has risen from about 22 percent a quarter-century ago to 35 percent today, adding billions of barrels to known reserves. Even so, a field that is now considered exhausted still holds 65 percent of its oil, waiting for future technological advances to make it profitably recoverable.

Consider the term *proved reserves,* a key measure of the oil world's always-fluid future. In its most general sense, the term refers to the accessible oil in a field that hard data suggests has a 90 percent chance of being profitably pumped out. This assumes no drastic setbacks in economic, political, or technical conditions; if drilling technology improves, the proved reserves figure will rise, too. Determining the amount of proved reserves, then, is more art than science. Geological and engineering surveys are analyzed and production from nearby wells assessed to come up with a reasonable figure. But as even Roger W. Bentley, secretary of a depletion-oriented group of scientists called the Association for the Study of Peak Oil and Gas, has acknowledged, "Proved reserves have been very conservative numbers, indeed. They do not reflect the total oil that has been discovered, but only that small portion for which definite plans are in place for current access." Some of the world's largest oil fields have been only cursorily measured. In Iran and Iraq, for instance, wars and political turmoil have prevented almost all exploratory drilling since the early 1980s, and modern technology has never been used to assess reserves.

Varying rules and methods of measurement also complicate the issue. In the United States, the Securities and Exchange Commission (SEC) insists that a very narrow definition of proved and recoverable reserves be used in measuring an oil company's financial health. The SEC reporting standards are so narrow that they discourage investors and prevent financial markets from correctly assessing the results of exploration. In Canada, meanwhile, companies are allowed to report both proved and probable reserves, which may better reflect the true potential.

A Cambridge Energy Research Associates report—released in February 2005 and funded by oil industry heavyweights ranging from production companies themselves to their law firms, auditors, and investors—points out that new technology like 3D seismic mapping has not only made oil in remote locations accessible and economically feasible to extract, it has also made estimates of these reserves far more accurate. If investors are to be enticed to finance production from these new sources of oil, the report adds, they need a better calculation of a company's reserves than the current SEC guidelines provide.

The problem, as critics see it, is multipronged. For one thing, the SEC does not allow companies to include in their reserve reports any oil at all from "unconventional" deposits such as deepwater wells or oil found in Canada's tar sands, even though the Canadian deposits have attracted billions of dollars of investment and are estimated to contain more oil than is buried in the Arabian desert. Never mind that gasoline derived from oil sands is already powering cars on U.S. highways.

In addition, the SEC alone uses year-end product prices to calculate reserve estimates, which, critics charge, distorts the numbers and forces oil companies to forgo many promising expansion opportunities. Exxon Mobil, ConocoPhillips, and others were forced to excise from their 2004 SEC reports millions of barrels of extra-heavy oil deposits after a last-minute slide in prices made these sources uneconomical in the eyes of the SEC. The heavy oil prices subsequently rebounded, but too late to change the annual reports. Partly because of pressure from oil companies eager to attract investors, the SEC may revise rules that many consider unnecessarily restrictive and also outdated—they were adopted in 1978.

Then there's the problem of a company's internal auditors attempting to apply SEC rules that don't mesh with the policies of many of the countries where the fossil fuels are located. Right now, though, as this and the succeeding chapter show, oil-producing nations aren't required to document their reserves at all, and they don't. In an attempt to remedy the confusing and often market-roiling lack of transparency, the Group of Eight (G-8) industrial nations, which account for two-thirds of the world's economic output, are urging producing countries and oil companies alike to lift the veil of secrecy and share data on output and reserves. "Transparency and data is [sic] key to the smooth operation of markets," the finance ministers acknowledged in a statement issued after a two-day meeting in February 2005.

"We need more information about oil reserves," declared Gordon Brown, the United Kingdom's chancellor of the exchequer, whose country hosted the talk. Brown suggested that international financial institutions work with industry groups to devise worldwide accounting standards for oil reserves, and he also advocated that producing nations release exact figures on supply. Brown had previously issued a statement at the October 2, 2004, meeting of the International Monetary Fund saying that transparency was needed "to ensure lower and more stable prices" and that "a lack of transparency in oil markets and pool quality information contribute to volatility and uncertainties." Reliable information would relieve traders' fear of the unknown, which so persistently sends market prices spiraling upward.

In countries like Libya, where Occidental Petroleum, Marathon Oil, Amerada Hess, and ConocoPhillips are scrambling to explore— a sure sign that significant reserves are thought to exist there—and in Iraq, Iran, Kuwait, Saudi Arabia, and every other place where secrecy rules, transparency would surely deal a significant blow to the myth of scarcity. In Libya alone, the estimate of reserves nearly tripled, to 100 billion barrels, after the big Western oil companies were recently invited back in and began probing the desert.

Is it any wonder, then, that the G-8 proposal was quickly denounced by the Saudis? Ihsan Bu-Hulaiga, an economist and adviser to the Saudi government, was quoted by the Bloomberg news service as saying: "Western nations are not dealing with oil producers as partners. Why should they have the advantage of knowing details of oil producers' reserves? Data on reserves is information, and information is power."

True enough, and that power might even include the ability to resist price increases. The question is, why must the world's consumers be denied it? This is a question we should ask every time we stand at the pump and see that the cost of gasoline has ticked upward again.

For all the basic ignorance about reserves and the lack of international standards of measurement, however, the "experts" never hesitate to make prognostications. Early in 2004, the generally accepted estimate of global proved reserves was 1.2 trillion barrels. Not everyone accepts these numbers without question; it is hard not to be suspicious, particularly when the estimates come from people with a vested interest in the oil business—some of whom have reason to exaggerate their reserves, while most of them seek to hide the true extent of their reserves. And apart from conflicts of interest and problems of standards, just how much credence should one put in a "global" estimate that excludes figures from one of the globe's largest oil producers? Russia, ranked second behind Saudi Arabia in the estimate, doesn't divulge its reserves—the numbers are literally a state secret. And the petroleum data that *are* available from the former Soviet Union are so poor as to render it impossible for an outsider to make a reasonable guess.

Then there's OPEC. Knowing the true size of the cartel's proved and probable reserves is critical to gauging with any degree of accuracy how long the world's oil will last—and the supply would not be difficult to determine. But because scarcity pays, Saudi Arabia and its OPEC brethren have reason to minimize their treasure. The Saudis alone sit on top of eighty known reservoirs, allegedly holding 261 billion barrels of proved reserves. But the desert kingdom currently taps just eleven of those basins, having opened two new fields ahead of schedule in August 2004, when fears of shortages sent prices on one of their periodic one-way elevator rides. Reprising their well-practiced, self-serving song, the Saudis professed to be opening the new fields in order to meet market demand and protect the world economy.

The newly opened fields are said to contain a total of 14 billion barrels, but given that they were discovered more than forty years ago, how can the estimates be considered credible? Until recently, the kingdom had for years done no exploratory drilling to ascertain how much more oil remains to be found. Most experts believe there is a lot.

Moreover, recent developments indicate that the Saudis know much more about their already proved reserves than they have been disclosing. On December 27, 2004, the Saudi minister of petroleum and natural resources, Ali al-Naimi, in a statement issued after opening new oil fields in eastern Saudi Arabia, said that those 261 billion barrels still waiting to be pumped might actually turn out to be 461 billion barrels. "There are big chances to increase the kingdom's producible reserves by 200 billion barrels," he said. "This will either come through new discoveries or through increasing production from known deposits."

No one bothered to ask al-Naimi how he could predict with such precision the number of barrels still waiting to be discovered. Or why he chose that moment, when rumors of OPEC production cuts were roiling the markets, to make his announcement. He gratuitously reiterated that "the kingdom is keen to ensure a balance between supply and demand and the stability of the market . . . so that producers benefit and consumers do not lose." Never mind that world consumers had already lost trillions of dollars to the OPEC manipulators. Al-Naimi's obviously calculated dispensation of significant "new" information could only reinforce the sense that the Saudis had deliberately been hiding reserves. But why should the Saudis rush to divulge their secrets? Why admit to having an underground ocean of petroleum that will only weaken your leverage in the market?

Iraq is usually reckoned the world's number four depository of petroleum, with an estimated 115 billion barrels of reserves. But given Iraq's war with number-three Iran in the 1980s, its invasion of Kuwait in 1990, its status as an international pariah barred from normal oil trade, and the neglect of the industry's infrastructure by Saddam Hussein's regime, exploration has languished and the industry has fallen into decay.

After the fall of Saddam's government, American engineers inspecting Iraq's oil fields were appalled at what they found: rusted valves, patched-up pipelines, chattering turbines, and ancient control rooms with dangling wires. Much of the working equipment had been looted, but it was clear that there had been little or no investment in the industry for years. And when the Americans tried to repair and modernize the facilities, insurgents regularly disrupted operations again by sabotaging wells, pipelines, and pumping stations. Iraqi oil production peaked in 1979, before the war with Iran, at 3.7 million barrels a day. Before the U.S.-led invasion in 2003, daily output was 2.5 million barrels; three years later, it hovered below 2 million barrels.

For all the guesstimates of reserves, no one really knows how much oil lies beneath Iraq. In August 2004, the country took steps to find out when it began soliciting bids to determine the size of some of its reserves, the first time since the Iran-Iraq War that modern exploration technology will be used to size up Iraq's oil fields. The fields to be examined are Rumaila and Kirkuk, Iraq's oldest and biggest producers. Kirkuk began producing in the 1920s, and even the Iraqis realize that applying updated exploration technology there is long overdue. But the continuing hostilities have delayed the work, and no updated reserve estimate has been announced.

Iran's situation is similar. The commonly accepted figure for its reserves is 125.8 billion barrels, but supposedly knowledgeable estimates run all the way from a ridiculously low 37 billion barrels to an astronomical 500 billion. No one knows because no one has tried to find out.

The entire dilemma can be summed up in one contradictory set of figures: In 1970, non-OPEC oil producers had 200 billion barrels of proved reserves among them. In the next thirty-three years, they pumped a total of 460 billion barrels. Now they say they have 209 billion barrels of proved reserves remaining. OPEC members, which supposedly had 412 billion barrels of reserves in 1970, have since produced 307 billion barrels and now claim to have 819 billion barrels in reserve. In a world where pumping billions of barrels out of the ground paradoxically seems to increase the billions still remaining, we are left to wonder where the real truth lies—or whether the concept of "proved reserves" has any relation to the world's supply of oil.

So what is the ultimate global potential? Who knows? Any answer requires crystal-ball forecasts of future developments in science and technology. All we have now is a bare framework for conjecture. Since the first well was drilled, a total of slightly over 1 trillion barrels has been pumped. Most doom-saying theorists, led by Colin Campbell and Jean Laherrere, a retired deputy exploration manager for French-based Total S.A., estimate that perhaps 2 trillion barrels of ultimately recoverable reserves (URR) are left.

Campbell and Laherrere, it should be noted, arrived at their estimate using closely held proprietary figures and their own arcane formulas. Meanwhile, the U.S. Geological Survey (USGS), after making its own analysis in 2000, pegged URR at 3 trillion barrels, 50 percent more than the Campbell-Laherrere estimate. For what it's worth, the

CEO of Saudi-owned Aramco, Abdallah S. Jum'ah, came up with a similar figure in the fall of 2006. On top of the 1.2 trillion barrels of currently known reserves, he predicted that future discoveries would turn up 1 trillion barrels of new profitable reserves, and that another 1 trillion barrels would be recovered from existing fields by advanced production technology, for a total of 3.2 trillion barrels.

What is more, three major discoveries of recent years—the previously mentioned Kashagan field in Kazakhstan, the Jack field in the Gulf of Mexico, and the Azadegan field in Iran—together account for nearly 55 billion barrels that were not included in the USGS or Campbell-Laherrere estimates. It seems unlikely that so much of a supposedly scarce resource would be found so quickly. Indeed, these discoveries throw the whole theory of scarcity even deeper into question.

But even as more and more oil is found and pumped, the depletionists refuse to quit muttering about a petroleum Armageddon. As further evidence that the world is fast running out of oil, they point to the fact that announced discoveries have been diminishing in size ever since the 1970s. There have been major discoveries since then in Iran and Kazakhstan, as well as in the Caspian Sea, offshore Africa, and the deepwater Gulf of Mexico. But none of them, the depletionists claim, is remotely comparable to the vast reservoirs in the Persian Gulf region. In fact, these naysayers flatly assert that no more major basins remain to be found.

Even in the Gulf of Mexico, Laherrere has argued, the pace of discovery is rapidly declining. He has claimed that 1,920 wildcat wells drilled in the region prior to 1980 located a total of 723 billion barrels of oil. In the next two decades, he said, another 1,720 wildcat wells discovered only 32 billion barrels of crude.

Chevron's "elephant" in the Jack field can be taken as rebuttal enough for this argument, at least in the Gulf of Mexico. But beyond this narrow point, the basic thesis of dwindling discoveries is deeply misleading. First, as mentioned earlier, Saudi Arabia stopped exploratory drilling after 1980, despite straddling the world's largest oil reservoir. Why? Because the Saudi princes saw no point in spending money to find reserves that would not be needed for years.

Second, Iran and Iraq also stopped exploratory drilling around the same time because they were at war with each other and mired in political turmoil. With the region's three biggest potential sources of discovery calling a time-out, wildcatting was stepped up in less likely places like Oman, Syria, and Yemen. Not surprisingly, the reservoirs of oil found in those countries were smaller. Even so, the odds are that the announced size of the discoveries isn't the last word on the subject. Experience shows that reserves are almost always revised upward as fields are thoroughly explored and new technology is applied to production.

The supposed dwindling pace of new oil discoveries is simply a red herring. It proves nothing about the amount of oil left to be found. While it seems unlikely that other fields as large as those in the Persian Gulf remain to be discovered, a large part of the world has yet to be thoroughly probed. The record of Russia, where huge discoveries since 1970 make outsiders rank it number two in reserves, proves this point. And, as the huge Gulf of Mexico find in 2006 demonstrates, no one can rule out the possibility of equally significant discoveries in the future.

Oil Doesn't Come Only from Wells

The Cassandras also ignore another major factor—the vast reserves of oil to be found that are not liquid petroleum. Besides that conventional oil, there are also huge reservoirs of oil in tar sands and oil shale. These deposits are admittedly more difficult to tap than conventional oil, which can be pumped without further processing or dilution. Tar sands, for example, are really deposits of bitumen, a heavy black viscous substance that requires a good deal of processing to turn into synthetic crude oil that can then be refined. The sands must first be strip-mined, which doesn't cost much, but then the bitumen has to be melted out of the sand and clay encompassing it. That can add anywhere from $10 to $15 to the price of a barrel of oil. While the cost of mining varies depending on the depth of the deposits and the density of the bitumen, at least some new operations can recover oil for $20 a barrel—providing a hefty profit at the current world price of $50 and up.

By rights, estimates of oil reserves thus ought to include the 1.6 trillion barrels in the tar sands of western Canada, finally economic after forty years of dogged effort. The legendary Texas oilman T. Boone Pickens is a significant investor in this area, giving credence to its growing potential. China is interested as well. In January 2005, the Chinese and Canadian governments announced preliminary agreements that are expected to lead to joint energy ventures. In addition, Enbridge Inc., a Canadian pipeline company, is working with Chinese refiners on plans for a $2 billion pipeline project stretching from Edmonton, Alberta, to the northern coast of British Columbia.

No one yet counts the equally vast heavy oil deposits of Venezuela's Orinoco belt, another 1.6 trillion barrels of reserves, even though they may be technically closer to conventional oil and easier to process than tar sands, and already yield 500,000 barrels a day.

An even larger amount of oil—estimated at 2.5 trillion barrels or more—is locked in the oil shale of the American West, still awaiting economic extraction. Three corporate groups have recently been granted experimental leases to try new ways of getting at the oil. The most advanced process, researched for years by Shell, would use electric heaters in deep holes to cook the rock slowly to 650 degrees Fahrenheit or more, which would separate oil and gas molecules to be pumped to the surface. Shell says this might be done for as little as $30 a barrel, and the resulting synthetic crude would need even less refining than today's best natural petroleum.

OPEC's Secret Weapon

But extracting unconventional oil from hard-to-reach deposits is risky for another major reason: The real cost of lifting oil from beneath the Middle Eastern sands is small, thought to average as little as $1.50 per barrel. What's to stop the Saudis and their OPEC brethren from suddenly flooding the market by pumping more of their cheap oil, to put this new competition out of business?

Would OPEC actually make such a move? Recent Saudi behavior adds credence to the notion and increases suspicions about the actual size of the kingdom's reserves. Abandoning two decades of strategy, Saudi Aramco said in February 2005 that it would have more than 70 drilling rigs operating by the end of the year, up from 34 rigs operating a year earlier.

Before the 1973 oil crisis, Aramco produced a ten-year plan that projected 1983 production of 20 million barrels a day, more than double what the kingdom currently pumps. Over the past twenty years, however, through all the ups and downs of the cyclical oil market, Aramco has maintained it would only preserve its daily capacity, not increase it. Like the Saudi reserves, production capacity is shrouded in mystery; there are some indications that the Saudis can already pump more than their announced maximum of 10.5 million barrels a day. But now the G-8 is pressing for more transparency, and the cash-rich oil majors are coming under pressure to beef up their budgets to find and pump oil. It hardly seems coincidental that the Saudis have announced a big push to increase their own output sharply. Early in 2007, the oil minister, Ali al-Naimi, announced an $80 billion investment to increase pumping capacity to 12.5 million barrels a day, to double the kingdom's refinery output, and to explore for more natural gas.

The kingdom's real agenda is surely to placate the G-8 and dissuade Western oil companies from using their cash windfall (the top ten companies together earned more than $100 billion in 2006) to open up exploration elsewhere in the world.

For all the risks, today's high market prices and technological breakthroughs make unconventional deposits increasingly tempting—and as we have seen, major players are jumping into the game. Adding up the unconventional sources—1.6 trillion barrels of tar sands in Canada, another 1.6 trillion barrels of Venezuela's heavy oil, 2.5 trillion barrels from oil shale—and adding them to the conservative estimate of 3.2 trillion barrels of conventional reserves, we get 8.9 trillion barrels of oil. At today's rate of use, which can and should be reduced by conservation even as the world economy expands, that store of oil would last for well over a century. That's far longer than it should take us to find alternative sources of energy and convert to them, in the cause of stopping global warming and saving the only planet we will ever have.

Bell Curve versus Plateau

Let's state the facts clearly and forcefully: The world is not running out of oil, as alarmists insist. On the contrary, the industry is likely to run out of markets long before the supply of oil peters out. So say experts like Morris A. Adelman, a respected oil analyst and a professor at the Massachusetts Institute of Technology. "Just as the Stone Age did not end for lack of stones," Adelman wrote in his 1995 book, *Genie Out of the Bottle* (paraphrasing, ironically enough, the former Saudi oil minister Ahmed Zaki Yamani), "the Oil Age will not end because of the scarcity of oil. Rather, oil will inevitably be surpassed in convenience by a new source of energy in the future."

In other words, we will never use it all. We began by using up the easiest oil to find and the cheapest to produce, and we are progressing to increasingly more difficult and costly deposits as the inexpensive fields are drained. Earth's last drop of oil will never be pumped, because extracting it would cost many times its highest conceivable value as fuel. Whatever the scenario, however, we will reach an inevitable point where what remains isn't worth the cost of bringing it out of the ground.

How soon? This question generates competing answers, notably "too soon" and "stay tuned."

"Too soon" is the refrain of the rapid-depletion school, devotees of the "Peak Oil" ideas of M. King Hubbert, a Shell geologist. In the 1950s, Hubbert set out to predict production trends in America's lower forty-eight states. He made the assumption that oil output would follow a classic bell curve, beginning a gradual rise in the nineteenth century, ramping up rapidly in the first half of the twentieth, leveling off as production began to match new discoveries, then plunging quickly as reservoirs were exhausted and discoveries dwindled. The final leveling-off on the far side of the bell is known in mathematics as an "asymptote," a curve always approaching but never quite meeting a straight horizon—reflecting the fact that the last drop will never be pumped.

In 1956, Hubbert predicted that oil production in the lower forty-eight states would peak in 1970. When his forecast came true right on schedule, his methodology seemed triumphantly vindicated. Colin Campbell and his latter-day colleagues—principally Jean Laherrere,

David Goodstein (a professor at the California Institute of Technology), and Kenneth S. Deffeyes (a petroleum geologist and the author of *Hubbert's Peak: The Impending World Oil Shortage*)—take Hubbert's theory as gospel. They are convinced that after world production peaks, the curve will fall nearly as precipitously as it rose. The depletionists don't agree precisely on the date when oil output will top out, or on the steepness of the declining curve. But most of them say production will peak in this decade and then plunge at a rate they liken to falling off a cliff.

The other side of the debate—the side this book argues—is made up mostly of economists specializing in energy. They do not disagree that oil production will someday reach a maximum level and begin to decline. But they think that day is at least two decades away and probably more, and that the decline will be long, slow, and relatively painless.

It is instructive that two hundred years ago, when European dominance depended on coal, Europeans worried that their primary energy source would run out. But although Europe's coal production peaked in 1913, there are billions of tons of coal in the ground today that are still being dug out, because it is economically feasible to do so. By the same token, there are even more billions not worth digging out—in large part because oil came along.

"Is there an imminent oil peak? The short answer is no," said Thomas Ahlbrandt, chief of the World Energy Project with the U.S. Geological Survey, as reported in the *Oil & Gas Journal* in 2003. "I believe in the plateau concept. The symmetric rise and fall of oil production is not technically supportable." Ahlbrandt then asked, "Why is there no accountability for these failed forecasts?" Why indeed?

Call Ahlbrandt a "straight-liner," someone who believes that the Hubbert curve analysis is simply too static to encompass all the variables of the hyperdynamic oil market, in which constant change shapes the market as it responds to innovation and regulation. We straight-liners point out that maximum production is more often than not followed by a plateau formation or a long-term trailing-off that makes the whole production curve asymmetrical and anything but bell-shaped. The slow plateau of gradual change, or even comebacks, is a function of improvements in drilling or refining.

Today's technology makes it possible to drill deeper and to recover more oil from a reservoir than geologists initially thought possible. New computers chart potential undersea fields with an accuracy that slashes the high cost of exploration wells. Holes can now be dug at angles in any direction, enabling companies to use fewer platforms and establish oil wellheads on the sea floor. Using multilateral drilling, one North Sea operation cut drilling costs by 75 percent in three years.

The real-world slow dwindling of the underground pools in a long-tail pattern, as opposed to the steep drop envisioned by the depletionists, is especially evident in North Sea production, which has repeatedly refuted bell-curve forecasts over the past two decades. In the Gulf of Mexico, which now produces 30 percent of U.S. crude, pumping from offshore wells has helped lengthen the long-tail patterns for the past thirty-five years, thus keeping production at previously unimagined levels.

The depletionists, who have joined forces as the Association for the Study of Peak Oil and Gas (ASPOG), tend to be ambivalent about these nettlesome facts. They claim to have developed new techniques that correct some of the more obvious flaws in the Hubbert model, and they have begun to acknowledge that the bell curve isn't invariable. In fact, Laherrere reduced the doctrine to a truism when he conceded at an OPEC seminar in Vienna in 2001, "The important message from Hubbert's work . . . is that oil has to be found before it can be produced." Still, the depletionists continue to use a steep curve in predicting future declines in output.

Worried in Public, Cool in Private

One great petroleum paradox is that the industry's biggest worry has always been abundance, not scarcity. When supply far exceeds demand, prices tumble—and that spells grief for producers. "We're in a cyclical business," Chevron Texaco's chief executive officer, David J. O'Reilly, told the *New York Times*. "History tells us that what goes up also goes down." Avoidance of oil gluts is thus among the industry's main preoccupations. In the summer of 2006, when oil was selling for $70 a barrel, Reuters reported that the major oil companies were not investing in any new production that would cost more than $25 a barrel. What does that tell us about the inexorable depletion of the world's oil?

Similarly, the whole point of OPEC's creation in 1960 was to safeguard member nations from overproduction and its attendant price wars, which threatened to bring down their revenues. By curbing production in major oil-exporting countries, such as Iraq, Iran, and Saudi Arabia, the cartel caused petroleum prices to balloon.

All in all, this is not the record of an industry fearful that its core resource will vanish. Quite the opposite. It is the story of an industry determined to curb supply in order to milk expanding demand at maximum prices. That means a level somewhere between inflation and extortion, but one also calculated to allow the golden goose to go on honking.

Most of the Hubbert modelers and their alarmist colleagues work for major oil companies, energy consultants, or governments of oil-producing nations. It is in their employers' interest to keep the world in a fluctuating state of alarm over the oil supply, since looming shortages are invariably invoked to justify high prices.

If the major corporations really foresaw the near-term peaking of production followed by an abrupt decline, it would also be in their interest to prepare for sharp price increases. They would be signing long-term leases on drilling rigs, investing in high-cost production technology to exploit oil shale and the like, and borrowing to buy proved reserves that they could hoard until prices went up. In fact, they are doing very little of this, and their investment in unconventional oil may be seen as mainly hedging their bets. Flush with cash from record-high oil prices, they are instead using the bulk of their bankrolls to buy back stock and pay dividends to shareholders. One can only conclude that they are far less worried than they let on.

There is objective evidence to support this conclusion. For twenty years starting in 1982, Dr. G. Campbell Watkins, an internationally recognized expert in energy policy who is joint editor of the *Energy Journal,* has kept track of all the sales of proved U.S. reserves of oil still in the ground. If the cost of finding and developing new reserves had really been rising, or if companies were expecting sharp cost and price increases in the future, the value per barrel of known reserves would have risen in anticipation. In fact, Watkins found no such price increases. Investors who bought reserves in 1982 would have lost money selling them twenty years later.

Don't misunderstand. This thesis is no reason for comfort and certainly not for complacency. While there is no realistic prospect of running out of oil, this news is as troubling as it is reassuring. The truth is that oil, like all fossil fuels, is bad for us. "The devil's excrement," as an early oil minister called it, is ruining the earth.

Our first priority must be to do everything possible to cut down on the oil we burn. For openers, this means getting better mileage from our cars and trucks. The federally mandated Corporate Average Fuel Economy (CAFE) mileage standard for new U.S. vehicles worked so well that it doubled actual mileage between 1973 and 1985, to a national average of 27.5 miles per gallon. When oil prices fell in the late 1980s, the federal government abandoned any further increases in mileage standards. Merely resuming the previous rate of improvement—which would not be difficult—would get the average to 40 mpg by 2015. Accelerated production of hybrid cars could push the average to 50 mpg, which would cut our use of automotive fuel in half and block millions of tons of greenhouse gases—not to mention the impact it would have on OPEC. If the public demands fuel economy, automakers can and will do even better without any orders from Washington.

Some have argued that imposing much higher taxes on gasoline, as most European countries do, would spur demand for more efficient cars and lower our use of oil. That's true. But, besides being a heavy-handed exercise of government power, higher taxes would impose an unfair burden on disadvantaged Americans who are already being punished by the devastating rise in gasoline and fuel-oil prices. It's especially unfair to the rural poor, who have no choice but to drive long distances. There are better ways to conserve, including (as I note in more detail later in this book) a mandated ceiling on the consumption of gasoline so the burden is shared equally by everyone.

After conservation, our next priority must be switching from fossil fuels to alternative energy sources. Advanced nuclear power plants are both safe and economical; France today gets 80 percent of its electricity from nuclear power. We have already tapped most of our potential hydropower, and there is probably a ceiling to the use of wind and solar energy. But a breakthrough in ways to store electricity could raise that ceiling. There is already an opening for hydrogen power in such stationary uses as power plants, and hydrogen fuel cells will be more efficient than any combustion process when they are made small and light enough to power cars. In sum, banishing fossil fuels is far from a pipe dream—but we need to expend the effort and have the conviction to make it a reality as soon as we possibly can.

In the meantime, we need to fear the right thing—the slow death of our planet—and shrug off the oil-shortage doomsayers whom one writer has called a "catastrophist apocalyptic cult." Scarcity is part of the human condition and heritage, a crucial motivator for both good and ill. We know that nothing lasts, but exaggerated fear of the end of oil can only leave us in thrall to whoever exploits our fears. That means OPEC and the entire oiligopoly. It is time to quit flinching at an oil famine invented by fear-mongers.

2

Hysteria Premium

The date was May 29, 2004. Over a year had passed since jubilant Iraqis, with the assistance of U.S. Marines, sent a towering, twenty-foot likeness of Saddam Hussein crashing into the streets of Baghdad. Over a year had passed since President George W. Bush announced the end of major combat under a "mission accomplished" banner on the flight deck of the aircraft carrier USS *Abraham Lincoln.* Hussein himself had been caught, as Major General Raymond Odierno put it, "like a rat" in a hole in the ground less than six months before. But still the Iraqi insurgency ground stubbornly on, part of a war that seemed always to have at least as many setbacks as victories.

The world was uneasy, and the price of oil reflected that unease. It included what traders call a "fear premium," a measure of the market's worry that hostilities might disrupt supply lines and choke off a significant part of the world's oil supply. The specter of possible supply interruptions, a remote possibility that is tirelessly promoted by the oiligopoly's public relations apparatus, hovered over trading on the New York Mercantile Exchange (NYMEX), where the price, which had averaged $20 for a decade, soared to $35.80 leading up to the war. Then, amid expectations for a quick victory and the actual fall of Baghdad, the price slid back to $30 and below.

But zigs and zags in the months afterward had pushed the oil price steadily higher. On May 1, terrorists burst into an office in Yanbu on Saudi Arabia's Red Sea coast and opened fire. Five Western oil company workers, including two American engineers, were slain. Four weeks later, on May 29, terrorists struck for the second time in what had once been the safe haven of Saudi Arabia. The attacks on a Khobar office building that housed major oil companies and an upscale residential complex killed twenty-two people, including four Saudis, an American, and workers from Asia, Africa, and Europe. When U.S. oil trading resumed on June 1 after a long Memorial Day weekend, fear gripped the market. The price of oil was driven to a record high of $42.33.

The reaction to the Saudi attacks was a perfect example of how bouts of often-irrational panic have come to rule the petroleum markets in the early twenty-first century. No matter how dramatic the raids and how tragic the deaths, the incidents were, in truth, minor hit-and-run skirmishes. Although the assaults were clearly intended to drive away Western workers, damage the Saudi oil industry, and hurt the U.S. economy, there was no evidence that al-Qaeda or any other terrorist group could do any real damage to the massive Saudi oil infrastructure or seriously interfere with shipments to Western refineries. And whatever disruptions did occur would be short-lived, as the attacks proved. In fact, an Aramco oil analyst pointed out that company operations have continued without interruption since the 1950s.

More to the point, at any given moment the world oil industry has inventories of millions of barrels of oil at every stage of production, making any glitch in the pipeline just that—a glitch or inconvenience, not a life-threatening event. Beyond that, the world's industrial nations keep 1.4 billion barrels of crude oil stashed in strategic reserves to cope with any serious disruption. This amount of oil would fill the gap should Saudi Arabia produce nary a drop for 166 days—nearly half a year.

So rather than a fear premium, it was a hysteria premium that spawned the market gyrations. Unwarranted emotionalism continued to convulse the trading floors, thanks in no small part to the OPEC propaganda machine. "OPEC cannot control prices," said Abdullah bin Hamad al-Attiya, the Qatari minister of energy and industry, in the *New York Times.* "It cannot control the fear factor. It cannot control politics. We can only increase supply to calm the markets."

As subsequent events would show, it effectively couldn't (or wouldn't) do that, either. After the post–Memorial Day panic, the price fell back below $40, only to leap again in early July when the color-coders at the U.S. Department of Homeland Security issued a warning that al-Qaeda planned to disrupt the American presidential election. The election was still five months away; nonetheless, the price shot up more than 3 percent in a single day.

Irrationality ruled. Hysteria had traders in a headlock. There were no shortages. Inventories were actually rising. But none of that mattered. As Fadel Gheit, senior vice president of oil and gas research at Oppenheimer & Company, rightly observed to the *Wall Street Journal,* "Whether or not more disruptions to oil supply are likely to happen, it's perception that's moving the market, not inventories at all."

Less than a week later, perception bested reality once again. Shipping sources reported that a South Korean tanker had refused to load up at the southern Iraqi port of Basra because the captain was afraid of terrorists. Naturally, the NYMEX futures price jumped to $41.05 a barrel, as normally savvy traders wrung their hands and shook their heads over the prospect of a lone Korean tanker captain bypassing Basra and setting off a serious stampede of likeminded seamen.

How big is the fear factor in the oil markets? At various points during 2004, traders reckoned it added as much as $15 a barrel, or about 36 percent of the price. Since the world uses 85 million barrels of oil a day, the price of fear could thus be pegged at $1.3 billion every day, or $459 billion a year. And the fear could be triggered by nearly anything, no matter how trivial the impact on world oil supplies. Prices spiked on news of a cut pipeline resulting from an ethnic squabble in Nigeria, the evacuation of drilling platforms during a hurricane in the Gulf of Mexico, political upheavals in Venezuela, and insurgents blowing up a pipeline in northern Iraq. In each case, the flow of oil was soon restored, yet the price still slithered upward.

Two of the most telling incidents came in August. In one, an attack briefly shut down Iraq's offshore facilities, affecting less than 2 percent of the world's flow of oil for just a few hours. But it was enough to send the New York price further along its record-breaking path, reaching $44.34 that day. Equally outrageous, a fire at a single BP refinery in Whiting, Indiana, pushed the New York price to another new record, $46.58. The unceasing speculation and irrational overreaction to every blip on the world screen finally drove the price for a single barrel of oil past $50 in October.

Throughout the entire year, no significant disruption in the supply of oil occurred anywhere in the world system. This indisputable fact, the equivalent of Sherlock Holmes's dog that didn't bark in the night, is key to understanding the oil markets. Even when disasters *have* disrupted production—as when two major hurricanes closed down much of the Gulf of Mexico for months in 2005, or when insurgents in the Niger Delta forced a 20 percent cut in Nigeria's total output for most of 2006—no actual shortages of oil have resulted. But hardly anyone notices, and for good reason.

This market is the culmination of OPEC's prime strategy over the years: carefully fostering the illusion that the oil supply is incredibly vulnerable and that any kink in the pipeline can bring the industrial world to its knees. It is a shell game, with OPEC hiding the pea of truth in a series of walnuts that it switches around in an intricate shuffle to fool the untrained eye. The basic premise is transparently untrue; throughout modern industrial history, the only real interruptions in the world's oil supply have come when OPEC leaders purposely closed the spigots. Yet, as this chapter explains, the fabrication has been woven into the tapestry of conventional wisdom through years of repeated "expert" warnings, the collusion of Western governments and the oil industry, and credulity on the part of the media.

Despite the relentless propaganda, the truth to be remembered is that oil is a plentiful commodity. There are billions of barrels of it lying just below the surface of the Arabian desert, where it can be found and produced for less than $1.50 a barrel.

In a free market, competition would drive the price down to the cost of extraction and production plus a fair profit. That would be a major boon for the world economy, freeing it of the burden created by the transfer of literally billions of dollars to OPEC countries. Lower prices would also speed growth and raise living standards for everyone. But the cartel keeps the price indecently high, and the OPEC nations' outrageous profits of 3,000 to 4,000 percent, based on stated production costs, come at the expense of virtually every other person on the planet. This truth makes OPEC the world's biggest parasite, feeding on the lifeblood of humanity.

OPEC wins as much by controlling production (even though its smaller members often exceed their assigned quotas) as by persuading everyone that the peril is real and could bring the world to a standstill overnight.

Sleight of Hand

In the oil industry, the most basic facts are hidden deep from public view. In shifting them around, OPEC's hand is quicker than most people's eyes. What the industry relies on as basic data on petroleum production is gathered not from audited reports or government figures, but from networks of secret informants furtively monitoring flows and counting tankers at oil terminals around the world. The figures these spies come up with are neither dependable nor transparent. Their notorious unreliability, coupled with the Securities and Exchange Commission's antiquated and vexing policy on booking reserves, leads to endless debates about basic facts, and also to occasional sudden shocks.

The Royal Dutch/Shell Group rocked the markets in 2004 by announcing that its reserves of oil had been overstated by 23 percent. But while the Shell discrepancy, which was exacerbated by the financial accounting rules, grabbed headlines and was seized upon by the depletionists as an example of eroding oil reserves, hardly anyone took note of equally startling news from Yukos: The publicly traded Russian oil giant, not bound by the government's penchant for secrecy, said its reserves had increased by 500 percent. But skeptics cast doubt on the claim, noting that Yukos was fighting to prevent a cheap sale of its assets in a tax dispute with the Kremlin. At both ends of the measuring stick, confusion prevailed.

To begin with, as we saw in Chapter 1, no one knows exactly how much oil even exists, let alone how much of it is readily accessible. The best we can do is estimate reserves, and these estimates are always subject to revision as history shows our guesswork to be limited and fraught with error. Additionally, OPEC has been careful to obscure exactly how much oil it can produce on any given day. Politics plays a big part in the obfuscation, and individual OPEC members often understate their production figures to make it easier to exceed quotas.

Here's the way it works: You claim to be pumping more than you really are, so as to inflate your baseline production figure. Then, when the cartel mandates that you cut a specific percentage from that baseline, you can appear to be going along without actually hurting your revenues too much.

Everyone involved in the global oil industry knows that OPEC members exceed quotas and lie about production levels, yet accepted wisdom in the summer of 2004 held that OPEC's production of 28 million barrels a day represented near-maximum capacity. Given that the cartel had produced more than 30 million barrels a day in the late 1970s, this assumption was dubious at best. Does anyone really believe that the member nations have not added to their capacity in a quarter of a century? Nonetheless, it was taken as gospel that Saudi Arabia was the only OPEC member not pumping flat-out.

Industry analysts said the Saudis, then pumping 9.3 million barrels a day, might be able to add another 1 million to 1.5 million barrels, but it would be low-quality, high-sulfur oil. These figures, too, are open to challenge. The Saudis tend to say whatever suits their purpose at the moment. When they are pushing for higher prices and trying to create the illusion that the oil supply is insecure, they stress their limitations. But when hysteria is getting out of hand and driving prices too high, thereby encouraging competition from alternative sources and causing political discomfort that might threaten to upset their carefully concocted plans, they embrace an entirely different point of view. Suddenly, ramping up production is simple—and even more, a gracious move intended to keep the world economy from needless disruption.

So in the summer of 2004, when hysteria-prone traders were near panic, the Saudis soothed the markets by disclosing that they were tapping new fields and raising capacity to 12 million barrels a day, and might possibly be able to do 15 million if necessary.

Interestingly, this claim was promptly discounted by the industry, brainwashed as most participants are by the illusion of scarcity. But in truth, the Saudis were almost surely still downplaying their real production capacity. This notion was given more than a little credence in December when, seemingly out of nowhere, the oil minister, Ali al-Naimi, let slip to reporters that Saudi oil reserves might increase by 77 percent in "a few" years. He hinted that there were "big chances" to boost producible reserves by a whopping 200 billion barrels. It is hard to imagine a supposedly dying energy source suddenly coughing up that kind of bonus. Little more than two years later, however, al-Naimi again announced a plan to increase capacity, this time to 12.5 million barrels a day. Which shell hid the truth? It was anyone's guess.

Even among OPEC's smaller producers, capacity figures are by no means a given. This uncertainty sets the stage for the kind of three-act farce performed by cartel members before a world audience in August 2004. When the New York price hit a new record at $44.34, Indonesia's oil minister, Purnomo Yusgiantoro, who then held the rotating title of OPEC president, nudged it higher by confirming what everyone thought they already knew: Saudi Arabia had some spare capacity but could not tap it right away, while none of the other members could pump another drop. "The oil price is very high, it's crazy," he told reporters in Jakarta. "There is no additional supply."

The very next day, Purnomo was back with a different story line. Now the cartel *did* have extra capacity. "OPEC continues to hold, at present, a spare production capacity of around 1 million to 1.5 million barrels a day, which would allow for an immediate increase in production," Purnomo declared. He didn't say which OPEC members had unearthed the extra barrels, nor did he explain why these anonymous donors could pump immediately when Saudi Arabia could not.

The following Monday, OPEC's official mouthpiece tried to explain things yet again: OPEC members were pumping the allowed quota of 26 million barrels per day, Purnomo said, while Iraq was kicking in 2 million barrels more, and "2 million others [were coming] from OPEC's overproduction [read 'quota cheaters'] in the field." What is more, OPEC was "ready to add another 1.5 million barrels a day." For those paying attention, Purnomo had placed the cartel's real capacity at 31.5 million barrels a day, well above the figure it dispensed for public consumption.

The audience at this theater of the absurd was still scratching its head when yet another cast member, Rafael Ramirez, the Venezuelan minister of energy and oil, stepped out from behind the curtain a few days later to contradict Purnomo. Ramirez insisted that OPEC was already pumping at its maximum capacity and had no way to respond to increased demand.

There was no telling who was correct. No matter. Oil industry observers and analysts, gullible as always, could reach only one conclusion: The supply buffer obviously was perilously thin.

Where did the real truth lie? We may never be able to penetrate OPEC's pronouncements, but we can look at the bottom line of experience to get a better sense of what is really going on. All through 2004, the world's output of oil rose and fell; there were disruptions large and small in Nigeria, Venezuela, Russia, the United States, and, above all, Iraq. Consumption soared in China. Longtime OPEC member Indonesia, beset by mismanagement, corruption, and underinvestment, couldn't even meet its production quotas. In 2004, Indonesia was a net *importer* of oil. Yet, there was never a real shortage of oil in the world arena. Whatever production and capacity figures were bandied about by OPEC and its member states, the cartel had no problem keeping the market supplied.

More to the point, OPEC was still amassing huge profits—the member states' oil export revenues shot up 42 percent in 2004, to more than $338 billion—while taking pains to reassure its victims that its motives were pure. Saudi Arabia's Crown Prince Abdullah had long promised that his country was "willing and ready" to pump any amount of oil "necessary to stabilize the world oil market." The new wrinkle was the war in Iraq; but right from the beginning of the U.S. crackdown on Saddam Hussein, OPEC ministers promised they would not profiteer or use oil to retaliate for such an attack. If the war were to disrupt supplies, vowed Algeria's energy minister, Chakib Khelil, "We will satisfy the demand in the market, whatever the reason."

In between dispensing such soothing words, the oil barons liked to argue that OPEC was "unfairly blamed" for high prices. During the 2004 run-up of record prices, al-Naimi had the gall to declare to reporters, "People in power know that crude supplies have nothing to do with the current gasoline prices in the U.S." He said the real problem was a shortage of refinery capacity in the United States— in other words, the victim was cutting its own throat. Previously, at an OPEC meeting in September 2000, Crown Prince Abdullah had outrageously proposed that Western governments "share the sacrifice" with producers by cutting their taxes on oil.

Prince Bandar bin Sultan, Saudi Arabia's gadabout ambassador to the United States, chimed in to rebut those "politicians and media commentators [who] have attempted to score political points by misrepresenting" Saudi motives. In a *Washington Post* op-ed written during the middle of the hotly contested U.S. presidential campaign, Bandar tried to beat down speculation that the Saudis' summer pledge to increase production was part of a "secret deal" to boost President Bush's prospects. Bandar stuck to the party line: "Saudi Arabia has always stood by America and the world when our intervention was required to stabilize oil prices . . . [and] maintain strong national and global economies."

Whatever the Saudi *raison du jour,* the drill was the same: Stoke fears of insecurity when prices begin to weaken; rush in to assure adequate supplies no matter what when runaway prices threaten to hurt long-term demand and political relationships.

Riddles, contradictions, and concerted efforts to confuse and obscure the relevant issues are the stock-in-trade of the Saudis and their OPEC fellows. In their constant obfuscation over prices, these apologists often argue unconvincingly that oil is somehow a more uniquely political commodity than, say, wheat or copper. They love to float the phony notion that the "inflation-adjusted" price isn't even all that high. In their distorted view, the real record price was reached back in 1981, when the oil price of $38 was equivalent to $72 a barrel in 2004 dollars. This is a particularly exasperating kind of doubletalk that is not applied to any other commodity. The fact is, the price of anything is determined by its value in the present economy; thus no commodity's price can be usefully compared with whatever its price happened to be in some other era. Why don't we hear about the "inflation-adjusted" price of wheat, copper, or steel?

But don't think doubletalk and obfuscation are reserved solely for outsiders. They are a staple of relations among OPEC members themselves. For instance, the cartel's price mechanism relies on production quotas to keep the oil price in a predetermined narrow range. But in 2004, as throughout much of OPEC's history, these quotas were a hollow fiction. Everyone knew, even before Purnomo's August admission, that most members were exceeding their preset limits. This meant that any sure-to-be-trumpeted increase in the formal quota would simply legalize what was already being pumped, without adding a single drop to actual production.

What was really happening? In theory, the cartel's official target price was still in the range of $22 to $28 a barrel. Below $22, OPEC would supposedly cut its production quota enough to raise the price.

Above $28, it allegedly was committed to pumping more oil to soften the market and bring the price down. But even though the target was never officially changed, the price averaged $30 a barrel between 2000 and 2004. Who could doubt that member nations relished every added nickel they raked in as the market soared toward $50?

As the price charged ahead, even the Saudis seemed to abandon their well-rehearsed worrywart act about pushing the price too high, which could trigger a recession and encourage the West to look for alternative energy sources. Al-Naimi told reporters at an OPEC meeting in December 2004 that the price band was still in place—quickly adding, however, that investors, producers, and consumers all seemed to agree that $30 was a fair price. Then, with the market price over $42, al-Naimi proposed to cut the cartel's production quota by 1 million barrels a day on the ground that the price might drop soon. If any further proof of OPEC's rapacity were needed, that move alone provided it.

A few weeks later, al-Naimi finally dropped all the pretense. Speaking to a Reuters reporter at the World Economic Forum in Davos, Switzerland, in January 2005, he said, "My view is the world is not suffering. . . . The price today doesn't seem to be affecting economic growth negatively." Translation: full speed ahead toward a higher target and baseline price, the upwardly mobile market-price starting point from which OPEC calculates its price band. Saudi Arabia, OPEC's most powerful member and once the self-appointed voice of reason against hotheaded price hawks like Iran and Venezuela, was itself championing a target price closer to $40 a barrel.

Just where the new price band would eventually settle remained unclear following OPEC's late-January meeting in Vienna. Iran reportedly had wanted $30 to $40, while Nigeria proposed $45 to $55, and Libya's representative suggested $60 a barrel. The only issue not in dispute was the dramatic change in the Saudi position. Whatever it had become, Saudi Arabia was no longer the voice of moderation.

Amid all the confusion, concealment, OPEC-induced panic, and self-serving Saudi doubletalk, a number of questions begged for answers: How often do the OPEC producers deliver on their promises? What had become of the Saudis' new capacity of 12 million barrels (maybe even 15 million), disclosed at the height of the hysteria in the summer of 2004? No one seemed to know. Talk turned once again to cutting production quotas and raising the OPEC price band. Apparently there was no need to offer soothing words. Higher oil prices (the NYMEX crude price hit $57.79 in April 2005) seemed to have been cravenly accepted by consumers and governments.

And it didn't stop there. Fueled by the continuing turmoil in Iraq, political unrest, and a bad 2005 hurricane season—all of them, of course, relentlessly exploited by OPEC's and the oil industry's propaganda mills—the price rose jaggedly all year and kept on jumping. Except for the chronic Iraqi oil woes and the Nigerian insurrection that cut off 20 percent of the country's production, nothing really calamitous occurred in the first half of 2006. But as spring became summer, the good-cop/bad-cop routine continued, the markets were panicky, and speculators in hedge funds helped push the price even higher. In July, it reached what is still at this writing its all-time record: $78.40 a barrel. And with that, predictably enough, the oil price fell back; OPEC knew when it had gone far enough to test the limits of political tolerance. After another spike triggered by the closing of a pipeline on Alaska's North Slope, the market drifted down through the $70s and then the $60s. There were the usual explanations, as thin and unconvincing as the ones justifying higher prices: Inventories were high and demand was down. The winter was unusually mild.

But when the price for a barrel fell below $55, OPEC voted for enough production cuts to hold the price above $60—presumably, the floor of a new target range, with the ceiling who knew where? Some of the members cheated on their new low quotas, and early in 2007 the price fell briefly below $50. But it rose again, hanging at this writing around $60 a barrel. How high would it go? Some traders guessed the price would stay where it was for the rest of the year; some were betting it would go back to $70 or more. And as always, the peak theorists were predicting the imminent crash of production and oil selling for $100, bankrupting the world economy.

Whatever the level turned out to be, OPEC still had us over its barrel. Now all it had to do was sit back and collect the money.

A Little Help from Our Friends

We can't blame OPEC alone for fleecing the world economy and taking an intolerable toll on our future. The oil-security shell game would have collapsed long ago were it not for the collusion practiced by the oil industry and major governments, most notably the United States.

The time has long passed when OPEC nations were at war with the oil industry, trying to break the monopoly of the infamous Seven Sisters, the major oil companies whose treaties with desert sheikhs cemented their dominance in the oil fields. The companies discovered years ago that the high prices OPEC craved were good for them, too, fattening profits all along the pipeline, from the oil fields through the refineries to the gasoline pump. That's why, when crude oil prices climb, there tends to be only token protest from the industry; applying their traditional margins to the new price structure, the oilmen can chuckle all the way to the bank.

The industry also prefers price "stability," even at high levels, to sharp fluctuations that could change the basic calculus of energy investment. After the first great "oil shock" in 1973, when the Arab nations embargoed oil bound for the West, the industrialized nations set up the International Energy Agency (IEA) to encourage the search for new oil outside of OPEC and explore alternate energy sources. But as soon as serious investments were made in more expensive production from fields like the North Sea and Alaska's North Slope, the IEA began to fear that a return to cheap OPEC oil might make these efforts worthless, whereupon it joined the rest of the industry in becoming a cheerleader for high prices and promoting the illusion of a fragile supply.

In support of that cause, the industry gives remarkably little scrutiny to OPEC's fuzzy production numbers. When all is said and done, the supposedly independent analysts and consultants, who typically parrot OPEC's party line in the media, are mostly on the payroll, directly or indirectly, of the oil industry or those who benefit from high prices. So it isn't surprising that they accept, with straight faces, whatever fictions they are fed by the people who give them their consulting assignments and award them contracts. It was a rare acknowledgement of reality when Kyle Cooper, an analyst at

Citigroup Global Markets, commented on the evident mismatch of supply and demand in the oil market in the fall of 2004. "We now are 8.3 million barrels above last year in terms of gasoline [inventories]," said Cooper. "Yet we are 50 percent higher in terms of price. I'd like someone to explain that to me."

The clear explanation was that the price had been pushed to irrational levels by cultivated panic. But, of course, no one thought to offer the truth.

On the face of things, OPEC's unlikeliest ally might seem to be the United States government. Why should Washington collude in a highway robbery that costs the American people billions of dollars a year? Part of the answer is the excuse that the government, like the industry, favors stability in the energy markets. But it seems reasonable to question whether stability is worth the enormous premium that American consumers pay.

Be that as it may, we can be forgiven for suspecting that a larger part of the reason for our collusion with what can only be called an economic adversary has to do with political alliances. President George W. Bush, an oilman and the son of an oilman, has lifelong ties to the industry. As detailed later in this book, it was his father, Vice President George H. W. Bush, who flew to Saudi Arabia in 1986 to make the deal that put OPEC back together and began the price spiral that has fattened oil patch profits at the whole world's expense ever since. And in the 2000 election that put the current president in the White House, individuals and political action committees from the oil industry ponied up some $35 million in contributions, the lion's share going to Bush and his Republican colleagues. Over the six years from 1998 to 2004, the Center for Public Integrity reports, the oil and gas industry showered more than $440 million on political parties and politicians, and on lobbyists whose job it is to influence those very same politicians. If you believe this has nothing to do with government energy policy, please clap for the tooth fairy; she needs your help.

Again, let's go to the bottom line: Throughout the price gyrations and near-panic in the oil market in 2004, George W. Bush refused to follow the example of two former presidents, Bill Clinton and his own father, by releasing oil from the Strategic Petroleum Reserve (SPR) to damp down soaring prices. When consumer advocates urged tapping the reserve, the administration, citing genuine national security concerns after 9/11, said such an action would be inappropriate except in a major disruption of supply. There was surely a case to be made for using the reserve to prevent high prices from damaging the nation's economic security. Instead, President Bush chose to increase the SPR from 600 million barrels right up to its newly expanded capacity of 700 million barrels, thus compounding the problem. With demand high and supplies tight, every drop sent to the SPR depleted the available stocks of oil and sent prices still higher. The president authorized briefly tapping the reserve only after Hurricane Katrina decimated oil output in the Gulf of Mexico in August 2005.

Apart from the impact that the release of even small amounts of oil from the SPR could have had on market psychology, the president also passed up the opportunity to send an unmistakable message to OPEC: Had he pointedly suspended adding to the SPR when the price rose past $35 a barrel, he would have made clear the limits of our price tolerance.

Adam Sieminski, an energy analyst for Deutsche Bank, spoke for many of us when he asked, in the *Christian Science Monitor* of June 3, 2004, "Why are we buying oil at $40 a barrel when most people think it's going back to $30 a barrel?" Of course, after the president failed to change the market mindset or signal our displeasure with OPEC, $30 a barrel became nothing more than a fond memory.

What the president did was give OPEC both a kiss and a conspiratorial wink: First, the show of affection said, in effect, we don't care how much your oil costs just as long as you let us keep buying it from you; and, second, we can rationalize paying these prices as long as we all pretend this is really the free-market price. In other words, President Bush gave OPEC every incentive to keep inflating the price. So all through the two-year escalation of the oil price, until April 25, 2006, our own government was adding to the demand by buying oil on the market, at prices up to $60 a barrel, to pump into salt domes in the Gulf of Mexico. Had it not been so insanely costly, this unfathomable policy might have been the stuff of comedy.

If any doubt remains that our president is solidly in OPEC's corner, consider what has happened in Iraq. After toppling Saddam Hussein and taking over his government, the United States could easily and sensibly have ended Iraq's membership in OPEC. Doing so would have removed the nation's vast reserves of crude oil from the cartel's arsenal of weapons arrayed against the West and the world economy, measurably weakening OPEC's power.

No such luck. The Bush administration named Philip J. Carroll, a former Shell Oil executive, to head up a modest "advisory committee" to the Iraqi oil ministry. Carroll insisted that he was there only to make suggestions and claimed to have no veto power. Pointing out that Iraq had been a founding member of OPEC, Carroll said Washington had no business trying to influence that relationship.

Carroll's successor, Rob McKee, another old hand in the oil business, was even more obliging. A former ConocoPhillips executive who had become chairman of Enventure, a Halliburton drilling-supply subsidiary, McKee set to work building a strong Iraqi national oil company that can go along to get along in the OPEC cartel. The state-owned assets would be operated by international oil companies, whose profit motives mesh so perfectly with the exorbitant prices forced on oil consumers by OPEC. The April 2005 edition of *Harper's* describes how McKee turned to a select handful of "Big Oil" consultants and executives to draft a 323-page plan for Iraq's oil industry, "even if he had to act over the objections of the Iraqi Governing Council." In short order, Iraq was back at the OPEC table, gleefully helping tighten the noose around our neck.

Just how gleefully became evident in January 2005, when Dhiaa al-Bakka, the head of Iraq's State Oil Marketing Organization (SOMO), said Iraq would slash exports from its southern region by 10 percent. The cutback was scheduled to last five months, until the end of June. SOMO blamed insurgent attacks or bad weather for the cutbacks, but how could it have known about these problems in advance—or known that they would last for five months? It seemed more likely that the Iraqi agency was bowing to OPEC demands to cut oil production in order to tighten the market and drive slightly weakening prices higher again.

Were this just another typical move by a short-sighted and self-serving OPEC member, we might shrug it off. But the fact that it came from Iraq, where more than three thousand Americans have lost their lives and thousands more have been gravely wounded, points up the utterly perverse nature of the oil situation we have helped create. While we are spending billions of American taxpayer dollars in an effort to bring stability to Iraq, it has joined forces with OPEC against us.

It is also a sad reflection on the state of our government and its allegiances that nothing has been heard from Washington about this betrayal.

Media Mayhem

In the end, no matter who promotes it, the reason for OPEC's success is the fiction of oil insecurity. But this doesn't discount the role played by the world's news media in cementing the myth. Far from it. With rare exceptions, the media have swallowed the myth whole and broadcast it with gusto.

In the summer of 2004, for example, when the market price stood well above $40, the *New York Times* ran a lengthy dispatch empathizing with OPEC as the cartel, in the newspaper's view, tried in vain to bring enough oil out of the ground to force the price back below $28 a barrel, then the high end of OPEC's ceiling. It was the OPEC party line taken at face value.

Beating the drum of conventional wisdom again, the *Times* followed up early in 2005 with another sympathetic piece that concluded: "Many of the issues that have vexed the oil industry in 2004 are expected to recur. Cheap oil increasingly looks like a thing of the past. . . . While demand has steadily increased each year, the industry's exploration efforts have not kept pace in new discoveries. . . . There is no cushion left in the system to weather a potential blow."

In yet a third piece, when NYMEX prices were edging toward $60 a barrel in mid-March, and just after OPEC had offered up a moderating 500,000-barrel increase in production quotas, the *Times* opined that "for OPEC, the situation is paradoxical since the group is uncomfortable with today's high prices. . . . But there is not much OPEC can do. Its 11 members are pumping close to 29 million barrels a day and do not have much more production capacity left to tap."

Nor was the *Times* alone in its fanciful assessments. Many publications hewed to the cartel's line. In January 2005, for instance, the *Wall Street Journal* duly reported OPEC drivel clearly designed to prepare the world for still higher prices. A *Journal* story asserted that "China's rising demand would increase dependence on the group in 2005. However, [OPEC] added that it would be able to meet global demand."

Sticking to its seesaw script, OPEC had bad news ready to counter the good. The reassuring report from headquarters was followed by a warning from Venezuela's oil minister, Rafael Ramirez, that the cartel would waste no time in tightening the spigot if need be. And just in case a reader had dropped in from Mars and didn't know that oil supply levels were precarious, the *Journal* reporter ended her dispatch with a foreboding pipeline bombing in Iraq, a strike threat in Nigeria, and, incredibly, news that fog had closed the Houston ship channel. Would rain in Spain be cause for worry next?

Occasionally, a reporter got the story at least partly right. Another dispatch from the *Journal* noted that, "to some extent," the oil market was "confusion by design."

But the media weren't altogether to blame. Journalists depend on their sources, and without reliable, audited, official statistics, they have no better idea of production capacity and security than anyone else. What is more, the people they usually talk to in the industry tend either to believe the myth themselves or to be part of the conspiracy. Journalists normally consult a source's detractors to assure credibility, but in this case even the opponents have fallen prey to the fallacy. Environmentalists and consumer advocates are among the firmest believers in the insecurity of the world's oil supply.

Ultimately, what members of the media seek are riveting stories, and the threat of imminent supply disruption will always trump a tale of business as usual. Why break your pick getting at the truth when the conventional wisdom is so much more accessible and interesting?

For the rest of us, though, the price of living in the shadow of fiction and deceit is intolerably high. Every glittery bauble and stretch SUV in Saudi Arabia represents wants and needs unfilled for those of us who spend good money for a cheap, plentiful commodity whose price has been artificially inflated. What we need is to admit the obvious, apply a dose of calm, rational thinking, and begin treating oil as a commodity like any other. At that magic moment, OPEC's power will evaporate.

3

Oil Poor

Nigeria is big, and it is diverse, stretching across an area of West Africa that would cover California twice over, with 137 million inhabitants who represent more than 250 ethnic groups and speak scores of languages. They reside in climates ranging from equatorial in the south and tropical in the midsection to arid in the north. They live and work in a land that contains a wealth of renewable and nonrenewable resources; rubber, tin, columbite, iron ore, coal, limestone, zinc, and natural gas are all abundant. Yet despite these many natural blessings, one resource alone rules Nigeria's economy: oil.

Nigeria is the world's sixth-biggest oil producer and a major member of OPEC. It is also the second most corrupt country in the world, according to Transparency International, an anticorruption watchdog based in Berlin. Financially, politically, and morally, oil is strangling Nigeria. How can a gift of nature cause such destruction?

As night follows day, so oil persistently fuels corruption in the poorly governed states where it is now most likely to be found. Initially, oil is hailed as a panacea for poverty. It is no panacea. Quite the opposite. In oil boom states from Chad to Angola to Nigeria, sudden wealth typically erodes initiative, weakens institutions, invites crooks, and entrenches despots. Oil is the Pied Piper of Third World hopes. A poor country that discovers petroleum under its barren land is like a lottery winner who squanders his windfall and crashes six months later. Nothing is more disorienting than the illusion that you have struck it rich for life.

Oil ultimately turns into a toxic substance, a curse to those nations "blessed" to sit atop it. A country with vast oil reserves has no incentive to put its human talents to work creating anything new, much less doing mundane chores like cleaning the streets or picking up the garbage. For those dreary tasks, one imports labor. All that the rulers of an oil-rich country need do is rent out the premises to foreign drillers and then cash their colossal checks for as long as internal combustion engines shall ferry the human race.

The plague decimating Nigeria is the result of an overabundance of oil, but the condition goes by the more general name "resource curse." It affects resource-abundant nations outside the OPEC circle, of course, but the devastation becomes even more horrific when the power and influence of the wholly corrupt oil cartel is injected into the mix. The combination of a weak domestic government and outside manipulation by an influential and self-serving force like OPEC prolongs and intensifies the suffering of a country's less fortunate citizens. OPEC is all about sustaining OPEC. This means maintaining the injurious status quo at whatever cost—a status quo that allows the cartel to continue robbing the world economy and keep its gang of thieves firmly in control in each of its member nations.

Consider the effect that the resource curse has on a country's leaders. There is no need to tax anyone, no need to protect property rights, no need to worry about accountability or pay even the slightest attention to the ordinary citizenry (the only exceptions being the usual few hotheads plotting revolution). For their part, the untaxed find little reason to complain. They need not do any work if they live in one of the earthly paradises staffed by poor Filipinos or Pakistanis brought in as virtual indentured servants. Those few citizens who do grumble, perhaps irked by the elite's self-indulgence, have no real way to make the government answer for its failings.

In the end, all the oil remains firmly in the hands of a few unchecked rulers, who, aided by OPEC, inevitably abuse their power. It seems unavoidable, a basic paradigm of human existence. When a country runs on a single resource, or suddenly discovers one, and this treasure is controlled by a select few, the winners spend huge amounts of time and money eliminating rebellious losers and making sure that nothing like a free press, dissident political party, or independent judiciary gets in the way. Should it be deemed necessary to hold an election, if just for appearance's sake, the incumbents in an oil state are sure to win, since they control not only patronage and the police, but also who gets to vote (relatives, party hacks, state employees) and who doesn't (critics, ethnic outcasts, women).

A neglected and ill-functioning economy, massive corruption, and human pain inevitably follow when oil is in abundance and the policies of OPEC hold sway. This chapter surveys the devastation wrought by too much oil and the money it attracts, using Nigeria, Venezuela, and Saudi Arabia (OPEC members all) as sad examples. But every OPEC nation displays the symptoms of the same disease. Indeed, Josef Joffe, the publisher of *Die Zeit* and a research fellow at the Hoover Institution, has described Saudi Arabia as a "pious kleptocracy." And if not all its OPEC brethren exhibit the same degree of piety, they are all well and truly kleptocracies. As the pages ahead reveal, dishonesty, bribery, and immorality of every sort are the oozing sores of a society awash in oil wealth.

Poisoned by Oil

Countries that should be rich by virtue of their oil wealth are, in fact, poor. A well-known 1995 study by economists Jeffrey Sachs and Andrew Warner, both Harvard professors at the time, discovered that some of the biggest economic breakdowns in recent memory came in countries where oil and other natural resources are plentiful. Studying ninety-seven developing countries, Sachs and Warner found that the bigger the role played by a natural resource in a country's economy, the lower the country's rate of economic growth. At its simplest, the explanation boils down to too much of an ostensibly good thing distracting a nation from nurturing the other resources and talents needed to support a productive society and economy.

To understand the curse of oil, it helps to look at the evolution of modern development theory as it pertains to economic and political advancement in non-industrialized nations. In the 1970s, the experts, taking their cues from the astounding success of Europe's Marshall Plan, sought to help poor countries by financing their physical infrastructures (dams, roads, power plants). Such hardware, it was thought, would work quickly to shore up fledgling governments in newly independent nations. But the policy failed. So in the 1980s, with little progress against poverty to show for the many billions of dollars spent, the global policy wonks switched to a model known as the Washington Consensus. The idea was to promote generous economic incentives to attract foreign private investment, the benefits of which would, in turn, seep down to the masses.

But that approach also failed to pan out as the lifeline for sub-Saharan Africa. Nor could the theorists explain why Asian countries, notably China, followed a very different model and blossomed. So development policy took yet another turn. The experts discovered the importance of all the intangible assets that sustain markets and save them from damaging swings: the traditions of trust, reliable contracts, property rights, honest courts, social loyalties, and so on—all the things noticeably lacking, whether by coincidence or by design, in the OPEC nations.

It is the longtime presence of such checks and balances, it turns out, that allows a democratic country to take sudden oil wealth in stride, as the United States did in the late nineteenth and early twentieth centuries, and as Norway has done more recently. It is their absence in less-developed countries that can turn an oil windfall into a cyclone that sweeps away every incentive for growth and development, leaving only a few tyrants and crooks preying on a nation of paupers. In the OPEC nations, we see the consequences of such corruption writ large.

History suggests that human and social assets are better indicators of national success than natural resources. In the 1500s and 1600s, "poor" little England and Holland outdid mighty Spain, despite all the gold and silver its conquistadors had stolen from New World indigenes. In the early 1900s, Japan, rich in culture, poor in resources, readily defeated Russia, an autocracy with huge natural resources but a tottering political system. In our time, tiny Singapore, with no oil but blessed with an educated and skilled population, has greatly overshadowed oil-rich Nigeria and Venezuela, both of which are wallowing in political and economic chaos.

According to a 2003 study sponsored by the financier-philanthropist George Soros, growth in resource-poor countries began to outrun growth in resource-rich countries in the 1970s. By no coincidence, 1970 marked the upsurge in world oil discoveries that have since bedeviled their beneficiaries.

Just why oil wealth seems to corrupt and impoverish nations is a question with multiple answers. The boom-and-bust cycle of natural resources is one explanation. Global prices for oil, copper, natural gas, and the like traditionally fluctuate depending on which way the global economic winds are blowing. Problems arise when the governments of resource-rich nations spend their windfalls and more, only to find themselves strapped for cash and forced to make drastic cutbacks when prices retreat. Even if official corruption is not draining off funds from health, housing, and education programs designed to lift the masses, the unreliability of resource income makes lasting gains difficult, if not impossible, to achieve.

Economists also cite "Dutch disease" when explaining the resource curse. Named for the malign effects of natural gas discoveries in the Netherlands in the 1960s, it broadly refers to the destructive consequences of rapid increases in a country's income. This theory holds that a sudden boom in oil, or any other resource from gold to coffee, causes a jump in foreign revenues that inflates a country's currency and crowds out other economically valuable activities. In a country awash in money from natural resources, everything begins to cost more, including labor. Starting up a factory, say, to make shoes for Nike or Reebok, becomes economically unviable. High labor costs would make the shoes too pricey to compete in a global market. Rising prices also make it harder for domestic producers to sell their goods; they simply can't hold their own against a flood of cheaper imports in the home market.

With capital and labor mostly siphoned away into the booming resource sector, existing manufacturing and domestic farming begin to shrivel. This decreases technical skill, management know-how, and on-the-job training. Exports dwindle, and the nation's trade balance tips to the negative. Growth fades in just about every area except bankruptcies and jobless workers. Entrepreneurial drive itself withers because no other wealth-creating mechanism seems as easy and attractive to tap as the prevailing natural resource industry.

So instead of spending time trying to invent new wealth, people are focused on trying to get their hands on some of the existing resource lucre. The most common way is by getting a job in the industry or—as in Saudi Arabia, where few citizens work in the private sector—by procuring a government sinecure that is directly supported by oil money. To understand the debilitating effects of such a mindset, one need only contemplate, by way of contrast, the immense wealth created in America by railroads, automobiles, and computers, none of which was there before someone did the hard work of invention.

When a single resource rules, economists become particularly worried that the loss of opportunities to "learn by doing" will stifle the development of skills, thus inhibiting long-term growth potential. If a country's manufacturers can't even get into the competitive race, the experts argue, how can they ever gain the experience needed to stay and win? Economists put great store in manufacturing because it develops the finance, production, marketing, and distribution skills needed for success in many other areas of global business. An economy based solely on the export of raw material, on the other hand, gets back little knowledge from abroad and is not exposed to the ongoing technological innovations that propel the modern world of business to ever-greater accomplishment.

Not to be overlooked in the search for answers to oil's corrupting influence is the inherent power of abundant natural resources to stymie a country's desire and ability to construct strong, workable political institutions. Typically, natural resource wealth is controlled by an elite group that selfishly opposes democratic reform, or by state-run monopolies that foster bureaucratic incompetence and invite official corruption because of the huge sums of money flowing from the booming resource. Having no reason to tax the citizens and no incentive to safeguard property rights in order to generate new sources of wealth, governments can rule without restraint. When there is no one to answer to, muscular and democratic political institutions cannot take root.

Nowhere is the toxic fallout of a natural resources boom more apparent than in the OPEC nations, all of which began to rake in enormous sums during the 1970s. In the decade following the organization's decision to ignite an explosion in oil prices, the price of a barrel of oil tripled to $30. While consumers suffered, the OPEC nations spent recklessly on government boondoggles, which are detailed in the chapters ahead. As political power became concentrated in the hands of a few, political problems, civil wars, worsening poverty, and corruption became the order of the day.

One of the founders of OPEC, Venezuela's Juan Pablo Perez Alfonso, sensed early on that oil wealth would be fraught with danger and famously labeled oil "the devil's excrement." Nigeria, though certainly not the only country drowning in a cesspool of oil, so completely reveals the sad and sometimes appalling effects of the curse as to make it a prime case in point of Perez Alfonso's prophetic wisdom.

Nigeria Sickened by a Diet of Oil

In its first thirty-five years as a petro-power, from 1965 to 2000, Nigeria took in roughly $350 billion of oil revenues. Yet during that time, the number of poverty-stricken Nigerians living on less than a dollar a day soared from a dispiriting 36 percent to an alarming 70 percent.

Long ruled by generals who failed to diversify the economy, Nigeria saw its domestic industry collapse; capacity utilization rates plunged from 75 percent to 30 percent. The agriculture sector crumbled as well, transforming a food exporter into a net importer. The environment was degraded by oil pollution, with an estimated four thousand major oil spills since 1960 in the Niger Delta, which sits above most of the oil. That's an average of seven spills every month, and cleanup efforts have been mostly perfunctory. As non-oil business plunged, so did the average Nigerian's purchasing power; per-capita gross domestic product stood at only $320 per year in 2003, putting Nigeria in the bottom tier of World Bank rankings.

What is more, violence has flourished and crime has run rampant over the decades. Since the late 1960s, disputes over controlling Nigeria's oil have triggered ten coup attempts (six of them successful), the assassination of two national leaders, three decades of military dictatorship, and a civil war that killed a million people. Carjackings and kidnappings are commonplace today, as are daylight muggings and robberies.

In the Niger Delta, oil riches have brought nothing but poverty and misery to the local Ogoni and Ijaw people. The labyrinth of rivers and creeks that used to teem with fish is now polluted and largely depleted. Repeated promises of local development have been broken; many schools and health clinics are empty shells, and unemployment in the region tops 90 percent. In 2006, an angry insurgent movement has kidnapped foreign oil workers, triggered car bombs, sabotaged pipelines, and killed at least thirty-seven Nigerian soldiers and several guards at oil facilities. For most of the year, the insurgency cut Nigeria's oil production by up to 500,000 barrels a day, more than a fifth of the total capacity, costing the government and the big oil companies $30 million a day.

An especially brutal mix of poverty, crime, and resignation to wrongdoing among Nigerians allows for a thriving international trade in people—young people, mostly girls recruited for prostitution in Europe, Saudi Arabia, and neighboring African countries. The girls are beholden to "sponsors," who charge them thousands of dollars for the privilege of working outside the country. (Some victims are duped into thinking they will be working in legitimate jobs or going to school.) They sometimes find their way back home, but not all are welcomed with open arms. Parents have been known to berate a daughter for escaping her captors instead of continuing to prostitute herself until she can repay her sponsors and then bring home extra cash that will make her a neighborhood somebody. Nigerian children also fall prey to domestic trafficking, in which impoverished parents readily send their girls and boys into slavery.

Oil so dominates Nigeria that it is almost the sole medium of power and wealth. The country is divided between those in the oil business—whether buying, selling, or stealing—and everyone else. Nigeria professes to be a democracy, but corrupt politicians raise campaign funds by hiring armed thugs to steal and sell crude oil from pipelines. An estimated 7 percent of the country's daily output of 2.5 million barrels of oil disappears this way. The proceeds are used not for television campaign commercials, but for buying weapons and goons to intimidate voters. And the political battles are escalating; the weapon of choice as the April 2007 presidential election approached was the AK-47 assault rifle.

Oil provides 90 percent of Nigeria's foreign-currency earnings and two-thirds of the federal government's revenues. This flood of cash evaporates, however, long before it reaches the masses, leaving nothing but toxic fumes. It is usually reckoned that federal and state governments have stolen or wasted $380 billion since 1960, even more than the total of oil revenues, with at least $100 billion in the pockets of corrupt officials. Bribes—known as "kola nuts," "brown envelopes," or "welfare packages"—are a way of life, from the highest government offices to traffic cops manning checkpoints. When Fabian Osuji, the education minister, was caught buying votes from lawmakers for $400,000, his defense was that this was "common knowledge and practice at all levels of government." It was also a good deal, he said, since he paid only half what was demanded. He was fired anyway.

Most of the money lubricates the corrupt godfathers of Nigeria's 36 state governments and 774 local governments. Late in 2006, no fewer than 31 of the 36 state governors were under investigation for crimes and corruption. The governorships are so lucrative that three candidates running for the office were killed during the year, and the *Economist* reported that "political mafias in some parts of the country have been buying up thugs and unleashing them on each other in anticipation of a bloody race for power." Those who have achieved power blithely raid the public treasury to maintain their iron grip. They constantly squander oil revenues on patronage schemes, buying off political opponents, hiring armed gangs to beat up stubborn rivals, and funding such absurdities as the huge Ajaokuta steel plant. This boondoggle ran up a tab of more than $5 billion over twenty-five years before ever producing a ton of steel.

A full member of OPEC since 1971, Nigeria is one of the world's oil giants, with reserves of light, sweet crude oil now estimated at 40 billion barrels. Yet its inflation rate (now 20 percent) is rising so fast that millions of people can't afford to buy the oil they need for cooking and heating. Many Nigerians have taken to stealing from pipelines, and many lose their lives in the resulting fires and explosions. The Nigerian populace, already rent by ethnic and religious conflict, has become increasingly enraged at its oil-induced poverty. In May 2004, hundreds died in sectarian massacres that were exacerbated by oil inequities. Christian mercenaries butchered Muslims, who then slaughtered Christians in turn. Alarmingly, many politicians inflame such religious and ethnic grievances to win votes, sparking fears that another Rwanda might be in the making.

In what might be seen as a bit of poetic justice, the crony capitalism that the major oil companies have so long practiced in league with OPEC and the corrupt leaders of the countries in which they operate is coming back to bite them. Royal Dutch/Shell, for instance, which initiated exploration in Nigeria a half-century ago and today gets about one-tenth of its oil production there, is being pushed to the brink by the pervasive violence. Despite its admittedly "less than perfect" efforts at community building, the company finds itself battered by the effects of crime, corruption, ethnic feuding, and poverty—all part and parcel of the oil curse it helped spawn.

President Olusegun Obasanjo, who may or may not be a reformed sinner in a distinctly dishonest society, was once a cheerleader for the alleged blessings of oil in a poor country. No longer. In a recent public blast at Nigeria's deteriorating condition, which was reported by the *International Herald Tribune,* Obasanjo cried out, "Oil and gas have blinded us. Oil and gas have taken away from us the values we used to know. Oil and gas have brutalized us."

A former military ruler, Obasanjo won election in 1999 after he voluntarily gave up power. He ran on a platform of fighting corruption, and after two terms he had achieved some progress: In its first three years, the new Economic and Financial Crimes Commission has won convictions in 91 cases, sending some 2,000 people to prison. A drive is under way to cut 20 percent of Nigeria's civil service employees, many of whom are "ghost workers" who do nothing but collect their paychecks. But Obasanjo has made himself oil minister, limiting public scrutiny of the oil sector. He also tried to change the constitution to allow himself to run for a third term. Some $400,000 was reportedly paid in bribes to senators, but the senate voted down the change.

Venezuela Gags on the "Devil's Excrement"

When Venezuela's former oil minister, Juan Pablo Perez Alfonso, predicted that oil would bring ruin, people scoffed. After all, he uttered his famous forecast when petroleum production was filling Venezuela's coffers with unimagined wealth. But now, in a striking and oft-repeated economic paradox, Venezuela and most of OPEC's other members also suffer, to a greater or lesser degree, from the Nigerian syndrome. Fabulously rich in oil and natural gas, their societies have become distorted, ruled by a privileged few at the expense of the ever-poorer many.

Poverty in Venezuela has almost doubled since 1970, with 80 percent of national income going to business owners and only 20 percent to ordinary workers. In the decade between 1988 and 1998, the number of Venezuelans with twelve years of education who were living below the poverty line jumped from 2.4 percent to a shocking 18.5 percent.

During the oil price frenzy of 2004 through 2006, Venezuela's oil revenues leapt to $50 billion a year, touching off a boom of consumerism among the prosperous that has doubled auto sales and tripled mortgage loans. The country's leftist, populist president, Hugo Chavez, has distributed much of the oil wealth to the poor, fattening government programs in health care, education, and housing. But the curse persists: There are ever-more poor who need help. In the Lake Maracaibo area, which boasts one of the world's largest concentrations of oil, a growing contingent of unemployed oil workers tries to cope with rapidly escalating living costs. It is a losing battle. Venezuela, like most of the world's resource-dependent economies, suffers from the Dutch disease.

Venezuala struck oil in the first decade of the 1900s. But it took more than five decades under the rule of two dictators, one military junta, and assorted legally elected presidents before Venezuela evolved into a relatively affluent country. In the early 1960s, it was a functioning democracy with the highest per-capita income in South America.

Then in 1973, thanks to the inevitable fight over the control of its suddenly exploding oil wealth, Venezuela became a cauldron of anger, corruption, national labor strife, attempted coups, and quasi civil war. The struggle has sapped the country's political and economic institutions, allowing strong-arm factions to take over and leaving Venezuela with a lower per-capita income than it had in 1960.

Chavez, the current president, insists that he is the champion of the poor and has threatened to nationalize large chunks of the Venezuelan economy. He has moved aggressively to assert control over the oil industry, renegotiating contracts with major companies and demanding state dominance in the development of huge deposits in the Orinoco Basin. Chavez has also demanded the power to rule by decree, bypassing his legislature, and he reportedly wants to be made president for life. But he has not moved to diversify Venezuela's industrial base and reduce its dependence on "the devil's excrement."

With estimated reserves approaching 1 trillion barrels (including the extra-heavy oil in the Orinoco belt), Venezuela had long been considered a reliable and relatively close source of oil for the United States. Chavez shattered that assumption in 2002 and 2003, when a series of strikes erupted in protest of his efforts to control and manipulate the oil sector. Eventually, 18,000 workers at the state-owned oil company were thrown out of work, and the production, refining, and export of oil came to a standstill for three months. Some 200 million barrels of oil and gasoline were withheld from the world market, and neither the Venezuelan economy nor its citizens were allowed to benefit from a potentially huge injection of export earnings. Never before had Venezuela's oil shipments been halted completely, and never before had a Venezuelan leader willingly cut off his country's lifeline simply to impose his political will.

Then there is Chavez's controversial arms buildup. The former army paratrooper turned politician has decided to spend hundreds of millions of Venezuela's petrodollars not on badly needed social programs, but on high-tech military equipment. Plans include the purchase of twenty-four multipurpose combat planes from Brazil, at a cost of $170 million, and 100,000 assault rifles and military helicopters from Russia. Chavez reportedly has also been negotiating a $4 billion purchase of Russian-built MiG fighter planes.

No one disputes that Venezuela has the right to modernize its military, but observers like Miguel Diaz, a senior analyst at the Center for Strategic and International Studies in Washington, D.C., question the scale and timing of the purchases. Noting that Chavez's political career began when he led two unsuccessful coup attempts in 1992, Diaz worries that the always provocative leader may be "inclined to follow through on his often-repeated threat to arm his supporters for the purpose of intimidating the opposition." Others fear that he may be planning to arm leftist rebel groups in neighboring Colombia. Given that the number of Russian rifles Chavez is buying exceeds the number of legitimate Venezuelan soldiers, these fears are not unreasonable.

But whatever Chavez's real motives, one thing is clear: For all the talk about revolutionary social policies and development that doesn't leave the poor behind, nothing much has changed for the ordinary Venezuelan, who is still mired in poverty and unemployment despite the nation's enormous oil wealth.

As for the mood of the people, the cyclical swings that typify an unstable industry like oil have engendered a boom-and-bust mentality. The people have grown used to a government that behaves in schizophrenic fashion, spending wildly when times are good and abruptly pulling back when oil prices sour. The trouble is, many government programs can't be turned off and on at will, so the state is periodically forced to live beyond its means on borrowed money—tax hikes being out of the question. Venezuelans balk at paying any taxes, since the state is thought to be awash in petrodollars. As one former Venezuelan president famously remarked, "In Venezuela, only the stupid pay taxes."

Venezuela offers a broken-record replay of the stories that have spun out across the oil-producing Third World ever since OPEC began to tighten its grip on consumers and squeeze out maximum profits for member states. Venezuelans struggle in a fun-house economy that makes citizens of a richly endowed country dependent on government handouts and imports from abroad. The nation produces little in the way of exportable goods other than oil and allows its fertile land to lie fallow while foodstuffs are shipped in from foreign fields. Hobbled by a simplistic belief that God put the oil under their feet because he wanted them to be wealthy, many Venezuelans simply expect their government to redistribute the nation's existing riches. It follows that hardly anyone is interested in trying to create new wealth. As the public sector expands, the private sector shrinks. It is a deadly combination.

Saudi Royals Threatened by Terrorist Ties

No country has reaped more riches from oil than Saudi Arabia. In fact, it is fair to say, no other country even comes close. Yet Saudi Arabia is poor in innovation, poor in initiative, and poor in self-reliance. Increasingly, its citizens are just downright poor, as an exploding population vies for what little is left after the famously extravagant Saudi princes indulge their every whim.

In an oligarchy, the few rule the many. In the Saudi oligarchy, more than 100 male descendants of the founding patriarch, King Abd al-Aziz, hold sway in senior government positions over the other 22 million Saudis. All told, some 7,000 male descendants of the prolific king receive government stipends. The royals have long held the view that they own Saudi Arabia and its enormous stores of underground wealth. They can do with it as they please. Regarding the Saudi people as mere subjects, the ruling class metes out benefits from the oil riches in the form of royal charity. In the beginning of the great oil boom, average Saudi citizens received education and health-care benefits. Many received government sinecures.

In the 1980s, however, as the population grew rapidly while oil prices fell, economic troubles germinated. With nothing but oil supporting its economy, the government eventually slid into deficit and could not keep up with the demand for public sector jobs and entitlements. Spending on the ruling elite continued unchecked, of course, leaving the Saudi people to suffer the consequences of a bloated bureaucracy, gross fiscal mismanagement, and a dysfunctional, largely noncompetitive private sector dominated by the royal family and its cronies. Income per capita, which had reached $18,000 in 1982, was cut in half by 2006.

Economic problems are just the beginning. Despite archives of photos showing smiling Saudi princes being feted by fawning U.S. government and oil industry figures, Saudi Arabia has one of the world's most repressive regimes. Women are second-class citizens. Religious freedom is nonexistent, as the U.S. State Department belatedly recognized in a 2004 report. "Non-Muslim worshippers risk arrest, imprisonment, lashing, deportation, and sometimes torture," the report said, but even devout Muslims are not safe if they choose to practice something other than the state-sponsored Wahhabi brand of Islam.

Started by Ibn Abdul Wahhab in the mid-1970s, Wahhabism is an extremist Sunni sect that dictates strict observance of the prophet Muhammad's teaching based on a literal reading of the Koran. Among its precepts are the punctual performance of public prayer; modest dress, especially for women; and prohibitions against music, dancing, and the use of alcohol or tobacco. Many of Ibn Abdul Wahhab's teachings are similar to those of other fundamentalist sects, but where they differ is in the insistence on conformity under pain of death. Wahhabism also urges the faithful to commit acts of violence against nonbelievers. One of the sect's most famous adherents is Osama bin Laden, the exiled son of a prominent Saudi family.

The Saudis consider it a sacred duty to propagate the faith because Islam began in their country. Islam's two holiest sites, Mecca and Medina, are located in Saudi Arabia. Thus, the ruling Saudi princes have spent tens of millions of dollars exporting their intolerant religion around the world. They have helped create a tangled web of government-sponsored and private charities that aim to make puritanical Wahhabism the prevailing doctrine in the Islamic world. Thousands of mosques, Islamic centers, schools, and colleges have been financed with Saudi oil money. Reams of Wahhabist propaganda have been distributed. Much of the missionary work has been directed at the United States and Europe, where Islam is not the predominant religion and where nonbelievers are considered fair game by militant Wahhabists. Deadly terrorist attacks in Britain, France, Indonesia, the Netherlands, and Spain, as well as the 9/11 attacks in the United States, have been attributed to Sunni Muslim fundamentalists.

The activities at Germany's King Fahd Academy have drawn special notice. At this white marble structure built with $20 million donated by its namesake Saudi king, Muslim students hear calls for violence against nonbelievers and are versed in the glories of martyrdom as servants of Allah. Originally founded in 1995 on the pretext of educating the children of Saudi diplomats posted to Germany, the school wasted little time in reaching beyond its mandate and bringing the children of German-born Muslims under the influence of its dangerous theology. Indeed, the school defiantly ignored German law to recruit local children.

Parents of the students at King Fahd Academy, many of whom have themselves been accused of links to terrorist organizations, defend their academic choice as nothing more than an effort to educate their children according to their cultural beliefs, in the manner normal to schools in Saudi Arabia. No doubt, they are being absolutely truthful, which is what makes the situation so frightening.

There are schools like King Fahd Academy in numerous countries, where malleable young minds are being inculcated with beliefs that call for the destruction of the infidels. This means anyone who doesn't practice Wahhabism, including other Muslims. School curricula in institutions run by members of this extremist sect are almost wholly devoted to religious teaching, at the expense of math and science and the humanities, thus ensuring that graduates will be unfit for the modern world—and that hatred of the West and all it stands for will be dominant for generations to come.

The Saudis claim that the problem is not with the religion of Islam but with those who wrongly interpret it. They insist they have tried to stop the diversion of missionary funds to terrorist causes. And ironically, since the first Gulf War, the royals themselves have begun to feel threatened by the zealots they have financed—and in many cases continue to finance. Extremists have accused Saudi rulers of desecrating holy ground by bringing in the infidel Americans to defend them against Saddam Hussein. Internal discontent over government policies has been rising, and Islamic militants have killed scores of people in bombings and shootouts.

Saudi Arabia's ruling family has apparently decided that idle and increasingly poverty-stricken hands are the devil's workshop. It is now directing more of its oil windfall into new job training programs and other initiatives designed to put people to work. These efforts center around ejecting foreign workers from jobs that Saudis could do, including positions in the building and food trades and computer-related work.

Yet even as they grapple with massive unemployment, poverty, subpar housing, and insufficient social services, many Saudi citizens seem unwilling or unable to take advantage of the available opportunities. Long conditioned to having others do the work for them, or perhaps trained for more skilled jobs that do not exist in the Saudi economy, they are reluctant to take on what they consider to be demeaning labor. Meanwhile, nothing has been done to reform the private sector, where people of privilege operate through monopolies that largely exclude the average Saudi citizen and, because they are protected by Islamic law, pay no taxes on their earnings.

A few insiders are concerned enough about the growing discontent to push for economic and social reforms. *Okaz*, a Saudi newspaper, printed an article in 2002 that called for drawing "the sword of conscience in the face of the lazy and the crooks." But it is hard to imagine that the ruling princes, who believe the country's treasure is theirs to squander, will easily give up their control.

Funny Oil Money Turns Up at Riggs Bank

A select few may take command of oil wealth, destroy all rivals, and sell petroleum for as much as the market will bear, but these toll keepers do not act alone. Their corrupt behavior is aided and abetted by toll payers, notably the multinational oil companies that notoriously compete for extraction rights by buying off the toll keepers. At least thirty-four such companies paid to recover the Angolan government's oil in recent years. How much, to whom, and for what they paid are secrets to which even the companies' auditors are not privy.

Such is par for the course in a murky world that laughs at the notion of transparency, with no legal pressure to divulge the massive bribes that presumably win drilling rights in corrupt oil-producing countries like Nigeria. But the estimated $100 billion skimmed by Nigerian officials to date was not manna rained down from heaven. Uncovering shady deals is tough, but not impossible.

If George Soros has his way, it may get easier. As part of his campaign to address the rampant corruption associated with natural resource extraction, Soros and his Open Society Institute are promoting an international "Publish What You Pay" initiative that would force publicly listed oil and mining companies to divulge details of their payments to governments. "Sadly, U.S. oil companies have thus far resisted," the institute's Thomas Palley noted in an article posted on the Open Society website. "[They claim] that corruption is a government problem. The reality is that corruption is a systemic problem."

Unless and until the established system is changed, perhaps the most promising route is to trace the toll keepers' stash, which is presumably deposited in safe hideaways outside their own not-so-safe countries. Which brings us to the Riggs National Bank of Washington, D.C., a capital institution that counts Abraham Lincoln and Jefferson Davis among its past depositors. In more recent times, Riggs has drawn attention because of the large shadow cast by its former controlling stockholder and sometime chief executive officer, Joe L. Allbritton, a charming Mississippi octogenarian and patron of the arts. Allbritton's five-foot stature belies his towering presence on the Washington social scene, as well as his ownership of a personal fortune estimated at $500 million.

Riggs itself is pintsized as banks go, but its less-than-dazzling balance sheet did not dampen Allbritton's enthusiasm for its global cachet: The bank specializes in serving Washington's foreign embassies and U.S. consulates worldwide, a mission that fit like a glove on the hand of Allbritton's social ambitions. For some thirty years until he sold the bank to Pittsburgh's giant PNC in 2005, Joe Allbritton helped keep Riggs close to Washington's diplomatic and political elite, the black-tie-and-champagne crowd he favors.

Its longtime social prestige notwithstanding, however, Riggs proved an embarrassment in the years just before its sale. Banking regulators, congressional investigators, and federal agents were all searching its records for evidence of terrorist financing, money laundering, payment of bribes to oil executives, and collusion on the part of a bank examiner who became a bank employee. In the end, the bank paid civil and criminal fines totaling $41 million. Allbritton himself escaped censure, except perhaps for having paid more attention to the bank's social glitter than to its depositors' transactions. Indeed, Riggs's relaxed attitude toward banking rules and red tape was a major drawing card for wealthy clients.

Not everyone appreciated the bank's tastefully discreet manners, as it turned out. In July 2004, federal regulators, disturbed at the bank's laissez-faire policies, publicly rebuked Riggs and levied a $25 million regulatory fine for neglecting to follow rules aimed at stopping money laundering. Federal officials were investigating its role in handling deposits by the former (and now deceased) Chilean dictator General Augusto Pinochet, as well as officials of Equatorial Guinea. These disclosures were particularly embarrassing to Riggs, coming as Pinochet, who ruled Chile from 1973 to 1990, awaited trial on charges involving human rights violations. It turned out that Riggs's involvement with Pinochet went back to 1979—far earlier than originally suspected—when the bank began helping him move his money through accounts hidden from regulatory scrutiny.

In January 2005, Riggs admitted criminal negligence in the money-laundering schemes and agreed to pay an additional $16 million fine. Federal prosecutors called it the largest criminal penalty ever imposed on a bank of Riggs's size.

Another major Riggs client used to be Prince Bandar bin Sultan, who from 1983 to 2005 was the highly connected Saudi ambassador to the United States. Before September 11, 2001, Riggs bankers merely beamed when the prince and other Saudi diplomats routinely withdrew a few million dollars on their way to weekend parties in London. After the terrorist attacks, things changed. The FBI's suspicions that Saudi money might have bankrolled the hijackers led to scrutiny of Riggs accounts controlled by Bandar and his wife, Princess Haifa. No smoking gun has been found as yet, but subsequent bank activities by Bandar and his wife raised eyebrows. After a series of very large and very quick deposits and withdrawals in the prince's personal accounts, Riggs officials finally bestirred themselves to ask Bandar what he and his wife were up to. He refused to answer. The Saudis no longer bank at Riggs, a decision each party says it arrived at first.

As scrutiny of the global monetary mess intensified, it was probably only a matter of time before blue-chip oil companies, a corrupt African oil kingdom, and an enormous sum of suspicious money would enter the picture.

In 2004, congressional investigators began delving into Riggs accounts held by the notorious dictator of Equatorial Guinea, Brigadier General Teodoro Obiang Nguema Mbasogo. A Senate panel was particularly curious to know why Simon P. Kareri, the Riggs executive who handled the bank's Equatorial Guinea accounts, personally dragged a sixty-pound suitcase stuffed with $3 million in plastic-wrapped packets of $100 bills into a Riggs branch for deposit. Kareri refused to answer, invoking the Fifth Amendment.

Until February 2004, Riggs managed $360 million deposited by the once impoverished West African country, which is notable these days mostly for oil discoveries and human rights abuses. The tangled skein of shady deals, sloppy oversight, and money laundering started to take shape a decade earlier, the Senate committee said, when Riggs began opening and managing more than sixty accounts for Equatorial Guinea, its officials, and several of President Obiang's family members. Operating like a Swiss bank on the Potomac, asking few if any questions, Riggs "turned a blind eye to evidence suggesting the bank was handling the proceeds of foreign corruption," the panel found. At their peak, Equatorial Guinea's accounts at Riggs, largely stocked with royalties from oil production, are said to have totaled as much as $700 million, which would have made the country the bank's largest customer.

Equatorial Guinea has been the wholly owned property of Brigadier General Obiang since 1979. Before vast deposits of oil were discovered in its offshore territory in the early 1990s, hardly anyone cared much about the tiny nation tucked into what has been called the armpit of West Africa. But Obiang's predecessor, Francisco Macias Nguema, was a clinically insane despot who outdid even Uganda's Idi Amin with his record of unspeakable torture, murder, plunder, and self-delusion. (He once ordered the managers of his capital's power plant to stop lubricating the machinery, explaining that he would make it run by magic. After the plant exploded, the city went dark.) By the time Macias was overthrown and executed by Obiang, his nephew and chief enforcer, one-third of Equatorial Guinea's population was dead or in exile.

Obiang was an improvement over Macias, but that's not saying much. In his supposed democracy, any genuine opposition is harassed and assaulted. He has survived several attempted coups, including a farcical plot involving Mark Thatcher, son of the former British prime minister Margaret Thatcher. Obiang controls all television and radio broadcasts, and there are no newsstands or bookstores. Elections are open frauds, with vote counts supporting the president by margins in the high 90s. According to the United Nations and the U.S. State Department, arbitrary arrests and torture are routine in Equatorial Guinea. Before the International Monetary Fund insisted on some nominal controls, Obiang treated the national treasury as his family bank account. He has bought himself a Boeing 737 for $55 million, and his son and probable successor, Teodoro Nguema Obiang Mangu, once went on a shopping spree for cars in Cape Town, South Africa, springing for two Bentleys and a Lamborghini in a single afternoon.

That, of course, was after the oil was discovered and Equatorial Guinea became Africa's third-largest producer, pumping oil worth

$6 billion a year. The oil—and the prospect that China would surely move to grab it if the West didn't—also sanitized Obiang's unsavory image. He has visited with President George W. Bush in the Oval Office, and Secretary of State Condoleezza Rice has hailed him as "a good friend" of the United States.

Obiang began banking with Riggs in 1995. Taking personal banking to new highs (or rather, lows), Riggs opened a slew of accounts for Obiang and his relatives, set up shell corporations for them, and lent a helping hand when the general and his wife wanted to stash $13 million of cash in their Riggs accounts. In addition, some $35 million of government oil money made its way, via Riggs-sanctioned wire transfers, into "private" company accounts, at least one of which Obiang is thought to have controlled.

The United States had been on the outs with Obiang since the mid-1990s, but diplomatic relations were resumed in 2003 when the Bush administration and oil interests were trying to secure oil supplies outside the Middle East. Even before the resumption of formal ties, however, American oil companies including Exxon Mobil, Amerada Hess, and Marathon Oil had poured some $5 billion into the country. According to the *Los Angeles Times,* payments went to buy protection from a company owned by Obiang's brother; to lease buildings from other relatives, including a fourteen-year-old landlord; and to pay college tuition costs for scores of students from elite families, among other things. To be fair to the companies, they had little choice. Since Obiang and his family own nearly everything of any value in the country, it is difficult to find anyone else to do business with.

Exxon Mobil, a major player in the region, was the point man in some of Obiang's dubious dealings, supplying cash as part of a profit-sharing arrangement with the dictator's regime in exchange for drilling rights. Naturally, Exxon Mobil can't discuss the details of the deal; it is confidential. All the company will say is that the contract requires it to pay Equatorial Guinea income taxes, oil royalties, and something called "legal obligations." The deal provided much of the money in the regime's Riggs accounts, which were officially described as government treasury funds requiring multiple signatories, but which, in practice, were apparently controlled by Obiang.

All these arrangements should have raised red flags at Riggs. They didn't, at least not until September 2003, when federal investigators ratcheted up their inquiry. In reviewing their accounts, Riggs executives discovered that a company called Otong, controlled by General Obiang, had opened a Riggs account through which the company passed millions of dollars from suspect sources.

Riggs examiners questioned Kareri, the executive who oversaw all the bank's Equatorial Guinea accounts. Kareri said Otong's big money came only from foreign accounts elsewhere that Obiang had closed, transferring the funds to Riggs for safekeeping. This explanation fell flat with Riggs officials, who suggested that the money was derived from bribes or political graft involving American oil company executives.

In January 2004, Kareri's bosses at Riggs caught him in a peculiar impropriety. He allegedly asked Obiang's son in Washington to give him money to buy a car. The son reportedly handed over a signed but undated check for $40,000, leaving the payee line blank. Kareri is said to have changed the value of the check to $140,000, filled in the payee line with the name of a friend, and then managed to have the funds sent to his wife. Riggs subsequently fired Kareri.

Meanwhile, Riggs officials uncovered more unusual transactions in which Equatorial Guinea oil money was switched to offshore accounts for unknown reasons. Asked to explain, Obiang came to Washington to meet with Riggs officials, but then took offense at their questions and walked out. Riggs finally closed all of its Equatorial Guinea accounts, blaming the whole mess on the departed Kareri.

The corruption continues. Despite the recent IMF reforms of Equatorial Guinea's financial procedures, the State Department acknowledges that Equatorial Guinea's oil wealth is not being used for the public good. Spending on health and education is minimal, and life expectancy in the country has fallen to less than forty-four years. Under Obiang's leadership, law enforcement in Equatorial Guinea is said to include chopping off ears, smearing naked bodies with substances attractive to stinging ants, and murdering prisoners by smashing their skulls with iron rods.

Accursed by OPEC, but Too Blind to See

Perhaps the worst thing about oil wealth is that it seems to corrupt the minds and hearts of all complicit parties—government officials, oil companies, banks, and even entire countries and cultures. A black sticky substance pumped out of the ground provides a self-justifying excuse for valuing easy money over creativity and vital work, over true enterprise, over democracy, even over life itself. And as the 2004 scandal over the Oil-for-Food programs showed, it has corrupted everything from the United Nations on down. (The ignominious Oil-for-Food program is discussed in detail later in this book.)

It is hard not to conclude that oil and its corruptions have had a profoundly enervating effect on all too many countries, particularly Muslim ones. Instead of freeing young minds, male and female, to thrive in the modern world, these countries often seem to cultivate stagnation and inspire resentment against progress. Arab cultures that once pioneered key mathematical and scientific concepts now seldom invent or patent anything. They don't even bother to trade with one another.

The West may yearn to end its dependence on OPEC oil, but in many ways the OPEC nations are even more destructively dependent. The terrible irony is that countries seemingly blessed with reservoirs of underground wealth can become so completely addicted to a resource-based economy as to end up impoverishing their cultures and their people.

Unlike China, Japan, or Korea, which will grow in spite of their need to import oil, the OPEC petro-economies see their true wealth spiraling downward in spite of their richly abundant resources. Their oil dependence deadens minds, kills initiative, and numbs hopes. It leaves millions of people furious at—though well funded by—the West, unable to look inward at their own strengths and weaknesses, and unable to summon their talents to meet the West on a level playing field. For them, oil dependence is an abiding curse, the ultimate corruption, and OPEC is the master evildoer, the terrible genius that is choking the life out of its members.

4

Global Warming— the New Time Bomb

For a long time, I was agnostic with regard to global warming. Sure, I thought, the earth is getting warmer; the statistics are pretty clear. And probably the warming is being caused, at least in part, by human activity. But why rush to solve a problem before we're sure how bad it might be, or what's to blame? After all, the planet was even warmer 125,000 years ago, when humans were only rubbing sticks together to make campfires. Let's wait, I thought, until all the facts are in and a consensus is settled.

Then, early in 2006, I went to China and what I saw stirred me to change my mind. It was horrifying, a nation shrouded in a suffocating blanket of pollution. Yellow-brown smog hung over the new highways and boulevards, obscured the tops of the soaring new buildings, and hid the magnificent details of the ancient Forbidden City. China's air is so foul as to erode real estate values in Hong Kong, and particles of soot from the People's Republic can be found as far away as California. It left a constant rank taste in my throat and gave me a nasty, hacking cough.

One day in Beijing—when the wind changed direction—the pollution magically lifted, and I saw what China could be without it. From my hotel window, I gazed at actual mountains forming a real horizon. No more than twenty miles away, they had been invisible for days. Then, poof; the next day they were gone again. Somehow, that glimpse of what China had lost was even more striking than the smog itself.

I came home a convert, utterly convinced that if we don't stop fouling the planet, we will surely kill it. The sheer magnitude of what I experienced was enough to persuade anyone of the danger, and, as I knew, that was just the beginning. The breakneck pace of China's economic boom, already the wonder of the world, seems likely to continue, and China's leaders have shown little interest in doing anything to clean up their polluted air. Sure, now that Beijing will be hosting the Olympics in 2008, China is making a Herculean effort to clean up the capital city's air before the games begin. And China's leaders plan to build twenty to thirty nuclear power plants by 2020, generating no carbon dioxide, methane, nitric oxide, nor sulfur dioxide emissions.

But that doesn't change the fact that Chinese leaders argue openly that it's only fair they be allowed to emit at least as much pollution as the United States has produced while they race to catch up with us. That won't take long: In this decade, China is expected to become the number two economy in the world and the number one polluter, surpassing America as the biggest source of emissions.

I also knew that what I saw during my visit to China wasn't the worst of it. The smog was merely the visible token of the unseen mix of effluents, the greenhouse gases that are trapping heat in the atmosphere and inexorably raising the earth's temperature. Even if we could clean up every tailpipe and smokestack tomorrow, the gases already aloft would keep warming the planet for years to come. Even if we start immediately to defuse it and work as fast as we can, the world that our grandchildren will inherit risks being far different from the earth we know.

I'm not alone in this epiphany. In the past year or so, the accumulating weight of evidence seems to have produced a sea change in public attitudes about the dangers of global warming. Most significant is former vice president Al Gore's book, *An Inconvenient Truth*. It was a number-one bestseller in 2006, and his accompanying film won the Academy Award for best documentary. It has been speculated that he might be in line for the Nobel Peace Prize.

For its audiences—myself among them—the film was a powerful experience. Narrating it, Gore came across as a thoroughly believable advocate—by turns rueful, objective, impassioned, and funny, but always reasonable. He translated scientific facts and arguments into plain language, and he accompanied his words with ominous charts and striking graphics of melting glaciers, sundering icebergs, submerged shorelines, and the destruction wrought by Hurricane Katrina. He noted that ten of the last fourteen years have been the warmest on record and that the Gulf Stream and the jet stream have undergone portentous changes. He pointed to record-setting typhoons in Japan and the Pacific and core sampling of polar ice that shows the greatest level of carbon dioxide in the atmosphere in 250,000 years.

He acknowledges that the earth, as his critics are quick to point out, does indeed undergo cyclical patterns; atmospheric carbon dioxide has increased and receded over the centuries. But, standing in front of a graph charting the ups and downs, Gore traces the line through recent years as it rises higher and higher until it simply runs off the chart. The earth is headed for a tipping point, he says: "The world won't 'end' overnight in ten years. But a point will have been passed, and there will be an irreversible slide into destruction." What's more, he says evenly: "There is no controversy about these facts. Out of 925 recent articles in peer-reviewed scientific journals about global warming, there was no disagreement. Zero."

Of course there are other voices, but this carping is mostly disingenuous, an attempt to create the appearance of real debate in the face of a settled consensus. Just as the tobacco industry kept denying the dangers of smoking for twenty years after the surgeon general issued his warning, or just as the Iranian president Mahmoud Ahmadinejad staged his "scientific debate" over the reality of the Holocaust, Big Oil and those in its pay have continued to throw up a smokescreen to obscure the truth and only recently in the face of public condemnation are beginning to relent.

For most people the scientific clincher came on February 2, 2007, together with the report finalized on April 6, 2007. The United Nations' Intergovernmental Panel on Climate Change (IPCC), a group of scientists and reviewers from 113 countries that is recognized as the authoritative body of climate scientists, formally concluded that global warming is "unequivocal" and that human activity has "very likely" caused most of the rise in temperatures since 1950. In the dry scientific language of the IPCC report, "very likely" means a degree of certainty between 90 percent and 99 percent. The report went on to warn that the buildup of greenhouse gases would inevitably bring centuries of climbing temperatures, rising seas, and changing weather patterns. The scientists also declared that prompt remedial action could substantially reduce the damage.

According to the IPCC, the average temperature on earth has risen by 1.4 degrees Fahrenheit since the late nineteenth century, and the IPCC warned that in less than fifty years, greenhouse gases will probably heat up the global climate by another 3.5 to 8 degrees. Sea levels, which rose by 6 to 9 inches in the twentieth century, will be 7 to 23 inches higher by 2100, and the greenhouse gases already present will keep the sea rising for at least a thousand years to come. Heat waves and torrential rains will become more frequent. Hurricanes will intensify. More rain and snow will fall in higher latitudes, but droughts will worsen in already arid zones. Carbonic acid, formed as the oceans absorb billions of tons of carbon dioxide, will make the seas less alkaline, and the falling pH level could imperil corals and plankton and disrupt the aquatic food chain.

Bad as they are, the IPCC's conclusions were deliberately understated, since its charter prohibits anything approaching speculation. Left unanswered were major questions about the speed and extent of some looming changes—such as the impact of melting polar ice caps on sea levels, because there is no scientific consensus on how fast the polar ice caps may melt. Some climatologists complained that the report wasn't strong enough. But its restraint made it scientifically unassailable, and the panel itself noted that there was a 10 percent chance—a significant risk—that there could be much greater warming than it predicted. As Achim Steiner, executive director of the United Nations Environment Program, summed up the findings, "The evidence is on the table. The new report gives us a stark warning that the potential impact will be more dramatic, faster, and more drastic in terms of consequences than previously thought." Or, as the *Washington Post* editorialized, "For mainstream science, it's settled."

The issue even seemed to be settled at the White House, where President George W. Bush had for years been calling for definitive proof that the world was heating up and that our use of fossil fuels was to blame. Now the administration issued a statement mildly blessing the report as "a comprehensive and accurate reflection of the current state of climate change science." But the statement added that the administration "has put in place a comprehensive set of policies to address what President Bush has called the 'serious challenge' of climate change," and claimed that "the current set of policies are working." In other words, no change was needed—and the energy secretary, Samuel Bodman, underscored that message when he dismissed the notion that the United States should act promptly to impose its own limits on carbon emissions. "We are a small contributor to the overall, when you look at the rest of the world, so it's really got to be a global solution," Bodman said. This administration sadly always finds a reason not to take forceful action on this gathering crisis. Leading by example seems to be a foreign concept. Instead, the president suggests that voluntary, market-driven efforts will be enough to deal with the issue. That's somewhat akin to hawking life vests on the promenade deck of a sinking *Titanic*.

For the international community, which had been chafing for years at Washington's refusal to go along with the Kyoto Protocol to limit global warming, the IPCC report came as welcome ammunition for the diplomatic battle. The UN's new and energetic secretary general, Ban Ki Moon, warned that the danger posed by climate change was at least as great a threat as "the danger posed by war to all humanity—and to our planet." Ban promised to push the Group of Eight leading industrialized nations, including the United States, to take new steps to curb emissions and to write a new treaty to replace the Kyoto Protocol when it expires in 2012.

Europe was willing. A month after the IPCC report landed, the twenty-seven member nations of the European Union set tough new limits on greenhouse gas emissions, pledging to reduce their pollution to 20 percent below 1990 levels by the year 2020. The new agreement will require the EU to generate one-fifth of its power from renewable sources, and to replace 10 percent of its auto and truck fuel with biofuels. And in a pointed challenge to Washington and other noncompliant governments, the EU said it would raise its overall reduction in emissions to 30 percent if other nations would join the cause. The British government went a step further, proposing a bill in Parliament that would force a 60 percent reduction in emissions by 2050. Then the EU touched off a political firestorm in Germany by proposing speed limits on the Autobahn, a measure that would eliminate several million tons of carbon dioxide emissions per year instantly and at no cost. German drivers were outraged, but the pressure from the rest of Europe seemed likely to persist.

Many of America's political conservatives have derided global warming as an environmentalist fantasy and fought off efforts to curb it, but in the new Zeitgeist, many are rethinking their beliefs. Writing in a *Washington Post* op-ed piece early in 2007, South Carolina's Republican governor, Terry Sanford, warned his fellow conservatives that their stance had "conceded the high ground to those on the far left." The call for government action is resonating around the world, he wrote: "Make no mistake, the issue of environmental conservation sits squarely on the battle line between government and liberty. From light bulbs to automobiles, government will gladly expand its regulatory reach even if the result is a hamstrung economy and curtailed individual freedoms." Sanford argued that the right must reframe the debate in terms of responsibility and conserving resources, "treating our environment as an investment our future depends on." And I can only applaud his conclusion: "When corporations such as BP and Shell America pursue alternative energy sources, they not only cut carbon emissions but help cut our petroleum dependency on OPEC nations."

Sanford's comments are an indication of the sea change that is currently taking place. This is an issue that crosses party lines. The nation's citizens are far more aware of its implications to their lives and their children's lives than our political leaders, whose time frame extends to the next election and the vested interests to be serviced in the meantime.

Without leadership from Washington, state and local governments around the country are already taking steps to recycle, clean up, and prevent further damage to the environment. Led by New York, seven northeastern states have joined the Regional Greenhouse Gas Initiative aimed at creating a joint program to reduce emissions. Step It Up, an environmental activist group, has organized no fewer than 870 small protests featuring marches, walks, swims, parties, and prayer meetings in forty-nine states to push for an 80 percent cut in emissions by 2050.

And people are increasingly willing to spend their own money for a cleaner world. Sales of power-saving compact fluorescent bulbs and fuel-efficient refrigerators and air conditioners are soaring, and efficiency ratings on appliances of all sorts are becoming commonplace. Customers at Whole Foods Market, the national organic food chain, are adding "wind power cards" priced at $5 to $15 to their shopping carts. The cards pledge that Whole Foods will send the money to Renewable Choice Energy, which uses it to subsidize wind farms feeding clean power to the grid. Similarly, people booking a vacation can offset a portion of the jetliner stream by paying $10 to $40 to the Conservation Fund to plant trees, thereby offsetting the carbon footprint of their vacation.

Utilities are also getting into the act, offering their customers a chance to buy more expensive "green power" from renewable sources, including wind and solar. More and more companies are finding it worthwhile to make the offer. At least one, California's Pacific Gas & Electric, plans to add a line to monthly bills pinpointing how many pounds of carbon a customer's electricity usage added to the atmosphere and suggesting a dollar amount, usually less than $5, that would cover the cost of buying offsetting carbon credits from clean-power projects in the state.

In fact, what may be the most significant and surprising manifestation of the new response to global warming is coming from corporate boardrooms. (As the *New York Times* recently editorialized, "Each day seems to bring news of another prominent convert to the cause.") In a striking sign of this role reversal, no fewer than seventeen panels discussed the global warming issue at the 2007 World Economic Forum in Davos, Switzerland. Many companies, previously fervent deniers of the entire problem, are now in the forefront pushing for solutions and gainfully polishing their images as friends of the environment. To the point where ten of the nation's biggest companies—including Alcoa, DuPont, and General Electric—joined leading environmental groups in January 2007 to call for federal mandates aimed at reducing emissions by 10 to 30 percent over the next fifteen years. Then, Chrysler, Ford, General Motors, and Toyota, the country's four largest automakers, hitched a ride on the green parade by voicing their support for emissions caps, provided they apply to all sectors of the economy.

Another sign of changing times came when a Wall Street mergers and acquisitions consortium, responding to environmental concerns, forced its quarry, the TXU Corporation, to clean up its act and change its ways. The giant Texas utility was under fire from environmental groups for its plans to build eleven huge coal-fired power plants. The Wall Streeters, sensing a potentially enormous problem, approached TXU's critics, Environmental Defense and the Natural Resources Defense Council, to negotiate a deal: The environmentalists agreed to sanction the takeover if TXU would promise to forgo building eight of the plants, support an emissions cap, double its purchases of wind power, and plow $400 million into energy-efficiency programs. The transaction has not as yet been finalized, but these negotiations have broken new ground. Never has there been a better demonstration of the growing power of conservation issues and their impact on the industrial and financial concerns of the nation's and the world's economy.

For example, American Electric Power (AEP) is leading the development of a promising cleanup technique designed to capture carbon dioxide from coal-burning power plants and pump it deep underground. The company's process, to be tested in an $800 million project in West Virginia in 2008, uses chilled ammonia to liquefy the carbon dioxide and then pumps it 9,000 feet into the earth. A crucial question will be whether the gas finds its way back to the surface; but in other test projects, carbon dioxide pumped into oil wells to raise the pressure in aging oil fields has remained safely underground. AEP is also experimenting with a more complex technology that converts coal to a gas and removes the carbon before it is burned.

Major investments in alternative energy—OPEC's biggest nightmare—are already in the works. BP, for instance, is carefully repairing and cultivating its image as an environmentally friendly oil company. That image was badly marred when a long-neglected Alaska pipeline sprang a leak and had to be shut down, and safety problems caused a Texas refinery fire that killed fifteen BP workers and injured 180. Nevertheless, the company has committed itself to spend $8 billion over ten years on alternative energy and has already made several major wind- and solar-power acquisitions. BP says it has a potential 6.5 gigawatts of wind energy and expects $1 billion in revenues from solar power in 2008.

Even giant Exxon Mobil, an OPEC cheerleader that has long been a favorite target of environmentalists' fury, has apparently seen the green light—or enough of its reflection, at least, to soften the company's position on global warming ever so slightly. CEO Rex W. Tillerson, one of the movers and shakers at the Davos gathering, took pains to erase the line drawn in the sand by his predecessor, Lee Raymond. "It's not useful to debate [global warming] any longer," Tillerson said. But being the Exxon true believer that he is, Tillerson couldn't cast off the long-held party line quite so easily. Within a few weeks of his Davos performance, he was referring to ethanol as "moonshine."

Later, Exxon's vice president for public affairs, Kenneth P. Cohen, speaking on a conference call with reporters, denounced as "flat wrong" any assertions that Exxon was discounting global warming. Saying Exxon wanted "to be part" of the congressional debate on new measures, Cohen even labeled as "a definite maybe" a cap-and-trade limit on emissions, something the company had long scorned. The Exxon defender skewed the facts when he tried to claim that the oil giant had never denied global warming, but the message was clear: Exxon is moving away from its hard-line stance. And even if the $100 million it donated to climate research at Stanford University is modest for a company that took home an all-time record profit of $39.9 billion in 2006, it was still change tossed into the right cup, with the hope of more to come.

Giants like Exxon and Alcoa, Ford and GE have enormous potential to change the world, but giants move ponderously. Some of the most interesting and promising efforts to curb global warming are coming from small, lively businesses scattered around the country.

The Timberland footwear and apparel company, for instance, has analyzed extensively the "carbon footprint" it leaves on the environment. Timberland found that more than half the energy it uses goes to produce and process its raw materials. Its investigation extended to the point where CEO Jeffrey B. Swartz discovered how much methane came, believe it or not, from the flatulence of cows whose skins he buys. Remarkably, and to his credit, he worked with his suppliers to give the cows a less gassy diet.

Timberland has also developed what it calls "green index tags" for its boots and shoes. The tags alert customers to the environmental cost of producing the footwear, scoring each product from 0 to 10 on three key criteria: its use of chemicals; the proportion of recycled, organic, or renewable materials it contains; and the carbon emitted in its production. The lower the number, the smaller the impact. A carbon rating of 0, for example, means that less than 4.9 kilograms of carbon equivalent were emitted, while a 10 denotes 100 kilograms or more, the equivalent of burning eleven gallons of gasoline. In the long run, the tags will be more useful if they can be employed to compare shoes from several makers, and Timberland hopes to sign up rival companies to follow suit.

But even if competitors were to agree, consumers would still have only the manufacturer's word backing up the tag's accuracy. Another approach comes from Gary Hirshberg, CEO of the Stony-field Farm yogurt company. Hirshberg has helped found a nonprofit group called Climate Counts to act as a kind of independent auditor to verify corporate claims of greenness. Stonyfield itself says it has become carbon neutral in its manufacturing, meaning it has eliminated emissions from its production of yogurt to the greatest extent possible, offsetting what remains by buying carbon credits. Like at least a dozen other companies, Stonyfield has also committed to donating 10 percent of its profits or 1 percent of sales, whichever is greater, to environmental causes.

Some of the most ambitious and visionary efforts to curb global warming are happening in Silicon Valley, where, as the *New York Times* has noted, the "dot-com era may be giving way to the watt-com era." High-flying companies that were grounded by the bursting of the Internet bubble in 2000 are gearing up to revolutionize the trillion-dollar energy market, the *Times* reports, and "venture capitalists are pouring billions of start-up dollars into energy-related start-ups with names like SunPower, Nanosolar, and Lilliputian Systems."

The goals of the fledgling ventures range from improved batteries and more efficient solar cells to biofuels made from algae and exotic schemes to scrub huge quantities of carbon dioxide from the atmosphere. But many of these companies are secretive and warily competitive. Dan Whaley, head of a San Francisco company named Climos that aims to use an organic process to remove carbon from the air, says he won't describe "the thing I'm working on" except that it must have scientific credibility. His own entrepreneurial credentials are beyond question: Whaley's previous startup, a travel site called GetThere.com, was bought by Sabre in 2000 for a global-cooling $750 million.

The watt-com trend has already produced an industry trade group, Cleanup Venture Network, which reports that $474 million of venture capital poured into Silicon Valley energy startups in the first three-quarters of 2006. The shorthand term for the work, the *Times* reports, is not green, "a word that suggests a greater interest in the environment than in profit." Instead, the Valley that used to be high-tech now talks about "clean tech."

In the absence of leadership on the national level, state and city governments are taking the bit in their teeth and moving to curb emissions, impose energy-efficiency standards, and control waste. Both Colorado and the state of Washington have passed renewable-energy standards in ballot initiatives. And up in New Hampshire, the annual ritual of town meetings had a new theme in the spring of 2007: Fully 180 of the state's 234 cities and towns had on their agendas a resolution urging the federal government to deal with climate change and support research on alternative energy. The measure also called for local solutions to global warming and told town selectmen to consider forming energy committees.

But no state government has moved further, faster, or more effectively to deal with global warming than California, which has set the standard for cleaner living in the twenty-first century. Californians first began thinking seriously about energy conservation, along with the rest of the country, during the oil crisis of 1973. But when oil prices eased and most Americans lost interest, California kept working at it. As a result:

- ◙ While average energy use per person has jumped 50 percent across the country since 1974, per-capita energy use in California has stayed essentially even.
- ◙ The average American uses 12,000 kilowatts of electricity per year versus the 7,000 used by Californians.
- ◙ Carbon dioxide emissions per person in the United States have held steady since 1975, whereas California's per-capita emissions have dropped by 30 percent.

California has achieved this happy result with a canny combination of high prices, regulations, and flat-out mandates, and it's not done: new moves to cut auto emissions, develop solar power, and cap greenhouse gases are on the way. Perhaps the best news is that both consumers and utility companies are pleased with the results, and the state has managed to maintain its economic growth. "California really represents what the rest of the country could do if it paid a bit more attention to energy efficiency," says Greg Kats, who heads Capital E, an energy and clean-tech consulting firm. "And they've made money doing it."

California has led the nation in mandating mileage standards for autos, and it imposed its first building standards for energy efficiency in 1974. Also, California's solar-energy promotion program offers homeowners a $2,000 rebate on solar panels if they can beat energy-efficient building standards by 15 percent or more. A helpful tip for collecting that reward, and one freely shared by state officials, is this: Changing a roof's color from black to white may save as much electricity as the solar panels generate.

When electricity is expensive, people use less of it, so one of the state's tactics is to maintain rates that are among the nation's highest. California rejects cheap and dirty fuels in favor of cleaner and pricier natural gas and renewable energy. But California was also the first state to "decouple" a utility's regulated profit from the volume of electricity it sells. Now that their profits depend on increased efficiency, the utilities are spending $700 million a year to promote compact fluorescent bulbs and energy-saving stoves and water heaters, even if they use gas instead of electricity. And while the utilities enjoy not only profit but predictable returns that don't swing with the weather, Kats estimates that the average California family, even though it pays higher rates, spends about $800 a year less on energy than it would spend without the improvements in efficiency made over the past twenty years.

California's most important lesson for the rest of us may be this: Conserving energy and cleaning up pollution is not only possible, it's virtually painless. To be sure, California has lost some 375,000 manufacturing jobs since 2001, and employers complain that high energy prices are driving them to lower-cost states. But manufacturing jobs are disappearing all over the country; California's loss of 19.9 percent since 2001 is only slightly higher than the national average of 17 percent. And if we all take similar steps together, with national leadership to make sure no one gets an unfair edge, no state will be in better or worse shape than any other.

If the nation—and the world—doesn't move quickly to take similarly effective measures, a real catastrophe is not out of the question. The IPCC's conservative scenarios, as laid out in the February 2007 findings and the April report, relied only on proven facts and theories. The panel's report paints a gloomy picture. It predicts that hundreds of millions of Africans and tens of millions of Latin Americans, people who now have access to water, will run short in under two decades. By 2080, depending on the level of greenhouse gas emissions, water shortages could affect 1.1 billion to 3.2 billion people across the globe, and wars over water are a distinct possibility. Ecologies around the world are at risk. Half of Europe's plant species could become vulnerable, endangered, or extinct by 2100. "We truly are standing at the brink of mass extinction" of species, according to one of the report's authors, Stanford University's Terry Root.

Even that grim scenario assumes a more or less steady rate of global warming. But many scientists warn that the world is dangerously close to several points where "feedback loops" can come into play, reinforcing and speeding up the process in an irreversible spiral. One such loop could be set in motion by the melting of the Arctic ice cap. By some estimates, the Arctic Ocean could be free of ice in summer by late this century. Since ice reflects the sun's rays back into space while dark open water absorbs them, the feedback effect could cause even more and faster warming, leading to more melting and still more feedback.

Similarly, no one is sure how fast the major ice sheets may melt. Ocean levels won't be much affected by melting ice on the open seas or in Antarctica's ice shelves, since they are already displacing nine-tenths of their volume. But the melting of ice locked in Greenland's interior and on the Antarctic land mass would submerge shorelines around the world. A substantially increased flow of water from Greenland or Antarctica would produce another feedback loop, adding substantially to the IPCC's estimated rise in ocean levels.

It was recently discovered that water from melting ice at the surface of Greenland's vast glaciers can run through crevices to the bottom, where it lubricates the ice's flow and speeds its course to the sea. Potentially, the melting of the Greenland ice sheet alone could raise global sea levels by twenty-three feet. But even a few inches could be catastrophic in a low-lying, heavily populated nation like

Bangladesh. A severe storm sweeping into an already higher Bay of Bengal could force as many as 100 million people to evacuate flooded areas, an unimaginable humanitarian crisis.

Yet another fossil-fuel-generated feedback loop could be triggered in the immense boreal forest that circles the Northern Hemisphere in Alaska, Canada, Russia, and Scandinavia. Nearly half the carbon on land is held in the boreal forest, and warming releases it faster and faster. Permafrost, melting in warmer weather, releases methane trapped in frozen peat; then the thawed peat, dead wood, and pine needles all decay, emitting carbon dioxide. The additional greenhouse gases in turn speed up the warming process, and the cycle continues.

No one is sure how fast all these loops could spin, or what would be the impact on the world. "We are taking risks with a system we don't understand that is absolutely loaded with carbon," said Steven Kallick, a Seattle-based expert on the boreal forests for the Pew Charitable Trusts. "The impact could be enormous."

Many Americans of all political persuasions are uniting on this issue. Thankfully, it's becoming clear to nearly everyone that this is no longer an issue of political sides. We are all on the same side in this one. And in the end, that's precisely the point. Global warming is no longer a curiosity, a question mark, or an issue we can go on ignoring. At the very least, we now know for sure, it will change all of our lives. And with just a bit of bad luck, global warming could do far worse. It is a clear and present danger—to us, to our children and grandchildren, and to the only planet we will ever have.

So we must do whatever is necessary, starting right now, to disarm the time bomb sitting on our doorstep. This includes blocking the greedy and self-serving impulses of the oil producers and OPEC's collaborators, a group that will, without question, initiate predatory pricing campaigns once alternative energy policies begin eating into their markets. The only way to strip them of their power is for all of us to become fully aware of the enormous environmental, social, and political premiums we pay every time we use their products. If we can't open our eyes to the truth of the reprehensible and debilitating arrangement to which we have acceded these past decades, sad as it is to say, we will deserve what we get.

5

Energy Security Is National Security

I t was October 5, 2002, and the French supertanker *Limbourg* was cruising off the coast of Yemen. The giant ship was high in the water, with only 397,000 barrels of crude oil sloshing in its tanks; it was headed for the port of Ash Shihr to take on more. Then a junior officer saw a small boat, which looked like a fishing vessel, speeding toward the *Limbourg* on a collision course.

It was an ominous sight: Only two years before in the harbor at Aden, 350 miles west of where the *Limbourg* was steaming, just such a small boat, crammed with explosives, had nearly sunk the American destroyer USS *Cole.* Evasive action was out of the question for a ship that took half a mile to respond to the helm, and if the tanker carried small arms to repel the modern scourge of piracy, there wasn't time to break them out. When the suicide boat hit the *Limbourg,* its load of TNT ripped through the tanker's double hull, setting the cargo afire and spilling some 90,000 barrels of crude oil.

Tugs towed the burning ship into port, with one dead crewman and seventeen injured, and it lived to make other voyages. But the message was clear: Al-Qaeda and its terrorist brethren could strike the world's oil industry anywhere, and no part of the supply chain would be safe. Around the world, markets gyrated as nervous traders tried to lock in supplies of oil, driving the price higher.

It's safe to say that most Americans don't usually think of flipping on the lights or turning the ignition key of our cars as a matter of national security. If we did think about it, however, there would be a national alarm sounding. Every year, as we depend more heavily on imported energy to run the country, our economy becomes more vulnerable to disruptions in the supply, whether from terrorists, hostile governments, or natural disasters. And every year, as rising global demand for energy runs into real or contrived constraints on supply, our dependence makes the world more dangerous for everyone.

Threats are everywhere. Despite the U.S. presence in Iraq, saboteurs have kept what was once the world's third-biggest oil producer crippled for the past four years. Osama bin Laden and his al-Qaeda terrorists have not only hit the *Cole* and the *Limbourg* but staged an unsuccessful raid on the vast production facilities of Saudi Arabia. Mahmoud Ahmadinejad and Hugo Chavez, the presidents of Iran and Venezuela, have warned that they will disrupt oil supplies if the United States threatens them. Venezuela has seized oil fields from foreign companies; Ecuador expelled Occidental Petroleum over a contract dispute; and Bolivia nationalized its gas fields, ordering major oil companies to renegotiate their contracts. Even Russia has used its oil and gas as a weapon, twice interrupting supplies to Europe in disputes with Ukraine and Belarus—a bully-boy tactic that only adds to the overall geopolitical nervousness, while coercing foreign investors such as Shell to all but cede their interests in Russian gas and oil fields to Gazprom on patently trumped-up allegations of environmental transgressions.

Receding Goalposts

For America, the danger of being dependent on foreign oil producers was first driven home in the Arab oil embargo of 1973, with frantic industries vying for fuel and mile-long lines at filling stations. In his 1974 State of the Union message, President Richard Nixon responded by preaching the need to regain control over our destiny by achieving independence from foreign oil suppliers. But as time passed and oil production stagnated in the United States given the impediments to drilling in the continental shelf and the Arctic National Wildlife Refuge, imports kept rising and the goal of independence kept receding.

In 1980, President Jimmy Carter issued the Carter Doctrine, vowing to defend the Persian Gulf oil supply from any hostile Soviet moves. Ronald Reagan put teeth in that promise by creating an American military command in the Gulf, and later ordering the Navy to protect Kuwaiti tankers during the Iran-Iraq War of the 1980s. Over the past two decades, the U.S. commitment has been expanded to West Africa, and the deployment of armed forces to guard the oil industry's sea lanes (with the ancillary benefit to producers such as Saudi Arabia and Kuwait that they are being protected as well) has cost the nation tens of billions of dollars every year.

But energy independence, or anything like it, is still nowhere in sight. In 2006, when the United States was consuming 20 million barrels of oil every day, more than 60 percent of it was imported. In that year's State of the Union message, President George W. Bush set a new and more modest goal: to replace more than 75 percent of our oil imports from the Middle East by 2025. But by his administration's own reckoning, even if we don't buy oil from the Persian Gulf, we won't be any less dependent on foreign producers. The Energy Information Administration (EIA) predicts that if all continues much as now, total U.S. consumption of oil will climb to nearly 28 million barrels a day by 2030, and 17 million of those barrels will be imported—still 60 percent of the total.

Since the twin oil shocks of 1973 and 1979, the nation has cut back on some uses of oil, replacing it with coal and natural gas in factories and power plants, while natural gas now heats many homes and commercial buildings. Some flexibility to switch away from oil still remains. But two-thirds of the oil we use goes for transportation, which is 98 percent dependent on oil—and the day is still distant when the whole U.S. fleet of cars, trucks, and planes will be powered by biofuels, fuel cells, or some exotic hydrogen technology. For the foreseeable future, we're stuck with oil. The bottom line, as a study by the Council on Foreign Relations concluded in 2006: Given the current construct of the oil market, energy independence is a distant mirage. We'll have to burn oil for at least the next few decades, and much of the oil we use will have to come from other countries.

Don't Call the Military

The perils of this predicament were driven home to Chuck Wald early in this decade, when he was a four-star Air Force general and deputy commander of U.S. forces in Europe, Central Asia, and Africa. Wald was the man, he realized, who was responsible for enforcing the metastasizing Carter Doctrine in an increasingly complex set of hazards, stretching from the Oresund Strait between Sweden and Denmark to the tiniest pipeline carrying oil to the coast of Angola. Huge new oil discoveries were being developed in the Caspian Sea, but their delivery would depend on a $3.9 billion pipeline being built across Georgia, Azerbaijan, and Turkey to the Mediterranean. It wasn't entirely reassuring that guards on horseback were being hired to protect that pipeline. Equally promising deposits were being found off the African coast, but on continental shelf belonging to nations including Sao Tome and Equatorial Guinea, notoriously corrupt and poorly equipped to defend any oil industry installations. How could Wald's Western Command step into a breach that enormous?

Wald figured he needed to know more about the oil business, so he brought in Paul Domjan from Shell's scenario planning department, which studies how wars, depressions, or natural disasters might affect the price of oil. Domjan ran the Western Command through some scary scenarios. In one, the Caspian pipeline exploded; in another, a terrorist attack on a gas pipeline in Russia blacked out much of Britain.

Soon Wald concluded that the Carter Doctrine needed amending: The job of defending all the oil in his sprawling command was simply too daunting. "You just can't call 1-800-dial-the-military," he said. "The oil companies themselves have to start stepping up." He began criticizing corporations for loose security and unguarded oil rigs, and exhorting top executives about the danger of relying on local police and armies to protect them. But then Wald overrode his own advice with an ambitious plan that his staff called the Caspian Guard. It aimed to train the security forces of Azerbaijan and Kazakhstan to keep a close eye on oil facilities in the Caspian region and improve maritime security by eradicating smuggling and piracy.

The project ran into trouble when the security forces began feuding with each other, and regional hackles were raised when pundits began speculating that U.S. soldiers would be deployed for the job. Funding from Washington dwindled, the Caspian Guard label was scrapped, and the security project dropped out of the news. But long after Wald retired, a spokesman for the Western Command said the program was still a priority.

Wald tried to launch a similar effort in the Gulf of Guinea, where the impoverished island nation of Sao Tome and Principe was turning into a bonanza of offshore oil, but the country's sheer backwardness defeated him. The Sao Tome coast guard had no seagoing ships at all, and when Wald visited an army post, he saw meals being cooked over open fires. His energy-security program had to begin with setting up a modern military field kitchen and sending Navy volunteers to rehabilitate a school. How long would it take to get Sao Tome to the point where it could protect its own oil?

Whatever the Carter Doctrine proclaims, the American military can't defend all the U.S. energy interests around the world; and even if we enlisted all our allies to bear part of the burden in an international energy police force, the global oil and gas system would still be vulnerable. Robert Gates, who would later become President Bush's secretary of defense, got a powerful demonstration of this reality in the summer of 2006 when he played the role of national security adviser in a war game in Washington. In this game, unrest and terrorist attacks had disrupted oil production in Alaska, Nigeria, and Saudi Arabia. At one point, Gates asked whether Washington could send troops to Nigeria to help restore order. "We can't do it. We don't have the forces," said P. X. Kelley, a retired Marine Corps general who was playing chairman of the Joint Chiefs of Staff. Later, Gates complained that America lacked enough resources even to defend its domestic energy industry. The lesson he took away from the game, he said, was simple: "The infrastructure is too big to protect as a whole."

By the time he retired to Washington in 2006, Chuck Wald had reached the same conclusion. He switched focus, joining a group of former policymakers and military officers who have decided that no amount of military effort or diplomacy can achieve energy security. The problem has to be redefined, they argue, and the only solution will be to end all oil imports through a combination of energy conservation, increased domestic oil production, and a long-range push for alternative energy sources. That's also the program of the Energy Security Leadership Council (ESLC), a group of former military officers and top business executives.

The president himself, however, has been cool to most such proposals, despite his pronouncement in 2006 that the United States is addicted to oil. He has consistently resisted higher mileage standards, and in recent months he has focused mainly on promoting biofuels, primarily corn-based ethanol.

But it's important to raise a flag here: All measures under discussion will take years before they provide any dividend in energy security, and all of them have limits. Take fuel conservation. In the ESLC wish list, federal mileage standards for new cars and trucks would rise by 4 percent every year, with an "off ramp" if that proves too difficult. That steady annual rise of 4 percent would make cars twice as efficient twenty-five years from now. But by the council's own estimate, that would save just 4 million barrels of oil a day, a goodly amount but less than a quarter of what we'll be importing by then. As for added drilling, as we saw above, the chances are it won't produce a flood of oil; the best hope for a big added supply within the next two decades probably lies in ramping up the flow of synthetic crude now being profitably steamed out of the tar sands in western Canada and seriously developing perhaps the largest fossil fuel reserve in the world, the vast oil shale deposits of Colorado, Wyoming, and Idaho, which hold some 2 trillion barrels of oil equivalents.

A Global Quandary

Energy security, of course, is not just a problem for the United States. It's a geopolitical crisis for nations big and small, developed and developing alike—and one for which there are no easy or obvious answers.

It's not that the world is running out of oil. As this book makes clear, the "peak oil" theorists have been all but discredited; there's plenty of oil, in fact, a lot more than mankind should burn if we want to keep the planet livable. The devil is in the details: who has it, who needs it, what it costs, how it gets from here to there, and who can disrupt its flow. And to this must be added a new calculation: What are the hidden costs of consuming oil in terms of the foreign commitments it entails in blood and treasure, as well as in the existential risk of global warming?

Internationally, demand for oil and gas is growing quickly, with the booming economies of China and India leading the charge. In countries already industrialized, growth in oil consumption promises to be relatively restrained; in the United States, for instance, demand is expected to grow by a total of 22 percent by 2030, which is only about 1 percent a year. But by most forecasts, within twenty-five years the world as a whole will need nearly 40 percent more oil than it uses today. According to the International Energy Agency (IEA), global consumption in 2030 will have risen from today's daily average of 85 million barrels to 115 million barrels if things continue as they are without any fundamental change.

Irrespective of climatic and environmental issues, the matter of access, transport, and security will be an ongoing problem for those nations and economies whose well-being is tied to a seamless supply of oil. As one example, Saudi Arabia is still sitting on an underground ocean of cheap oil, and according to an article in the *New York Times* on March 5, 2007, the Saudis are claiming that their reserves are much higher than the previously broadcast figure of 260 billion barrels. They claim that with new drilling techniques and seismographic technology, reserves can now be calculated as approximately 716 billion barrels, and possibly as much as 1 trillion barrels. Yet Saudi Arabia has shown itself to be a singularly unreliable supplier, cutting its production again and again to push prices of crude oil higher and higher. Given their past performance, one can assume they will continue to do so. Given their quixotic pricing policies and the precariousness of their lines of supply, they are a source that cannot be counted upon. One never really knows for sure what cards the Saudis are holding or how they will play their hand. Other big potential suppliers—including Iran, Libya, Venezuela, and Kuwait—are equally opaque, while Iraq is fraught with its own problems.

The producing nations also have a tough new awareness of oil as a diplomatic weapon—and they don't hesitate to brandish it when the West tries to pressure them. Venezuela's Hugo Chavez is leading a Latin American pushback against U.S. dominance in the hemisphere, openly threatening to cut off supplies to his biggest customer. And Iran, under pressure to end its nuclear weapons program, has been even more belligerent. Supreme Leader Ayatollah Ali Khamenei warned recently that oil shipments will be "seriously jeopardized" if Tehran is punished in its nuclear standoff. His spokespeople pointedly reminded the world that Iran constitutes one side of the strategic Strait of Hormuz, which has to be negotiated by every tanker carrying oil from the Persian Gulf. "We have control over the biggest and most sensitive energy route in the world," the Iranians boasted.

Western officials still talk about their military options for preserving energy security. In May 2006, Secretary General Jaap de Hoop of the North Atlantic Treaty Organization told the European Parliament that NATO would consider using force to defend Europe's energy supply. "As far as oil and gas is concerned, I think NATO could play a role to defend the sea lanes," he said. In practice, however, any detailed scenario for such a defense can only come to the conclusion that Robert Gates reached after his war-game experience: The oil infrastructure is just too big and complicated to protect. As long as we are dependent on imported supplies of oil, energy security is a myth.

PART TWO

How OPEC Put Us Over a Barrel and Where We Go from Here

6

OPEC's Bludgeon

History is littered with the ironies of revenge. The narcissistic tyrant becomes easy prey for the courtier's stab in the back. The avenging victim of injustice becomes a brute himself. The early communists derided capitalists as so greedy that they would willingly profit from their own hanging. Vladimir Lenin allegedly sneered, "We will find a capitalist who will sell us the rope." (It didn't exactly turn out that way.) All these ironies and more abound in the bizarre story of OPEC, a Leninist script in which the oil cartel drapes a hangman's noose around the global economy's neck and the world not only cheers but actually collaborates. If OPEC now has the strength and means to throttle our economy, it is only because we supplied the rope, along with instructions for using it.

It will take several chapters to explain just how the world's nations managed to become hostage to the market manipulations of eleven contentious oil producers, most of them located in the Middle East. This chapter tracks the cartel from its obscure origins in the vast Arabian desert through the first "oil shock" in 1973. It is a convoluted tale of twists and reverses, advances and declines, culminating in the emergence of a new global force with power over billions of lives.

Starting as a grab bag of Third World countries, sheikhdoms, and emirates, OPEC came together only when its members joined in smoldering resentment at the diktats of the Seven Sisters, as the biggest oil companies collectively had come to be known. OPEC gradually remade itself from a pawn of the corporations into their partner, and finally their unchallenged master. By the end of this chapter, you will see how, over the last four decades, oil has been used by OPEC as a bludgeon to make itself a major player on the world's political and economic stage.

The long saga has its roots in the nineteenth century, when the British Raj (Great Britain's rule of the Indian subcontinent) dominated the Middle East as a means to secure its routes to India. In those days, the barren tribal kingdoms and sheikhdoms were of little importance, their rulers surviving only on what they could skim off their subjects' meager income from fishing, pearl diving, camel herding, and regional trading.

Before World War I, it was the British resident in the Persian Gulf, an imperial official comparable to the Roman proconsuls, who largely dictated the terms of the first oil "concessions" that gave the major companies exclusive rights to find and pump the region's oil. As was so often the case when oil was involved, fear played a part in Britain's dealings. The British government decided to revamp its naval fleet to run on oil rather than coal. Top government officials (most notably Winston Churchill, First Lord of the Admiralty) wanted to make sure the Royal Navy would not be caught short in its burgeoning naval arms race with Germany. With the resident's backing, the world's major oil companies held a distinct advantage in bargaining with their host governments in the Middle East.

The concessions were designed to benefit first the multinational corporations, whose officials wrote contracts on their own terms and set up an interlocking network of national and regional operating companies in which the local governments had no share at all. The Iraq Petroleum Company (IPC), for example, was a holding and operating business jointly owned by the Anglo-Iranian Oil Company (later British Petroleum and now BP), Compagnie Française de Petrole (now Total), Royal Dutch/Shell, Standard Oil of New Jersey (now Exxon Mobil), and Socony-Vacuum (later Mobil, now part of Exxon Mobil). The other members of the group that would come to be called the Seven Sisters were Gulf, Standard Oil of California (now Chevron), and Texaco (now part of Chevron). That actually adds up to eight sisters; the list of "seven" depended on who was doing the listing.

Partnership and percentages in the operating companies varied from country to country, but the major players had shares in concessions all over the Middle East. They were often joined by another partner, Calouste Gulbenkian, the legendary oil field operator known as "Mr. Five Percent" for his ability to cut himself in on such deals. Gulbenkian, the son of an Armenian oilman, got his start when he took the lead in forming the Iraq Petroleum syndicate to drill for oil when Iraq was still part of the Ottoman Empire. The syndicate tapped gushers and Gulbenkian clung like a limpet to his partners, shrewdly insisting that any exploration anywhere be conducted through IPC itself.

But for all its wealth of oil reserves, the Middle East remained a backwater until the end of World War II. Then, during the Cold War, U.S. strategists feared that the stricken nations of Europe would fall into the Soviet camp. Under the Marshall Plan, Washington worked to accelerate Europe's economic recovery by using a modern, oil-based model to rejuvenate the continent's industrial base. Obtaining the needed oil meant building up the oil industry in the Middle East, which was then the only region of the world with known reserves cheap and plentiful enough to fuel Europe's modernization. Washington pushed the major international oil companies to move aggressively into the region. With U.S. and British diplomatic backing, concessions were expanded and rapidly developed in the postwar years.

This strategic decision, in tandem with the postwar boom in America and the speedy recovery of Europe, paved the way for the golden age of oil. From 1948 to 1972, world oil production would mushroom by 500 percent, and no one would benefit more than the Seven Sisters.

The key to the Sisters' lucrative arrangement was the so-called "posted price" of oil, an arbitrary per-barrel fee named for the sheet that was literally posted at a producing field. The posted price was set unilaterally by the big producers. They used it to market the crude oil output to their own refineries and parent companies, as well as to determine what they owed in taxes and royalties to the governments of the areas from which they pumped the crude.

Naturally, the Sisters kept the posted price low. This maximized their profits from both ends. By paying a cheap price for the petroleum acquired from the host governments, and then padding the prices of the refined products they produced downstream and sold to consumers, the Sisters minimized the royalties to their hosts and created huge margins that fattened their bottom lines. Later, when a free oil market did develop, the true market price took into account the differences in the oil's quality and accessibility from one oil field to the next. Often the market price would vary widely from the one posted by the Sisters.

For each barrel pumped from its pool of reserves, a host country received royalties and taxes totaling 50 percent of the posted price, minus half the cost of finding and pumping petroleum. Middle East oil was exceptionally cheap to locate and produce. Industry wags liked to say that if you just poked a straw into the Saudi desert, oil would come out. At the time, it cost just 20 cents a barrel to produce Mideast oil, versus 80 cents a barrel in Venezuela and 90 cents in Texas. So at the longstanding posted price of $2.04 a barrel, a host government received 92 cents and the oil company took $1.12.

At first, it seemed like a winning proposition for all parties. The majors profited handsomely, while a torrent of revenues transformed sandy sheikhdoms into centers of opulence. Architects designed striking monuments and built modern cities. Water from new desalination plants irrigated gardens, flowed from fountains, and created oases of green golf courses in the desert. Middle Eastern potentates and their sizeable retinues emptied barrels of oil money in the shops of London, Paris, and New York. Back at the palace, meanwhile, armies of migrant laborers—Egyptians, Indians, Pakistanis, and Palestinians—tackled the menial work that suddenly wealthy natives could now afford to avoid.

From the beginning, though, the arrangement chafed. It was the major companies alone that determined the posted price of the oil, and the host countries had a stake only in the "upstream" drilling and pumping part of the crude oil industry. The Seven Sisters, meanwhile, had their own separate "downstream" refining and marketing networks that let them gear production to ultimate demand in the countries where the products were sold. By keeping the price of drilling and extraction operations low, they made sure that most of the profits emerged later in the refining and marketing end. If the host governments wanted additional revenue (and they did), the only way to get it was to pump more oil.

Even that decision, however, was not one the individual producing nations had the power to make. The Seven Sisters had the right to allocate production to favor one government over another. The interlaced corporate structure of the operating companies meant that the Sisters could concentrate production in whatever country they chose, effectively playing one government off the next and dictating the flow of income to the hosts.

Restive voices soon began to grumble that oil barons in faraway places were draining the wealth and controlling the destinies of proud oil-producing nations. As the boom of the 1950s spread, two men in particular became vocal critics of the Seven Sisters: Abdullah Tariki and Juan Pablo Perez Alfonso, the oil ministers of Saudi Arabia and Venezuela, respectively. Their discontent would ultimately strike a chord among the rulers of the other oil-rich countries and lead to the creation of OPEC.

The Sisters Begin to Lose Their Grip

The deal that the majors had dictated was too good to last. Independent oil companies looking for new sources of crude oil began playing by their own rules, offering better terms for concessions than the Sisters gave. A limited free market sprang up for buying and selling oil beyond the Sisters' control. Most important, a giant new player stepped out from behind the Iron Curtain to enter the game.

Russia had been a pioneer and early leader in the oil industry. The world's first oil well was drilled in 1846 at Bibi-Aybat near Baku, fifteen years before drilling began in Pennsylvania, and Russian oil fueled most of Europe through World War I. But the Bolshevik Revolution in 1917 and the subsequent confiscation and nationalization of privately owned fields brought the industry to its knees. The bloody birth pangs of the Soviet Union and the struggle for power within the Communist Party kept Russian oil infrastructure neglected and output below pre-revolutionary levels for more than a decade. In 1930, Josef Stalin, having largely consolidated power, moved to reverse the damage and decay.

But it was World War II that really kicked Soviet oil production into high gear. After the war ended, Stalin's enormous investment began to pay off in major discoveries in the Volga-Urals region. By the late 1950s, Soviet oil exports were beginning to become a major factor in international markets, particularly in Europe. Moscow was aggressively undercutting prevailing prices to woo new customers, stoking fears among the Seven Sisters that they would be plunged into economic turmoil. The Central Intelligence Agency was prompted to warn that the Soviets were "a force to be reckoned with in the international petroleum field."

In 1960, the Soviet Union would displace Venezuela as the second-largest oil producer in the world, behind only the United States. Its production that year equaled 60 percent of all the oil pumped in the Middle East.

With a world economy much less thirsty for oil than it is today, it did not take long before there was far more petroleum sloshing around the marketplace than there were buyers ready to consume. Discounting was so fierce that at one point a barrel of oil could be bought at a Soviet port on the Black Sea for half the price posted by the Seven Sisters. Further exacerbating the situation, the United States stepped in to protect its own domestic producers from a flood of imported oil in 1959, when Dwight Eisenhower slapped limitations on imports by presidential proclamation.

The Mandatory Oil Import Program's quotas sharply limited access to the world's biggest market. As Robert L. Bradley reminds us in his book *The Mirage of Oil Protection,* Eisenhower expressed misgivings about the program, citing the "tendencies of special interests in the United States to press almost irresistibly for special programs" that conflicted with the idea of increased world trade. The quotas nevertheless remained in place until 1973, when Richard Nixon scrapped them in favor of yet another form of protectionism: higher tariffs on oil imports.

In this fierce competition, the Seven Sisters' dominance began to wither. Though their sales continued to grow, their rivals gained faster. Between 1950 and 1960, the Sisters lost one-quarter of their share of world refining capacity and one-sixth of their share of world production volume.

To keep their markets, the Sisters had no choice but to match the competition's discounts. Under the agreements with their host governments, however, the Sisters still had to pay royalties and taxes based on the predetermined posted price, not oil's real market price. Given the depth of the free-market discounts, the Sisters found themselves surrendering 60 percent or even 70 percent of their actual revenues to the host nations, instead of the 50 percent less half the production costs called for in their concession agreements. Accustomed to taking a heftier share of the revenues, the Sisters were not prepared to tolerate their demotion for long.

The Sisters Make a Bad Bet

Given the grumbling in producing nations about Western exploitation, the Sisters knew it would be politically risky to lower the posted price. Nevertheless, early in 1959, British Petroleum took the gamble. It slashed 18 cents, or nearly 9 percent, off its longstanding posted price of $2.04 a barrel. The other major companies followed suit. Ultimately, the move backfired. In hindsight, it's clear that the Sisters were providing rope for the hangman: Their ploy to maintain their revenues and profits at the expense of the host governments fertilized the seeds of anger and resentment that were already germinating and would eventually sprout into OPEC.

Predictably, the host governments reacted with outrage. Abdullah Tariki and Juan Pablo Perez Alfonso, the Saudi and Venezuelan oil ministers, began actively looking for ways to assert their independence and reclaim national pride. They knew each other only by reputation, but after the Sisters reduced the posted price, the two were united in their determination to play a larger, more rebellious role in the unfolding oil drama.

Even before the price cut, an Arab oil congress had been scheduled to open in Cairo in April 1959. Here, Perez Alfonso and Tariki would finally meet face to face. Perez Alfonso was attending merely as an observer, but he was armed with texts that outlined Venezuela's oil legislation, translated into Arabic for easy comparison with the concession contracts of the Middle East.

His go-between with Tariki was Wanda Jablonski, then a reporter for *Petroleum Week,* who used her charm, style, independence, and encyclopedic knowledge of what was happening and who mattered to make herself an influential player in the decidedly male-dominated oil industry. Tough and sardonic, she wisecracked and needled her sources to get scoops on almost every important story in the postwar industry. Her reports made for indispensable reading, particularly after she founded her own newsletter, *Petroleum Intelligence Weekly*, in 1961. Hands down, Jablonski was the most important journalist in the industry.

Neither custom nor convention stopped her. In the 1950s, for instance, she was one of the first journalists of either sex to tramp through oil fields in the Middle East, Latin America, and Africa. On a trip to Saudi Arabia to interview King Saud, she found herself lodged in the ruler's harem. As related by Daniel Yergin in *The Prize*, Jablonski wrote a friend that it had been "a perfectly gay 'hen party.' ... Forget what you've seen in the movies, or read in the *Arabian Nights*. None of that fancy, filmy stuff. Just plain, ordinary, warm home and family atmosphere—just like our own, though admittedly on a considerably larger family scale!"

It was also on this trip that she met Tariki, an angry young man who voiced his extreme displeasure with California Standard, Jersey Standard, Mobil, and Texaco, who were the American owners of Aramco, the Saudi holding company. Struck by Tariki's determination and dedication to changing concession policies in the Middle East, Jablonski pegged him as someone who would be a key player.

At the conference in Cairo, Jablonski introduced Tariki to Perez Alfonso. The two formed an almost instant bond, cemented by a shared mission. Young Turks from different corners of the globe, they quickly agreed that Cairo presented the perfect opportunity to hold secret talks with a few of their colleagues about what they perceived to be the growing menace of the sisterhood. They invited delegates from Kuwait, Iran, and Iraq to a private boating club on the Nile in Maadi, a southern Cairo suburb near the hot springs resort of Helwan. Held in the off-season, the meeting at the club drew no particular attention.

From the outset, there was little chance the five men could form an official pact. The Iranian delegate said he lacked the requisite authority from the Shah to commit his country to any agreement. The Iraqi representative, much like Perez Alfonso, was nothing more than an observer, since Saddam Hussein's new regime was boycotting the conference because Saddam was feuding with Egypt's Gamal Abdel Nasser. Nevertheless, the group reached a gentleman's agreement that included recommendations to their governments on how to level the playing field in the increasingly cutthroat oil game.

The recommendations that came out of the secret Maadi talks outlined a common front against the Seven Sisters. Suggestions included creating an advisory body that would help defend the oil price structure with unified action, and a bid by all the governments to gain a share of the lucrative downstream refining and marketing business. This would be achieved by forming national oil companies, adding domestic refining capacity, and building integrated marketing structures. The group also urged the governments to junk the companies' unilaterally imposed 50-50 split of posted-price revenues and insist on at least a 60 percent share.

Observers for the Seven Sisters also attended the main Cairo meeting, which on its face produced little of importance. The Seven Sisters remained blissfully unaware of the Maadi gathering's agenda. British Petroleum's Michael Hubbard wired a report back to London assuring his supervisors that political issues had taken a back seat.

Hubbard also told his chairman that, even though Wanda Jablonski had helped arrange for him to talk with Tariki, nothing substantive was accomplished because the Saudi minister wanted only to harangue Hubbard about the inequities of the system. The clear implication was that Tariki was incapable of discussing the economics of the business. Tariki, however, had worked and studied in Texas, and he knew full well the inner workings of the industry. Those acquainted with him said he hated being patronized by what he perceived as arrogant Westerners whose knowledge of the oil business was, at the very least, no greater than his. He no doubt dreamed of the day when he could finally give them their comeuppance.

An Open Spigot Sinks Oil Prices

In the months following the Cairo conference, the recommendations presented by the rebel group gained little traction with the producing countries. The turmoil in the marketplace meanwhile intensified as more oil flowed, the Western economies began sliding into recession, and market-price discounts deepened. The Sisters became alarmed when Soviet crude began to make significant inroads with their primary customers in Western Europe. In fact, Enrico Mattei, head of Italy's state-owned energy company, was openly buying

Russian oil. American statesmen fretted that the Soviet premier,· Nikita Khrushchev, was using oil as an economic weapon in the Cold War. "Khrushchev has threatened to bury us on more than one occasion," said Senator Kenneth Keating of New York after the Soviets had succeeded in doubling production between 1955 and 1960. "It is now becoming increasingly evident that he would also like to drown us in a sea of oil if we let him get away with it."

The Sisters understood they had to fight harder if they were to survive the discount war. Their posted price was still the basis for splitting revenues with the host governments and was a drain on their declining income. The benefits they had gained by reducing the posted price in 1959 were being eroded by the continuous discounting of the real market (or spot) price. Yet most of the group argued that it would be folly to cut the posted price again. They feared fueling the already considerable anger of their Middle Eastern hosts over the previous cut. But in New York, Jersey Standard's new chairman, Monroe "Jack" Rathbone, scoffed at such timidity.

Rathbone was a quintessential product of the oil patch— supremely self-confident, brusque, and not much interested in other people's opinions. He had proved himself both smart and gutsy when, as a young engineer in Baton Rouge in the 1930s, he developed the catalytic cracking process. He persuaded the federal government to sink hundreds of millions of dollars into this process to produce aviation fuel of better quality, despite having tested the process only in a small research unit. Fortunately, it worked, and Rathbone was credited with revolutionizing the refining process to make the fuel that gave the Allies an edge in World War II. During his early years in Baton Rouge as general manager of a Jersey Standard refinery, Rathbone had earned his spurs fending off the demagogic attacks of Governor Huey Long. Headstrong and self-assured, he zoomed rapidly to the top of the company hierarchy.

By 1960, Rathbone's opinion of the oil-producing countries was, to put it mildly, condescending. Unwilling to waste time consulting with people about whom, at that time, he knew little and cared less, Rathbone was now insisting on another cut in the posted price, with no conception of how it would be received by the host countries. Their reaction, in his view, would be irrelevant anyway.

Howard Page, Jersey Standard's Middle East negotiator, tried to argue with Rathbone. He even brought in Wanda Jablonski to explain the realities of Arab nationalism to the board of directors. Rathbone dismissed this woman, friend to Arab sheikhs and Texas wildcatters alike, as too pessimistic. He had just been to the Middle East himself, he said, and had heard nothing that sounded as threatening as Jablonski made out. Having experienced herself the extreme courtesy and generosity typically shown to guests, Jablonski shot back that Rathbone had merely been treated to a display of Middle Eastern manners. It was obvious to her, at least, that Rathbone had no clue what his hosts were really thinking.

At Rathbone's insistence, Page asked the Jersey Standard board to approve the cut. The directors gave their blessing only on condition that the Middle Eastern governments be consulted to work out some kind of compromise to share the pain. But Rathbone overruled them. He decreed that Jersey Standard would cut the price his way, with no consulting or dickering. On August 9, 1960, Rathbone made good on his promise: Jersey Standard knocked another 14 cents a barrel, or about 7 percent, off the posted price. With varying degrees of foreboding, the other majors followed Rathbone's lead.

Predictably, this unilateral action was met with shock and indignation in the Middle East. The lack of consultation or even advance notice of the price move added further insult to the grievous injury that the offended governments were already feeling. The Maadi strategists made hurried plans to meet in Baghdad to assess the situation.

Well aware of the blunder by the Seven Sisters and brandishing the telegraphed invitation in his Caracas office, Perez Alfonso could barely contain his glee. He gloated to his aides that the alliance he so wanted was now inevitable. Though Alfonso would later grow disenchanted with oil, in 1960 he brimmed with enthusiasm for the possibilities he thought it afforded Venezuela.

The major international oil companies, meanwhile, were about to meet a countervailing force that, given their five decades of swagger, they hardly could have contemplated. Scarcely a month after Rathbone's blustering move, representatives of the five countries that collectively produced 80 percent of the world's oil—Iraq, Iran,

Kuwait, Saudi Arabia, and Venezuela—gathered in Baghdad. The four-day conference in September 1960 gave birth to the Organization of the Petroleum Exporting Countries. Though it was destined to be one of the most important developments of the twentieth century, at the time it drew scant notice. In the *New York Times,* for instance, OPEC's formation merited only oblique mention in the back pages.

The group's mission, simply, was to defend the price of oil and win a bigger share of petroleum revenues. OPEC would insist that the major companies consult with its members on pricing matters, and it would work for a system of regulated production that allowed each member country to adjust supply to demand and that distributed revenues fairly. Most important, the members pledged themselves to solidarity should the companies try to divide them.

A Sob from the Sisters

The formation of OPEC amounted to open rebellion, and the Seven Sisters tried to damp it down with a show of groveling contrition. But their public repentance at a later Arab oil conference was nothing more than crocodile tears. The reality, according to Iran's Fuad Rouhani, OPEC's first secretary general, was that the companies still did not take the organization seriously. At first, Rouhani said, they behaved as if OPEC were a desert mirage, a figment of the producers' overheated imaginations.

Whatever his previous misgivings about high-handed treatment of the host countries, Jersey Standard's Howard Page later admitted that his company gave little credence to the oil producers' cartel. From Rathbone on down, Jersey Standard's managers thought it would never work because the notoriously quarrelsome members of the group would not be able to maintain a united front. Nor were the oil companies the only ones giving short shrift to the new alliance. Two months after OPEC was founded, the CIA wrote a report on Middle East oil that barely mentioned the organization.

And in fact, for the next decade, OPEC seemed like anything but a major factor in the industry. True, its membership more than doubled, but the members frequently quarreled and feuded. Some dropped out. Saudi Arabia and Venezuela, both under new leadership, allied themselves with the United States, relegating the firebrands Tariki and Perez Alfonso to the sidelines.

Whenever they could, which was often, the Sisters ducked negotiations with OPEC. They preferred to deal directly with the countries that had awarded them concessions. Amid all this, there was no change in marketplace realities: After the brief recession ended, both demand and supply continued to mushroom, yet intense competition was the order of the decade.

Although events of the time served mainly to strengthen the hand of the major oil companies, OPEC could still count some real accomplishments and practical gains in its first years. The cartel, in fact, benefited the companies and the producing countries alike. All sides had a stake in "price stability" and "orderly markets." These code words, when translated into day-to-day reality, meant high profits for the industry—a drain on the pockets of the world's consumers to the benefit of the producers. The real difference after OPEC came onto the scene was that oil-rich countries began to demand a bigger role in decision making, along with a bigger share of the revenue pie.

Their demands began to be met in the early 1970s, thanks largely to Colonel Muammar Qaddafi of Libya. In September 1970, he forced the independent Occidental Petroleum Company to increase the posted price and lower the production of Libyan crude. Cutbacks in the output of the high-quality and much-in-demand Libyan oil tightened supplies across the market, opening the way for OPEC to make changes as well.

In 1970, following Qaddafi's showdown with Occidental, OPEC negotiated a technical change in the tax-and-royalty formula used by the oil companies, increasing the host governments' share from just under 50 percent of the posted price to a minimum of 55 percent. At the cartel's conference in Caracas in December, members decided to use their power to push for a rise in the posted price itself. After several rounds of talks with the major companies, OPEC won an increase of about 35 cents a barrel, to $2.18. The camel's nose was under the tent.

Ominously for the world's consumers, the new agreement promised an additional increase every year, supplemented by an adjustment for inflation. A later amendment would call for yet another price adjustment to compensate for any depreciation of the U.S. dollar, the currency in which world oil prices are determined. The tables were finally turning. The posted price would now be determined by OPEC, not the Seven Sisters, and the price of oil would be pegged both to the rising costs of other goods and services and to the vagaries of the U.S. dollar.

In retrospect, it is easy to see that OPEC's first decade was a watershed. To be sure, the burgeoning free market for oil substantially increased competition and eroded the profits of both the cartel's member nations and the major oil companies. Nevertheless, OPEC had established itself as a unified power in the industry, a power that could negotiate and win on its own terms.

Just as important, the world oil market was changing, and to the cartel's advantage. The industrial world was no longer awash in oil. Demand had continued to increase at a rapid pace as the world economy expanded, and it was now outstripping new production capacity in almost every country except Saudi Arabia. Every OPEC producer was pumping without restriction to meet the growing demand. But with oil prices still historically low, there was no economic incentive for U.S. producers to explore for additional reserves that, inevitably, would cost more to bring out of the ground than the price of importing oil from the OPEC members.

This was only one example of shortsighted U.S. policy that helped turn OPEC from a minor player into an 800-pound gorilla. To be sure, Washington was preoccupied by the Cold War, the failed Bay of Pigs invasion, the Cuban missile crisis, and later by its entanglement in Vietnam. But by failing to devise a consistent oil policy, the U.S. government became an unintentional co-conspirator in making OPEC a dominant force in the world economy. Mesmerized by low, low prices, we didn't care that our own self-reliance and energy self-sufficiency were being stripped away. In a few policy forums and military and academic circles, there were warnings that the Arab nations now had an "oil weapon" that could be used to hold the world hostage. But Congress and successive administrations shrugged them off.

In the Kennedy, Johnson, and Nixon administrations, American energy policy decisions repeatedly lurched in conflicting and contradictory directions, usually to OPEC's benefit. U.S. policymakers had earlier encouraged the multinational companies to move into the Middle East. Now these companies were being forced to scale back their profit ambitions. The import quotas decreed by President Eisenhower in 1959 had been meant to protect domestic producers. By the 1970s, instead, they locked the Sisters out of the U.S. market and put more downward pressure on world prices, thus discouraging development of oil from non-OPEC sources.

All that was needed to bring the OPEC monster fully to life was a crisis of major proportions. The world's first oil shock, triggered by the Yom Kippur War of 1973, would provide the defining moment.

OPEC's Whip Hand

The war that began on October 6, 1973, offered dramatic proof of OPEC's nascent power. Spurred on by the Soviet Union, President Anwar al-Sadat of Egypt and President Hafez al-Assad of Syria took Israel almost completely by surprise with their sudden assault on Yom Kippur, the holiest day in the Jewish faith. Israeli forces reeled. Having miscalculated how much equipment would be needed to fend off enemies heavily armed with Soviet weapons and attacking on two fronts, Israel began rapidly running out of supplies. Prime Minister Golda Meir, in a secret letter to President Richard M. Nixon, warned that her country was in danger of being overwhelmed. When Syrian forces began to fall back, the Soviets undertook a massive resupply of goods and equipment for both Syria and Egypt, and urged other Arab nations to join the attack. Within the parameters of Cold War tit for tat, Nixon and his secretary of state, Henry Kissinger, arranged for a similarly massive resupply of armaments to be airlifted to Israel.

As it happened, just as the war broke out, OPEC was again holding talks in Vienna to increase the posted price of oil. Rising world demand had the industry pumping flat-out with almost no capacity to spare, and the soaring spot price had long since eclipsed the OPEC posted price. While OPEC was holding its talks, market prices spiked again on fears that the war in the Middle East would cause disruption throughout the region. Thus it was another shot heard round the world when OPEC made known its latest demand: The group wanted a staggering increase of 100 percent, which would have boosted the posted price well above the spot-market level.

Worse yet, President Nixon received a message from the chairmen of the four U.S. owners of Aramco—Jersey Standard, Texaco, Mobil, and California Standard—warning that any show of American military support for Israel would risk bringing on a serious oil shortage. The Arab "oil weapon" was being hauled out into the open. Moreover, if Nixon failed to heed their warning, the executives predicted, the United States might be shut out of the Middle East and replaced by other interests—Europe, Japan, perhaps even the Soviets.

The realpolitik of the Cold War, however, dictated Nixon's decision to come to Israel's aid in the face of the Soviet-supplied onslaught. The help from the United States enabled Israel's troops to halt the Arab offensive and mount a counterattack, but the cost was high. Arab leaders read the incident not merely as a proxy skirmish between the two superpowers, but as a deliberately dramatic show of American meddling in Middle Eastern affairs. Once again, they saw an insult piled onto an injury, further stoking their fury.

The talks in Vienna ultimately broke down, tabling the proposed doubling of the posted price. But officials from six key nations—Saudi Arabia, Iran, Kuwait, Iraq, the United Arab Emirates, and Qatar—reconvened shortly afterward in Kuwait to take action, with or without OPEC. The six nations issued a decree raising the posted price by a whopping 70 percent, to $5.12 a barrel, which matched the latest market price in the panicked world arena. Now OPEC—or its main players, at least—had completed the metamorphosis from subservient minion to reigning master. It was in full charge of the posted price, free at last from policy decisions made by the Seven Sisters. According to the *Guardian*, Ahmed Zaki Yamani, who in 1962 had supplanted Abdullah Tariki as the Saudi oil minister, gloated in Kuwait City: "This is a moment for which I have been waiting a long time. The moment has come. We are masters of our own commodity."

OPEC's Surprise Attack

But the war was still ongoing. Whatever its show of muscle so far, OPEC had yet to use the full measure of its clout in the oil market. Following the price-setting action in Kuwait, the delegates from the six Middle Eastern nations stayed behind to discuss future plans.

The retaliation most feared by the industry if Washington openly backed Israel was for Arab states to nationalize facilities owned by American companies. But now the Arab leaders couldn't agree on what to do. The sticking point was Saudi Arabia's new leader, King Faisal, who wanted to consult with President Nixon before doing anything drastic. Accordingly, Faisal sent Nixon a mildly worded letter, and a delegation from several Arab states paid a visit to Washington.

The Arabs were their usual courtly selves, and the cordial discussions left the Americans hopeful. Kissinger explained to the visitors that the U.S. airlift only incidentally concerned Israel and its enemies. He stressed pointedly that it was primarily a Cold War response. Nixon chimed in to offer Kissinger's services in mediating the dispute, assuring the Arabs that they could work with the secretary, soothing concerns over his Jewish background. In the Rose Garden afterward, the Saudi minister of state was suave and gracious. The Americans heaved a sigh of relief.

The very next day, however, the Arab oil ministers, meeting in Kuwait and led by Saudi Arabia, agreed on a surprise strategic wallop. They wouldn't nationalize the U.S.-owned companies; rather, they would withhold Arab oil from the companies' customers. States that the Arabs considered friendly would continue to be supplied. Those viewed as unfriendly would be punished progressively in 5 percent monthly increments—their oil supplies would be cut by 5 percent in October, 5 percent in November, and another 5 percent every month thereafter until the Arabs were satisfied that the miscreants had mended their ways. A secret clause decreed the worst treatment for the United States: even steeper cuts that would ultimately lead to a total embargo on shipments from every country signing the decree.

It was a shrewd plan, designed to split the industrial countries and force them to compete with each other for available oil, while encouraging them to make secret deals to placate the Arabs. For all the talk of an oil weapon, it was nationalization, not an embargo, that had worried oil executives. The Seven Sisters, like everyone else, were surprised by the news.

The embargo, without the secret clause punishing America, was announced on October 17. Two days later, Nixon unveiled a $2.2 billion military aid package for Israel. He explained that it was designed to restore military parity and encourage the warring parties to negotiate.

Unable or unwilling to grasp the bigger geopolitical picture, Arab leaders saw the aid package as further evidence of U.S. favoritism toward Israel, and took steps far more drastic than the limited 5 percent monthly cutbacks they had announced. Libya promptly announced an immediate halt in all oil shipments to the United States. Saudi Arabia and the other Arab producers followed suit a short while later. The total embargo on Arab oil shipments, first imposed only on the United States and the Netherlands, was later extended to Portugal, South Africa, and Rhodesia (now Zimbabwe).

OPEC was now firmly in the saddle and the world was in full crisis mode. As the next chapter reveals, however, the embargo was not the only oil shock the cartel would administer to the world. Nor would it be the worst.

7

Crude Squabbles

With the oil embargo of 1973, OPEC suddenly acquired unexpected power. Once patronized, its exotically costumed leaders were now courted and resented, flattered and despised. Apparently outflanked and outwitted, Western oilmen reacted like colonial rulers aghast to find the natives in charge. To OPEC members, it was hugely satisfying.

OPEC's new power was to prove fleeting. Unable to curb their fighting and bickering, the members would soon squander their advantage. They misjudged the economic forces they had loosed on the world and the new competition their success made viable. In short order, a petroleum glut crushed prices, shook the foundations of the cartel, and reshaped the oil-production landscape. OPEC survived, but only because of yet another misguided move by the West. In the name of "stability of supply" and to help the U.S. oil industry, Western interests forced an end to the price war. Not for the last time, the rope tossed out in rescue would wind up around our own necks.

But all that was yet to come. In October 1973 the embargo, aimed primarily at the United States, shook the whole world. Even though the oil shock lasted just a few months into 1974, it was still an enormous blow to the industrialized economies. Only a few alarmists had expected such a move, and no one was prepared.

Just six years earlier, when Israel's Six-Day War rattled world oil markets, excess U.S. stocks turned out to be the critical factor in meeting demand and stabilizing prices. In the intervening years, however, rocketing world demand for oil had forced the United States to move from protecting its domestic market against imports to using every drop of its own production capacity to cover demand.

Making matters worse, President Nixon had slapped price controls on domestic oil in March 1973 as part of his plan to stem spiraling consumer price inflation in the United States. In the absence of price controls, U.S. exploration and production might well have increased. As it was, 1972 marked the peak in production from the giant oil reservoirs of Texas. For the first time ever, with no more readily available spigots to open, the United States could not compensate for a shortage of oil from abroad by pumping more oil at home, and thus could not soften the embargo's impact on world markets.

Technically, the embargo failed in its stated goal of keeping oil from the United States. Oil being a fungible commodity, non-OPEC suppliers happily stepped into the breach when the Arabs refused to sell to the United States. In addition, "Arab unity" proved to be a contradiction in terms. Some of OPEC's fractious members quickly started surreptitious oil sales, and the embargo sprang leaks.

For example, Iraqi delegates had advocated even tougher economic warfare at the Kuwait gathering, then left in a huff after their ideas were rejected. Declaring Iraq unbound by the agreement, Saddam Hussein actually increased production. He explained his defection by assailing the regimes of Saudi Arabia and Kuwait, claiming that they were too close to the United States. Non-Arab Iran, where the Shah was hungry for revenues, also stepped up production to take advantage of the skyrocketing prices.

All told, the defectors managed to soften the embargo's impact by 600,000 barrels a day. Nevertheless, as the fateful year of 1973 drew to a close, the loss of world petroleum supplies totaled 4.4 million barrels a day, about 14 percent of all internationally traded oil at the time. In the thick of the crisis, however, no one could be sure how much oil was lacking, and this uncertainty produced panic in the markets. Inevitably, prices rose to new highs, topping $12 a barrel in 1974, quadruple the price prevailing in 1972.

Fear and Panic in the Industrialized World

Uncertainty and confusion fed the panic. How long would inventories last? Would the Arabs include more nations in their embargo? Would they go ahead with the threatened monthly incremental cutbacks? In the end, it wasn't actual shortages that drove prices into the stratosphere, but fear of them. Buyers became so nervous over the prospect of being caught short of oil that they were willing to pay almost any price—and each day's increase fed the certainty that tomorrow's quote would be even higher.

In the United States, the retail price of a gallon of gasoline jumped by 40 percent, and there were real shortages. On any given day, a filling station might be forced to close shop after putting up a sign announcing that it had no gas. At stations that still had gas to pump, lines of waiting cars sometimes stretched for a mile or more. Patience dwindled, anxiety thrived, and hoarding worsened. Fearful drivers kept topping off their tanks, lengthening already long lines, and burning nearly as much fuel in waiting as they were able to buy. Equitably minded station owners worked out rough rationing systems. Motorists with license plates ending in even numbers, for instance, might be allowed to buy gas on Mondays, Wednesdays, and Fridays; odd numbers could buy on Tuesdays, Wednesdays, and Thursdays.

For Americans, of course, the crisis of the embargo was playing out against the backdrop of another national drama: the slow unfolding of Richard Nixon's Watergate crisis. The actual burglary of Democratic headquarters in the Watergate Hotel had happened more than a year earlier, in the 1972 presidential campaign. It had become a political scandal only in March 1973. But by the time the embargo was declared, the White House was in a state of siege that was to last for ten months more.

As the fuel crisis ground on, government officials mostly fumed and blustered at OPEC members, issuing vague warnings of dire steps that might have to be taken if the embargo continued. In fact, according to diplomatic documents recently declassified in Britain, the Pentagon drafted a contingency plan for the 82nd Airborne Division to seize the oil fields in Abu Dhabi, Kuwait, and Saudi Arabia. But the plan came to naught, partly because it was exposed beforehand by U.S. media and partly because Secretary Kissinger took a long view of the nation's strategic interests. As he would explain two years later, getting rid of the Saudi ruling family and upsetting the political balance in the Middle East would only open the way for potentially more dangerous leadership that might derail U.S. economic objectives.

The psychological impact of the embargo shook the foundations of the developed world. The end of an era of plenty seemed at hand. Economists warned of lost growth, recession, inflation, international monetary crisis, and stagnation in the developing world. The Club of Rome doomsayers were hailed as prophets. Their prediction that economic growth would be stymied by a global energy shortage— we were supposed to run short of oil by 1990 and natural gas by 1992—seemed to be right on schedule.

An obscure economist named E. F. Schumacher, author of *Small Is Beautiful: Economics As If People Mattered,* which providentially appeared just in time for the embargo, was virtually beatified in the press. Schumacher's notion that a civilization built on renewable resources (forestry, agriculture) is far better and more sustainable than one built on nonrenewable resources (oil, coal, etc.) gained credence in the economic and psychological turmoil engendered by the oil embargo and the ensuing fear of life-altering energy shortages.

This turmoil roiled nearly every spot on the planet. The hard-won gains in Western Europe's recovery from World War II seemed imperiled by the fallout from the embargo; when the West German government tried to allocate oil supplies, it was besieged by industries clamoring for higher quotas. Japan's growing confidence as an economic power foundered on the realization that it all depended on a string of tankers continuing to ply the waters from the Persian Gulf to the Sea of Japan. Fearful American homemakers hoarded the supplies they lacked in World War II, starting panicky runs on common household items.

Suddenly, everything seemed up for grabs. People questioned whether the U.S. superpower was weakening, whether the West was in permanent decline, whether Russia might win the Cold War. Fears arose about the stability of the international trade and monetary systems. With OPEC in the driver's seat, new assessments were being made.

OPEC had never before had decisive leverage on the world oil market. When the Arab producers had tried to put an embargo on their oil during the 1967 war, for example, they quickly backed down as increased U.S. production pumped enough petroleum into the market to actually lower the spot price on oil for immediate delivery. Furthermore, OPEC had never developed a workable mechanism for regulating its production—its own charter forbade it from interfering in the sovereign members' decisions—so it could only jawbone its members to cut their output and thus push up prices. The members often refused, or only pretended to go along while selling as much oil as they wanted.

This time, though, things were different. Soaring market prices were lining producers' pockets with record revenues even as they were selling less oil. Now everyone could see the merits of curbing production. And none other than the recently converted Mohammad Reza Shah Pahlavi had become OPEC's most fervent advocate for higher prices and lower production, not just for the duration of the embargo, but for all time.

Fiercely determined to turn his country into a modern industrial giant, the Shah constantly searched for ways to fatten his oil revenues so as to provide the investment funds needed to boost Iran's economy. Previously, he had scoffed at the notion of curbing OPEC's output in order to raise the posted price of oil, convinced that it would never work. But in an apparent eureka moment, the Shah had a stunning change of heart and mind. He couched his argument in a new, pretentious conservation theory. Speaking at an OPEC meeting in late December 1973, he described oil as "noble fuel" and argued that it should be replaced by other sources of energy whenever possible. Oil, he said, should be saved for more important purposes, such as the manufacture of petrochemicals. And to the Shah's way of thinking, a commodity with such a noble purpose should carry a noble price as well.

At OPEC's year-end meeting in 1973, with the market price for oil still hovering at around $6 a barrel, the Shah pushed to make the posted price $11.65, more than double the $5.12 agreed on by the delegates in October. In the context of the times, it was an extraordinary jump. The Shah came up with this number after conducting an investigation of the cost of alternative fuels. The Saudis led the opposition, arguing that OPEC's actions should be seen as politically motivated for the good of the world economy, not simply a grab for more money—as if the House of Saud itself were somehow motivated by something other than the vast wealth and lavish lifestyles its underground stores of black gold bestowed.

The disingenuous prattle from the Saudi rulers was perhaps the genesis of the myth that OPEC is concerned about the economic vitality of the consumer countries. That idea, to put it mildly, is rubbish, a consistent fabrication of Saudi/OPEC public relations that has long deluded global leaders and numerous figures in the oil trade. At best, the Saudis' concern for global economies extends only so far as the ability of those nations to keep buying Saudi oil. Like the Mafia, the oil producers don't want to put their customers out of business, because they want to continue getting a check every month from those they extort. As noted in Chapter 2, though, the scales may at last be falling from some eyes following the Saudis' January 2005 admission of support for a sharp rise in the stated target price of OPEC oil. Make no mistake: The Saudis and all the other OPEC producers have always had just one goal, and that is to sell oil at the highest possible price to the largest possible market.

The Saudis had also voiced fears that a huge boost in the oil price might spur a real search for alternative sources of energy that could reduce demand for the vast Saudi reserves, making them less valuable. So, at the 1973 year-end meeting, Ahmed Zaki Yamani, the Saudi oil minister and a lawyer by trade, argued for raising the posted price only to $8 a barrel. Yamani was poised, articulate, and charismatic; but in the end, the Shah's new vision prevailed. Two days before Christmas, Yamani stunned the industrial world by announcing that world oil prices were about to skyrocket. At the beginning of 1974, the price for a barrel of oil would be pegged at $11.65, more than 300 percent higher than it had been only six months before. In only three years, the posted price had multiplied more than fivefold (from $2.18 a barrel).

In the White House, Richard Nixon welcomed the chance to show he was in charge and divert national attention from the recently discovered twenty-five-minute gap in a key tape of his Watergate discussions. He named William Simon to be the federal energy czar. Simon lowered the national speed limit to fifty-five miles per hour to save fuel, and he also ordered up rationing coupons (though they were never used). Nixon instituted "Project Independence," a drive to cut energy demand and increase domestic output in order to free the United States from foreign oil dependence. Exemplifying the behavior he wanted from Americans, the president turned down White House thermostats and doused the floodlights after 10:00 P.M. Patriotic citizens and businesses followed suit, with many eliminating holiday lighting and dialing down winter thermostats to a chilly 68 degrees.

The president also wrote to the Shah, predicting a global economic disaster and asking him to reconsider the price increase. But the Shah was adamant, lecturing the industrialized world about the end of the era of cheap oil. New energy sources must be found, he said, gratuitously adding, according to the *Middle East Economic Survey*, that "those children of well-to-do families who have plenty to eat at every meal, who have their own cars ... will have to rethink all these privileges ... and they will have to work harder."

In the next few months, as the United States moved to promote a peace settlement and new political relationships in the Middle East, the embargo continued. Henry Kissinger twice journeyed to Saudi Arabia for discussions with King Faisal, whom he would later describe as soft-spoken and given to making somewhat inscrutable comments. Nothing came of the talks.

Nixon courted Egypt's Anwar al-Sadat. A onetime hawk who now thought that both the war and the embargo had served their purpose, Sadat favored ending the embargo. He had already signed a cease-fire accord with Israel, but his ally, Hafez al-Assad of Syria, had continued the assault. With Saudi help, the Americans began negotiations with Syria concerning Israel's withdrawal from Syria's Golan Heights—talks that enabled Sadat to tell his Arab allies that Washington was working for a new political reality in the Middle East.

As the months wore on, however, the embargo came to resemble a sieve more than a stopper. With so much oil leaking through the porous wall of Arab unity, Faisal finally decided that the embargo had fulfilled its aim, and on March 18, 1974, the Arab producers moved to end it. Syria and Libya dissented.

Kissinger soon worked out a deal on the Golan Heights, and the "peace process" was in train. Richard Nixon took a break from his Watergate torment to pay a triumphant visit to Egypt, Israel, Saudi Arabia, and Syria, and was cheered deliriously by millions in Cairo.

For the Egyptians, it seemed to be the dawning of a new age. After suffering under the sway of the Soviet Union, they were now basking in the glory of the first-ever visit to their country by an American president and the renewal of diplomatic ties broken off during the 1967 war. Dreams of renewed prosperity filled the air and invigorated the happy crowds. For Nixon, who had ignored his doctors' advice and made the trip despite a dangerous case of phlebitis, the cheers were to be a last hurrah; in August that year, he resigned in disgrace.

In terms of OPEC, however, what mattered most was that the oil weapon had been used to even more devastating effect than its advocates could have predicted. The oil industry itself and the relations between producers and consumers had been reordered, while economic and geopolitical realities were transformed, not just in the Middle East but throughout the industrialized nations as well. The realization that oil could be used as a means of coercion now hung over the world like the sword of Damocles.

OPEC: *Master of the Universe*

OPEC's age of influence had finally dawned. The eleven nations that formed the cartel were now the putative masters of the universe. Diplomats hung on the results of the group's periodic meetings; international journalists shouted questions as the members emerged from their limousines to glide across hotel lobbies, and their cryptic answers made headlines around the world.

The new order brought forth by OPEC was one in which its members actually controlled the destiny of other nations; their actions could dictate prosperity or recession. Never before in history, Kissinger wrote, had such a weak group of nations been able to force such dramatic change in the way the rest of the world lived. What is more, by establishing sovereignty over the commodity that helped fuel world commerce, the producing nations had completely turned the tables on the Seven Sisters. As in the timeless tale *The Thousand and One Nights,* the king had become a beggar and the beggar a king. Symbolically, the Vienna office tower once known as the Texaco Building, which had become OPEC's headquarters in 1965 when it moved from Geneva, Switzerland, now bore the cartel's name in big, bold letters.

If there was foreboding in the industrialized world, there was euphoria in the Middle East. The Arab nations had avenged the insults and defeats imposed on them over centuries. Riches would bring power and influence. Nomads who not long before had been eating locusts in the desert would now bask in the blessings of wealth and technology. And with astonishing speed, the Arab nations sprouted emblems of luxury—grand cars, towering buildings, great hospitals, proud universities, and lush villas in the desert oases.

Ironically, OPEC's triumphs, like those of the Sisters before it, had planted seeds that would take root and sprout into a thorny problem. Although no one had yet noticed, what the Saudis feared when they argued against instituting a large price increase was coming to pass. Prodded by the oil shock, the West was exploring furiously for new oil deposits, building energy-efficient homes, seeking alternative fuels, taxing oil products at higher rates (especially in Europe), and forcing automakers to design more fuel-efficient cars. Each of these measures would limit the growth of the market for OPEC's petroleum.

The world's appetite for oil turned out to be price-sensitive after all. In Europe, where oil consumption had been growing at 8 percent annually, it now actually fell, from 15.2 million barrels daily in 1972 to 13.5 million barrels two years later. Although consumption later stabilized at a higher plateau of about 14 million barrels daily, the decoupling of petroleum from economic growth had begun. Oil would continue to be a factor, of course, but no longer would its overall consumption automatically increase in lockstep with GDP growth. Smarter, more efficient energy usage was, in effect, increasing supply. It would take another decade to prove out, but around the world, less and less oil was needed to support any given level of growth.

The four years from 1974 to 1978 were a time of complex crosscurrents, both in the world at large and within OPEC. The Shah, ambitious to turn Iran into an industrial superpower virtually overnight and fearful that its projected oil reserves would run out, craved ever-rising oil prices. He quarreled continuously with the Saudis, whose vast reserves dictated a strategy of long, slow exploitation that would keep the world hooked on oil.

OPEC still had no mechanism for regulating output. Though it was often called a cartel, it did not technically qualify as one. A cartel, by definition, must be able to restrict the supply of a commodity reaching the marketplace, as DeBeers, the South African diamond producer, has been able to do in its market through near-monopoly control of the supply of rough stones. In a true cartel, two or more companies in an industry collude to reduce competition and fix prices so as to increase profits. But within OPEC, when it came to cutting production to force up the price, there was no way to enforce discipline.

In the prosperous years of 1974 through 1978, not much discipline was needed. Most of the member nations were pumping at or near their presumed capacity, with only Saudi Arabia functioning as the swing producer and adjusting production to world demand. The Saudis relished being able to make this grand gesture, but they also resented the curb on their revenues.

Throughout the region, petrodollars were providing a mixed blessing. As we saw in Chapter 3, the new riches disrupted traditional values and customs, tilted the social balance, and sparked friction between the new rich and those left wanting. While some gladly embraced glamorous foreign novelties, others bewailed the loss of custom, tradition, and social order. American culture, it seemed, bred a resentful anti-Americanism.

In Algeria, the mounting discontent turned into a twenty-year civil war between the nation's rulers and insurgents who called themselves the Party of God but wanted mainly the bounty of oil. Saudi Arabia's royal family tried to buy off its restive critics or pretend they didn't exist—a pretense that would grow more and more hollow and dangerous as the years passed. In Iraq, Saddam Hussein brawled his way to the top and used oil money to foster state terrorism, wreaking havoc both in the region and around the world.

But it was in Iran that the backlash had its most dramatic impact. Although the Shah worked tirelessly to turn his country into the "Great Civilization" he envisioned, there was growing resentment against him and the small group of wealthy elites who benefited from his extravagance. Meanwhile, the political corruption and social upheaval spawned by petrodollars were feeding a conservative religious movement that sought a return to the principles of

fundamentalist Islam. A scowling, burning-eyed prophet, the Ayatollah Ruhollah Khomeini, led the movement from his exile in Iraq
and France. As more and more of the new middle class created by
the oil boom discovered its Muslim roots and flocked to Khomeini's
banner, the Shah's position grew more precarious.

Reporting from Saudi Arabia, the U.S. ambassador informed his
superiors that top Saudi officials considered the Shah to be a men-
tally unstable megalomaniac. Later, a *New York Times* report by Sey-
mour Hersh would quote a CIA analyst as saying much the same
thing, but the warnings went unheeded in Washington. As Hersh
described it, the assessments ran "contrary to U.S. policy." Sheikh
Yamani, the Saudi oil minister, is also said to have predicted—quite
accurately, as it turned out—that a brutal anti-American government
would most likely follow if the Shah were deposed.

For their part, the Western industrial powers, led by the United
States, didn't necessarily want low oil prices so much as stable, predictable prices unthreatened by crises and shock (a policy that would
serve as cover for OPEC's future excesses). In fact, as noted in Chapter 2, the International Energy Agency (IEA), formed by the industrialized nations in 1974 to try to prevent future oil shocks, soon came
to fear that a major drop in oil prices would jeopardize investment
in high-cost alternative energy ventures and such promising oil operations as the Alaskan North Slope and the North Sea reservoirs. To
safeguard these interests, the IEA actually discussed setting a floor
price for oil. Washington even flirted with a long-term deal to trade
U.S. wheat for Soviet oil. But talks broke down when Henry Kissinger,
now Gerald Ford's secretary of state, insisted on a lowball price for
the oil and a high level of publicity for the deal as a way to humili-
ate OPEC.

Within OPEC, the United States lobbied consistently in support
of Saudi Arabia and against raising the posted price. To pacify the
Shah, Washington sold Iran huge quantities of sophisticated weapons.
By the mid-1970s, fully half of all U.S. arms sales were to Iran. The
strategy seemed to work, at least when it came to the oil price: OPEC
made two relatively small increases that raised the price to $12.70 a
barrel in 1977.

Below the surface calm, however, new currents were developing. OPEC, which had produced 65 percent of the free world's oil in

1973, still accounted for 62 percent of it five years later. But global exploration and development triggered by the oil shock were beginning to pay dividends. Major new rivers of oil were about to flow from the North Slope, the North Sea, and Mexico's Reforma oil field. Within a few years, non-OPEC nations would out-produce OPEC.

Nevertheless, even as pumping from the three newest sources rose to nearly 7 million barrels a day, the overwhelming consensus in the industry was that another supply crisis was inevitable. Given what was assumed to be a still-critical need for oil to fuel economic growth, the experts predicted that demand in the second half of the 1980s would again outstrip supply, with the resulting energy gap triggering another oil shock.

As it happened, the experts were wrong. The decoupling of energy use from economic productivity, a trend that had begun in the mid-1970s, picked up speed in the 1980s for a variety of reasons. Not least of these was the developed world's transition from manufacturing to service and information industries, which tend to run on less energy. Then, too, global governments stepped in with taxes and regulations to encourage fuel efficiency and energy conservation. In the United States, for example, the Corporate Average Fuel Economy (CAFE) law boosted new-car fuel economy by more than 40 percent between 1978 and 1987. Accordingly, U.S. oil use dropped by 17 percent at the same time its GDP was rising by 27 percent.

Like many other people, however, Sheikh Yamani believed the experts. He began arguing that OPEC, to cushion the shock, should switch from trying to foster price stability to imposing a series of small, regular price increases. Even some in Washington were inclined to go along, reasoning that small, predictable increases were better than sudden massive shocks.

Ironically, Yamani and his allies were again at odds with the Shah, who had had yet another epiphany and now argued *against* higher oil prices. Money, he had decided, was not the cure for what ailed Iran, but its cause. Taking a page from Perez Alfonso's book, the Shah concluded that Iran's oil boom and the flood of petrodollars were creating chaos, waste, inflation, corruption, and political and social tensions that actually threatened his regime. He was right, but his latest insight came too late to save him. In December 1978, Iran erupted in mass demonstrations that finally forced the Shah to flee to the West on January 16, 1979. A few weeks later, Ayatollah Khomeini returned triumphant to establish an Islamic theocracy in Iran.

The Second Shock—and a Free-for-All

It was the unforeseen events in Iran, not any market shift or economic trend, that set off the world's second oil shock, and it was to prove even more disruptive than the first. Iran's production of 4 million barrels a day was sharply curtailed by the outbreak of revolution. But just as during the shock six years earlier, the worst damage resulted not from lack of oil, but from panic.

California, America's most populous state and often a bellwether for the nation, was the first to experience oil-shock difficulties. Early in May 1979, for instance, gasoline stations began cutting back their hours because of fuel shortages. Long lines materialized, accompanied by sporadic violence. The *Los Angeles Times* reported that one station attendant was beaten with a baseball bat, while another required fifty stitches to close a wound administered by a beer-bottle-wielding customer. Thieves hijacked a Shell Oil tank truck after pulling a gun on its hapless driver.

Hoarding was widespread, occasionally with tragic consequences. In a three-week period, Los Angeles fire officials blamed forty-four fires and four deaths on poorly stored gasoline or siphoning accidents. A number of large organizations were accused of worsening the crisis by stockpiling millions of gallons of fuel.

Mounting tensions prompted a dozen California counties to inaugurate gas rationing on May 9; motorists were restricted to alternate days at the pump. Before the month was out, President Jimmy Carter followed up with an executive order empowering other states to regulate gasoline sales until September 30, 1979.

As shortages spread to other states, so did anger and suspicion. In mid-June, a *New York Times*/CBS News poll found that 62 percent of those interviewed did not believe the crisis was real. Some even harbored convictions that U.S. companies and the federal government were in league to hold back gasoline. Paul Fieler, a postal clerk in Cincinnati, voiced that common skepticism when he was quoted as saying: "You can't say that they don't play hand in glove, footsie and patsie, with one another."

Iran's exports to the United States would not officially end until almost ten months later, on November 4, 1979, when Iranian students stormed the U.S. embassy in Tehran and took scores of Americans hostage. President Carter then halted all imports of oil from Iran; and Iran, in turn, canceled its contracts with the United States. Shortly after the disruptions began, however, the other OPEC producers had stepped in to pick up some of the slack, leaving a worldwide shortage of about 2 million barrels. That was less than 5 percent of overall daily demand, a shortage that could easily have been handled with a mix of conservation and use of stockpiles. Nevertheless, a scramble among the world's oil players to avoid getting caught short again intensified the market disruption. Long-term contracts were unilaterally canceled. Spot trading—in which the agreed-on price is for immediate, or nearly immediate, delivery of the commodity purchased—became dominant. Governments responded with conflicting signals, and the OPEC members, comfortably ensconced in the catbird seat, shook down their customers and manipulated supplies to push prices even higher.

The whole international system of fixed, posted prices for oil seemed on the verge of collapse. But there was another, even greater force at work: Many feared that the new power of Islamic fundamentalism might spread throughout the region. For a while, concern about the reach and grasp of the Iranian imams captured Washington's attention. But once the hostages were safely released (on January 20, 1981, the day Ronald Reagan was inaugurated), the threat seemed to fade from consciousness and an aura of complacency set in. Sure, the United States periodically slapped another economic sanction on Iran, as extreme anti-American propaganda and covert activities aimed at exporting the revolution continued undeterred. As we now know all too well, the United States would come to regret its complacency.

The immediate effect of the uproar in the oil market was to push up inventories. At any given time, several billion barrels of oil are stockpiled and in inventory around the world to ease the flow from the well to the refinery and to guard against shortages. Because inventories are expensive to maintain, no one holds more than is needed—

at least in normal times. But in the panic of 1979 and 1980, buyers at every level of the marketplace assumed that tomorrow's price would be higher than today's—and worse, that they might not be able to buy tomorrow at any price. Irrational behavior was the order of the day, from executive suites to celebrity mansions.

Some companies were actually holding oil in supertankers. This is a hugely expensive proposition. Most tankers are chartered, and every charter contract sets out a predetermined number of days for unloading cargo. Staying overtime subjects the tanker to demurrage charges, which can run to many thousands of dollars. Companies using supertankers as storage vehicles during the second oil shock were paying vast demurrage fees. The potential rewards, however, were also great. As prices went up, the value of the cargo shot up. Thus, traders who anchored loaded supertankers with tens of thousands of tons of oil offshore at major trading ports, like Rotterdam in the Netherlands, were more than willing to incur the cost, which paled in light of their profits.

The most notable of these traders was Marc Rich, who had long been making a fortune in the oil trade. Throughout the 1970s, Rich used his ties to the Iranian royal family to buy cheap oil, which he then sold for whatever the tumultuous spot market would bear, yielding him a cumulative pretax profit exceeding $350 million in 1976 dollars. When the Shah was overthrown, Rich, without missing a beat, changed partners and continued his trading with the new Khomeini regime and its radical followers. It was those transactions, made illegal by the U.S. restrictions against Iran, that later led to Rich's conviction for dodging domestic oil price controls. (Rich, who fled to Switzerland in an attempt to escape prosecution, received a controversial pardon from President Bill Clinton in his final hours in office.)

Prior to the Iranian crisis, Rich had had the good luck—or foresight—to sign contracts for inexpensive Nigerian crude oil. By the late 1970s, he reportedly controlled as much as 50,000 barrels a day of Nigerian production. That's how Rich came to have oil-filled supertankers incurring demurrage charges as they sat outside Rotterdam while the second oil shock roiled the markets. As the price climbed, Rich, an acknowledged trading wizard, increased his profits exponentially by docking his tankers and periodically selling the oil.

One avid customer was the Atlantic Richfield Company (ARCO), now a part of BP, which found itself in desperate straits in 1979 after the Iranian revolution and subsequent U.S. embargo stripped the company of 200,000 daily barrels of oil, or about one-fourth of what it needed to keep its refineries producing at full tilt. To fill the gap, ARCO signed contracts with Rich that required the payment of hefty premiums atop the official posted price of Nigerian oil. In a twelve-month period, ARCO paid many millions in such premiums, company officials later told the *Washington Post*. ARCO also paid a $315 million fine for its part in colluding with Rich to sidestep U.S. price controls, although its participation in the illegal maneuvering was categorized as unintentional.

All told, the rush to build inventories added an estimated 3 million barrels a day to normal world demand, which was already 2 million barrels higher than the available supply. Inevitably, the outsized demand again drove prices heavenward. In the final reckoning, the posted price would soar from $13 a barrel to a new record of $34 in January 1981.

The OPEC producers couldn't contain their natural urge to take advantage of panicked consumers. As Daniel Yergin recounts in *The Prize*, Shell Oil got a telegram from an oil minister one morning invoking *force majeure* to cancel a long-term contract to supply a daily quota of oil. *Force majeure*, which literally means "greater force" but is commonly translated as "act of God," is invoked to excuse one party in a contract from liability when an unforeseen, unavoidable, and uncontrollable event, such as a war or natural disaster, makes it impossible to carry out the agreed-to obligation. That afternoon, a second wire arrived from the minister, offering the same amount of oil at a spot price 50 percent higher than the contract price. Shell took it.

The oil minister's actions were disgraceful, but typical of the way the OPEC members operate. Where was the act of God? It was nonexistent. Pure and simple, this was a breach of confidence and a breach of ethics, not to mention an outright breach of contract. The oil minister pulled off a daylight robbery because he knew he could, and because Shell couldn't do anything about it.

Even after spot prices fell back following the revolution, when Iranian oil started to trickle back into the market, OPEC continued to milk the market for every penny it could get. Member nations unilaterally cut back production to keep the price up. When OPEC met officially in March, it gave its members permission to tack on whatever surcharges and premiums the traffic would bear. Obviously, this free-for-all did nothing to allay buyers' fears. The prevailing instinct was to buy now, no matter the price; otherwise, you'd regret it when the quote went higher tomorrow.

Saudi Arabia swam against the OPEC tide, insisting that it would stick to the posted price of $18 a barrel. But when only the United Arab Emirates followed their lead, the Saudis feared they were losing control of the situation. Back then, the Saudis were acutely aware that an overly voracious pricing policy could have political consequences.

Sheikh Yamani led a one-man campaign for conservation and price moderation, to little effect. Even Western leaders and analysts, whose countries had to bear the brunt of rising fuel costs, didn't seem as intent on encouraging their citizens to conserve energy as did Yamani. He stood practically alone in sounding the alarm, predicting that confidence-sapping oil price increases would lead to serious, long-lasting competition in the form of alternative fuels.

The panic sparked by the revolution in Iran in the spring of 1979 was compounded in November, when militant Iranians took more than sixty Americans hostage in an assault on the U.S. embassy in Tehran. In response to the growing tension on the world's political stage and President Carter's embargo on oil exports to the United States, spot oil prices spiked repeatedly, erasing record after record.

When the OPEC members next met, the Saudis reprised their voice-of-reason role and suggested that everyone agree to abide by a posted price of $24. No dice. Iran immediately jumped to $33; spot prices had continued to climb and were now running over $40 a barrel.

With no end to the price spiral in sight, Yamani warned that the inventory buildup would eventually end, and when it did, the excess stores would be dumped onto the market. The resulting glut would trigger a price collapse, thereby decimating the members' revenues. Few of the Saudi oil minister's colleagues agreed with him. In fact, most openly derided both Yamani and his unpopular notions. Marathon discussions failed to produce an agreement, and after the meeting, several members joined Iran in raising their posted prices to $33.

A few months later, in April 1980, the Carter administration's ill-fated Desert One raid to rescue the hostages sparked yet another bout of hysterical buying in the jittery oil market. Gloom settled over the industrialized countries after OPEC's long-range strategy committee recommended that the posted price should be raised every year by 10 to 15 percent. That strategy would lead to oil at $60 a barrel in five years. Clearly, the pundits concluded, the world oil economy was in massive danger, and the mood in the United States and Europe reflected this grim assessment. The humiliation of Desert One and the interminable hostage crisis only compounded the damage—and President Carter didn't help matters when he gave a speech counseling against the national "malaise."

Dire Prophecies Become a Reality

Prices averaged $32 a barrel when OPEC met again in June 1980. Sheikh Yamani, whom a Venezuelan delegate once described as "a charming genius," still couldn't convince his colleagues of their folly, although his dire prophecies were becoming reality. With inventories bulging, companies had no place left to store their excess petroleum stocks. Meanwhile, a recession was plainly developing in the industrialized nations, pulling down both demand for oil and its spot price.

By September, several worried OPEC members had agreed to cut production by 10 percent to support the price. Then they were saved by a bolt from the blue: In September 1980, as OPEC's ministers gathered in Baghdad to plan a glorious celebration of the organization's twentieth birthday, war broke out. Saddam Hussein sent Iraq's troops across the border into Iran in a dispute over control of the Shatt al-Arab, a waterway that both countries needed for access to the Persian Gulf. The war was to drag on for eight years before ending in a ceasefire mandated by the United Nations. It foreshadowed Saddam's grab for Kuwait in 1991, which in turn triggered the first U.S. invasion of Iraq.

With Saddam's foray into Iran, more than 3 million barrels a day again vanished from the oil market, and the spot price jumped to a new record of $42. In December 1980, OPEC reached a split-decision, two-tiered price structure: $32 for Saudi Arabia, $36 for everyone else.

Meanwhile, non-OPEC production was rising. Despite the continuing war, Iranian and Iraqi oil would soon reappear on the market. In order to defend its posted price, OPEC had to cut its own production, which meant accepting a lower share of the world oil market. At the same time, buyers, fed up with the high prices, began to tap into their massive inventories. As Yamani had predicted, OPEC was beginning to harvest the fruits of its ill-considered pricing and production strategy.

Finally, in 1981, OPEC announced a unified posted price of $34. This was, in effect, a price cut for most of the members. The posted price would go no higher for a decade. OPEC found itself pinned down by its own declining market share and the lower price offered by its non-OPEC competitors. By 1981, OPEC's annual production had plummeted by 26 percent from the 1979 level, to 22.5 million barrels a day. Revenues slumped, too.

The year 1982 provided no respite. Non-OPEC nations outproduced the cartel by 1 million barrels a day. Soviet exports were rising, and spot prices were running as much as $8 a barrel below OPEC's posted price. Now it was payback time for the oil companies. They, not the OPEC producers, were reneging on long-term contracts and playing the spot market. The choices were stark. OPEC could either cut its posted price to match the competition, or cut production to firm up the price. Fearing that another price cut would undermine their long-term gains, weaken their posted-price structure, and sap their political and economic clout, the OPEC nations reluctantly took the last step to becoming a true cartel. In March 1982, OPEC set a collective production limit of 18 million barrels a day, a whopping 42 percent below the 31 million barrels it had produced just three years earlier in 1979. (Today, almost a quarter of a century later, OPEC is producing 27.1 million to 29.1 million barrels a day, with no perceptible decrease in proved reserves. In fact, OPEC members now claim to have nearly twice as much oil in reserve as they had in 1970, and this after producing at least 300 billion barrels in the intervening years. Clearly, the numbers that OPEC distributes for public consumption just don't add up.)

Each member nation was assigned a daily quota, and Saudi Arabia was to act as the swing producer, adjusting its output to keep the price steady. The quotas were supposed to be a temporary measure while the market recovered, but the market price kept heading lower.

In March 1983, after twelve days of wrangling in a London hotel, OPEC cut its posted price by 15 percent, to $29 a barrel. The collective production quota was reduced to 17.5 million barrels a day. OPEC had now made itself the world's swing producer, propping up global oil prices at the expense of its own market share. It had come full circle from its glory days in the 1970s. No longer did buyers worry about getting supplies. Now it was the oil producers who worried about losing access to markets. Buyers who once competed to pay premium prices now expected huge discounts. Instead of "black gold," oil had become just another commodity, with too much product chasing too few buyers. The situation looked bleak for OPEC.

The cartel's troubles only deepened when the New York Mercantile Exchange opened an oil futures contract in 1983, hammering the final nail into the coffin of dictated prices. Now the price was being set on a minute-by-minute basis in thousands of independent transactions around the world, instantly reported and transparent to all players. OPEC's quota system was in a meltdown, with overpumping rampant and member countries defying efforts to verify their production figures.

By 1985, amid a still-soft world economy and a weak market for oil, booming non-OPEC production had cut the cartel's market share to just 37 percent. Saudi Arabia, the swing producer's swing producer, was pumping only 2.5 million barrels a day, or one-quarter of its presumed capacity. Its oil revenue, which had peaked at $119 billion in 1981, had dwindled to $26 billion four years later. The Saudis were forced to impose actual austerity measures, with pay cuts as deep as 30 percent for government workers, teachers, and hospital employees.

Austerity in corrupt, oil-dependent societies seldom if ever affects the ruling elite, however. In Saudi Arabia, the royal family felt no pain. The *Wall Street Journal* reported in 1985 that the Boeing Company was hard at work converting a 747 into a flying palace for the country's new leader, King Fahd. The plane was designed to mimic the Gothic architecture of the king's new palace, with arches, chandeliers, ceiling mirrors, gold-plated hardware, a three-story elevator, a medical room equipped with a surgical table, and a communication system that outperformed the system installed on Air Force One.

Frustrated by their falling revenues, the Saudis rebelled and adopted a complex new pricing structure worked out by Sheikh Yamani that let the kingdom cut prices and increase production. Predictably, their OPEC brethren jumped to do the same and prices collapsed: By the summer of 1981, benchmark light crude was selling for $8 a barrel. Within twelve and a half years, the OPEC producers had ridden a round-trip roller coaster that brought the price virtually back to where it started.

Looking outside their own house for the villain, the OPEC nations declared war on the non-OPEC producers, vowing to "secure and defend" the OPEC market share. What those words really meant was a no-holds-barred, cutthroat price war. To steal away market share from the non-OPEC producers, the cartel jacked up its production and hacked away at prices, undercutting the outsiders in hopes of forcing them to fall in line and cut their output to raise prices. "Join us or die" was the message.

Of course, the heavy-handed OPEC approach triggered another full-fledged oil shock—this time on the downside—and while buyers rejoiced, it was the producers and traders who felt the pain. The futures contract price on the New York Mercantile Exchange plunged to $10 a barrel, while actual spot prices in the Persian Gulf fell to $6. OPEC had increased its tangible production by only 9 percent, expanding the free world's oil supply by no more than 3 percent. But in an age of greater market volatility, that was enough to spark a sellers' panic. Exporters scrambled for markets and buyers jockeyed for ever-lower prices. The free market was calling the shots.

The clear winners were the world's consumers: Every nickel, centime, or pfennig they didn't have to spend for fuel was free to be spent on everything else. Economies were expanding as demand rose and sellers boosted their operations to meet it. People added on to their houses, vacationed abroad, sent their children to college, bought color television sets.

But not for long. As had so often happened during OPEC's tumultuous existence, the cartel would be rescued by its victims. But, this time, the consequences for OPEC's ever-willing protector would prove to be particularly threatening.

8

The Faustian Bargain

I t's an ancient story of misplaced values. Faust, a German school-teacher *cum* fortune teller and magician, allows his pride and thirst for power to tempt him into making a fateful pact with the devil. In this sixteenth-century German legend, Faust is first rewarded with twenty-four years of pleasure and power, after which Mephistopheles, the supreme spirit of evil, carries the suddenly repentant schoolteacher off to suffer an eternity's worth of pain and sorrow for his prideful mistake.

From this ageless classic comes the term *Faustian bargain,* a pact made for present gain without sufficient regard for future cost or consequence. George H. W. Bush made just such a bargain when, as vice president under Ronald Reagan, he arranged with King Fahd of Saudi Arabia to rescue America's domestic oil industry. By giving OPEC a reprieve and stifling competition, Bush helped saddle world consumers with a bill for hundreds of billions of dollars—money that was transferred from rich and poor countries alike into the coffers of the OPEC producers and their cronies. And it was all done under the guise of protecting the domestic oil industry. In essence, the United States became OPEC's cheerleader and defender. With the American government on board, OPEC oil producers had little to fear politically.

But for anyone not part of the oil game, Bush's efforts were a disaster. Here was the mother of all crony capitalism. Oil industry constituents inside the United States and out hijacked the national interest. Henceforth, our government would pay close heed to the opinions and well-being of the Arab states in the Gulf, rationalizing actions fraught with hypocrisy by cloaking them, as discussed in earlier chapters, in terms like *stability, security of supply,* and *finite resources.*

Washington Rides to the Rescue

In hindsight, the seller's panic and ensuing price plunge of 1986 was the world's last best chance to get the OPEC monkey off its back. The cartel was in tatters, its power vanquished. If its former victims hadn't come to its rescue, OPEC surely would have faded into history without the oil-buying nations ever having struck a blow. They could have just sat and watched as OPEC destroyed itself.

For consumers and their advocates, the selling panic of 1986 was an answer to prayer. The doomsday crowd, it seemed, had been mistaken: Oil was cheap and abundant, and the once-fearsome oil weapon was nothing more than a cardboard sword. Cheap oil would cut costs across the economy, and lower retail prices would mean faster growth and higher living standards for everyone. Betokening the bright promise, filling stations mounted their own retail price wars, and the only gas lines to be found were in Texas, where one entrepreneurial dealer came up with a unique loss leader: a one-day promotion offering gasoline absolutely free.

As far as the oil world was concerned, however, there was nothing either welcome or amusing in the situation. Chaos was the operative word. Even the industrialized countries discovered that rock-bottom oil prices were a mixed blessing. The higher-cost, non-OPEC producers were suffering—some North Sea oil fields were losing money on every barrel pumped because the market price had fallen below production costs. But it cost so much to mothball production platforms that their owners kept them going, hoping against hope that the price would rebound.

In the oil industry, there are fixed costs and variable costs. Someone drilling a well pays for the fixed costs of equipment, lease purchases, taxes, and interest—say, $100,000 a year—whether or not the well ever produces a drop of oil. So a driller with a producing well may decide to keep pumping even at a loss as a way of bringing in revenue to defray at least some of those fixed costs—so long as he can also cover his variable costs, including labor, fuel, royalties, and transportation.

But, of course, producers can't hang on forever in the face of loss-making economics. A group of non-OPEC producers tried, and failed, to start a dialogue with OPEC. In the United States, where production costs were rising rapidly and total production was plummeting, oil companies reacted to the crisis with massive cuts in spending, particularly for exploration and new production. The Texas oil business virtually collapsed; deep recession gripped the Southwest.

In Washington, President Ronald Reagan single-mindedly championed the free market and rejoiced over low prices at the pump, telling audiences in South Carolina in the summer of 1986, "Thanks in large measure to our decontrol of oil, we've seen energy prices tumble, including the price you pay for gas. Isn't it good to pull into a station today and watch the gallons on the pump add up faster than dollars?" But the domestic oil and gas industry and its backers in Congress were all clamoring for some sort of action to reverse the price collapse.

Leading the charge was Dick Cheney, who as a congressman representing energy-rich Wyoming championed a new tax on imported oil. He declared in October 1986, "Let us rid ourselves of the fiction that low oil prices are somehow good for the United States." What was good for America, Cheney's reasoning went, was higher prices in the domestic oil industry. Cheney failed to say a thing about the billions of dollars his proposed import tax would remove from the pockets of U.S. oil and gasoline consumers, who might have found cause to question just how good Cheney's tax plan was for their region of the country.

The backers of a tax argued that continued low prices might permanently cripple the domestic energy industry and bring a chronic flood of imports. A weakened U.S. energy industry was perceived as a threat to national security and American leadership of the free world. To safeguard domestic oil, President Eisenhower had imposed import quotas back in 1959. Now, the industry was seeking a tariff on imports to level the playing field.

Cheney's plan and ones like it were criticized by other lawmakers as snake oil that would lead to factory closings and put hundreds of thousands of people on the unemployment line. Senator John Heinz, Republican of Pennsylvania, said the legislation would cost his state's consumers another $1.3 billion a year in energy costs and would send inflation spiraling higher. Years later, when the Cheney plan was revisited by Democratic congressmen in the spring of 2004, Senator Richard Durbin of Illinois said the proposal, had it not been defeated, would have cost consumers $1.2 trillion over the intervening years.

What actually happened was much worse.

The industry plea for some kind of tariff had found a receptive ear in Vice President Bush, himself once an independent Texas oilman. When none of a variety of relief proposals for the oil industry made it through Congress, Bush began to press for coordinated production restrictions by the Gulf oil producers. He aimed to shift their focus from raising their market share to supporting higher prices. The vice president had long planned a visit to Saudi Arabia and the Persian Gulf states to discuss mutual national concerns, oil among them. When he actually made the trip in April 1986, it was in the wake of the price collapse and the resulting turmoil.

Ever since the first oil shock in 1973, OPEC and its allies had been imposing what amounted to a tax on the industrialized world's consumers. The price collapse, reflecting real market forces, was now repairing the damage, shifting $50 billion back to the consuming nations in 1986 alone.

When Bush set out to reverse the flow back to the producers, he drew fire from the free-market White House. At a news conference just before flying off to Saudi Arabia, the vice president said, "I think it is essential that we talk about stability and that we not just have a continued free fall, like a parachutist jumping out without a parachute." When this remark caused a spike in the spot oil price, a senior official in the Reagan administration acidly retorted that "poor George" had got it wrong; all things considered, falling oil prices helped the U.S. economy, and the best policy was to let the market do its thing. "It's a gaffe," the official said. "George is a Texas, pro-oil guy, but that is not the administration policy."

But even while denying any change in its free-market policy, the White House sent conflicting signals. President Reagan himself insisted at a press conference that he and the vice president were in agreement, but that oil prices should be "settled in the open market." Earlier that day, the president had told the American Society of Newspaper Editors that the plunging prices were a boon for many Americans but were hard on domestic oil producers. And he just hoped that the "whole thing will stabilize very quickly."

The energy secretary, John Herrington, further beclouded the administration position when he advised in a speech that the Saudis needed "to be aware of the dire straits the American oil and gas producers are in." This, in turn, prompted Congressman Philip Sharp, a leading House Democrat from Indiana, to accuse Herrington of trying to "talk up" the oil price "by urging the major player in the OPEC cartel to return to the tactics which have caused our economy such great damage in the past."

Bush was undeterred by the sniping, including an anonymous administration official's comment that the vice president was "off the reservation," and a *Detroit News* editorial headlined "Bush to Michigan: Drop Dead." At a news conference aboard the USS *Enterprise* in the Gulf of Oman, Bush shot back: "I think this [support for the U.S. oil industry] is administration policy. I think I'm correct. I know I'm correct. Some things you're sure of. This I'm absolutely sure of." Another thing he knew for certain, he told a group of U.S. businessmen at a breakfast meeting in Riyadh, was that at some point "the national security interest of the United States says, 'Hey, we must have a strong, viable domestic industry.' I've felt that way all my political life, and I'm not going to start changing that at this juncture. I feel it, and I know the president of the United States feels it."

At a dinner with several Saudi ministers, Bush warned Sheikh Yamani that continued low prices would only turn up the heat in Congress for a tariff on imports. He added pointedly that the administration would find it hard to resist.

Yamani—who was widely regarded as the shaper of Saudi, and therefore OPEC, oil policy—took Bush seriously. Whatever the White House was saying for public consumption, he reasoned, surely the vice president of the United States had to be delivering the real message. Nevertheless, the *Boston Globe*'s Robert Healy reported that Bush carried a letter from the president to King Fahd stating "the president's desire to maintain a free market and an unwillingness to intervene in the oil markets." (In reality, the whole dispute was moot, because, as Healy went on to note, "there is no free market for world oil, and there probably never has been." Whether Bush overstepped his brief and what might have happened had Reagan dispatched an emissary who spoke the party line are questions for the ages.

A Faustian Bargain with the Saudi King

Vice President Bush was later called to a private midnight meeting with King Fahd, after a day in which a Saudi tanker had been attacked by Iranian gunboats. The meeting was ostensibly about security in the Gulf and U.S. arms for Saudi Arabia. Oil was mentioned only in passing, according to official reports. But administration officials later told the *Wall Street Journal* that Bush had repeated his statement that national security demanded a strong domestic oil industry. He also told the king that "Saudi interests and U.S. interests aren't identical with regard to oil pricing." The king agreed that stability would be good, but, according to the *Journal,* neither Bush nor the king initially mentioned a desired price level.

Eventually, Bush and King Fahd settled on the notion of cutting back production and boosting oil prices by 50 percent to a target of $18 a barrel. The Faustian bargain had been struck, and its repercussions would be felt not only by American consumers paying higher prices to protect the domestic oil industry, but by consumers around the world.

Bush's trip to Saudi Arabia triggered a long debate within OPEC, as well as the emergence of a new concept: a "target price" for oil. The original rationale was that the price should be high enough to give the producing nations sufficient revenue for their support, but low enough that consumers could live with it, too. And it should be competitive with alternative energy sources, reducing the pressure to move away from oil or impose draconian conservation measures. Such a price would have to be enforced by quotas, which had proved problematic in the past. But perhaps the recent chaos had taught OPEC's truants a lesson about the dangers of cheating. If so, quotas might now be effective.

In the months that followed the vice president's visit, a consensus emerged that the "right" price would be one that fell within a range of $17 to $19 a barrel. Not coincidentally, this was right in line with the price brokered in the meeting between Bush and King Fahd.

In later years, OPEC adjusted the range to target a price somewhere between $22 and $28 a barrel, which held until the second war in Iraq touched off the panicky price spiral that peaked at $78.40 in July 2006. The next January, OPEC members seemed to be setting a new target, with suggestions ranging between $50 and $70 a barrel. The Saudis, ever the "moderates," appeared to be favoring a $50 to $55 level. Needless to say, any mention of maximizing OPEC profits is studiously avoided in the cartel's public statements about these negotiations. Discussions are typically described in terms of keeping markets well supplied and offsetting currency depreciation and inflation. But the elephant in the room is always the simple question of how much gold can be extracted without killing the goose.

Back in 1986 when enforcement of quotas was first being seriously discussed, Iran was still at war with Iraq and at first held out stubbornly. With war damage keeping it from raising its oil production, and higher prices its only option for bringing in more revenue, Iran was against the whole idea of price moderation—through imposition of quotas or by other means. Iraq, meanwhile, would have no part of any pact that included Iran.

But at an OPEC meeting held in Geneva in August, Sheikh Yamani had a surprise visit from the Iranian oil minister. He astonished Yamani by pledging Iran's support for the new system after all—but with a major caveat: Neither Iran nor Iraq would be forced to cut their level of output, while Saudi Arabia, Kuwait, the United Arab Emirates, and Qatar would carry most of the burden of reducing the cartel's production in order to stop the price bleed. The Saudis and their allies accepted the Iranian deal, giving in because they believed Iran was winning the war against Iraq, which would make it a power to be reckoned with in the Persian Gulf. An analyst in New York told the *Wall Street Journal* that he had detected a "subtle shift in power ... within OPEC," with the Iranians wielding more influence and the Saudis becoming more submissive.

For Yamani, whose price-war strategy was designed to regain OPEC's dwindling share of the world oil business by boosting production, it was the beginning of the end of a twenty-four-year run that had made him the man the king turned to in matters of oil.

Yamani was unceremoniously dumped a few months after the Geneva conference. Iran was accumulating power, and Yamani was the main obstacle blocking its way to higher oil prices. That and a push from Saudi royal family members resentful of his influence was all it took to retire Yamani and his perfect Oxford English from the corridors of power within OPEC.

But the deal had been cut: OPEC would set its target price and enforce it with production quotas. And the OPEC members insisted that some major non-OPEC producers support the new structure as well. Battered by the price war and tempted by the lure of high and stable prices, several signaled that they would comply. Mexico vowed to cut production. Norway announced it would slow its rate of growth. Even the Soviet Union offered to reduce its output by 100,000 barrels a day.

By the end of 1986, the new—albeit shaky—structure was in place. After its implementation, the quota system repeatedly seemed to be on the verge of collapse. Iraq temporarily seceded from OPEC, declaring itself unbound by OPEC's numbers. Many non-OPEC producers refused to take part. As for the Soviets, it was impossible to verify that Russia was living up to its commitment. At one point, the price fell to $15 a barrel. Nevertheless, the basic structure would stand for three years, despite its rickety foundation.

If not actually happy, nearly everyone was at least reconciled to the arrangement and its outcome. Drivers filled their tanks with more expensive gasoline, a reality that OPEC and its anointed analysts tried to camouflage with sweet talk about how the price compared "on an inflation-adjusted basis."

The spinners rightly assumed that consumers could be cajoled into emptying their pocketbooks so long as some arcane method of measurement reassured them they were lucky not to be paying even more. In exchange for losing the benefit of very low prices, consuming nations won the assurance that their investment in high-cost oil fields would be protected, and that decreased dependence on oil imports would make them less vulnerable to another crisis. Even the Reagan administration seemed to have been converted. A lower price might well generate higher growth and lower inflation, the president's men reasoned, with a touch of cynicism. But if the domestic oil industry could make a living at $18 and stop pushing for a tariff, the White House could sit idly by and boast that it was letting the market work. Of course, what was really working was the cartel, but the voters would hardly know the difference.

Fading Romance

For the oil industry, the 1980s ended and the 1990s began with a somewhat less colorful cast of characters than those featured in the 1970s. The whispery King Fahd of Saudi Arabia suffered a debilitating stroke in 1995 and was, as insiders knew, essentially replaced by his pragmatic regent, Crown Prince Abdullah. Mohammad Reza Shah Pahlavi of Iran, Venezuela's brooding Juan Pablo Perez Alfonso, and "Mr. Five Percent," the Armenian Calouste Gulbenkian, were long gone. The suave, tailored Ahmad Zaki Yamani and the oracular Henry Kissinger had both been sidelined by political reverses. Wanda Jablonski had long since printed her last scoop. But if the new characters were less flamboyant, the events they set in motion were no less significant.

Oil's image was beginning to match reality. It was increasingly viewed as a commodity like any other. Far from running out, proved reserves of crude oil had actually risen by 50 percent between 1984 and 1990, from 670 billion barrels to around 1 trillion.

But as usual in the oil world, the newly emerging impression would be distorted by events. Below the tranquil surface, the market was tightening. On the brink of the global economic boom of the 1990s, total oil consumption by 1989 had recovered to equal its high point of a decade earlier, though supply growth was thought to be lagging. Production at the operating wellheads in the non-OPEC fields of Alaska, Mexico, and the North Sea, according to the proponents of "peak oil," had already reached their zenith.

At least as important was the collapse of the Soviet Union and the end of the Cold War. Before their economy crashed, the Soviets had out-pumped even Saudi Arabia, hitting 12.5 million barrels a day in 1988 (most of it from what is currently the Russian Federation). But the industry's infrastructure had been neglected for years in the rush to produce, and it was rapidly decaying. By 1996, Russia was producing just half of its peak production, a drop deemed not to be easily reversible. Joseph Stanislaw and Daniel Yergin of Cambridge Energy Research Associates opined in *Foreign Affairs* that Russia would need to invest $50 billion in its dilapidated facilities just to maintain its reduced level of production, and another $50 billion to $70 billion in new technology to regain its 1988 capacity.

The global "security margin"—the gap between in-place production capacity and demand, which had been high enough in the 1980s to allow the world to weather the Iran-Iraq War—appeared to be dwindling fast. With each passing month, the world economy seemed more vulnerable to the kind of event that would give OPEC a new opportunity to squeeze the West. On August 2, 1990, that event occurred. Iraqi strongman Saddam Hussein shocked the world by massing 100,000 troops along his country's border with Kuwait.

As usual, Saddam was playing a devious and many-layered game. On one level, in the wake of the Iran-Iraq War, he was trying to rebuild his nation while Iran was preoccupied with its own internal political turmoil. Meanwhile, he was carrying on a border dispute with Kuwait over a large oil field and two strategic islands. But what is less well known is that he was also mounting a challenge to Saudi Arabia for the leadership of OPEC.

Saddam's million-strong army, the biggest and best equipped in the entire Middle East, already sparked fear in the region. Saddam had used chemical weapons to subdue rebellious Kurds in northern Iraq, and he made his menace loom even larger by nurturing suspicions that he was developing biological and nuclear weapons as well. Now he meant to use his muscle to displace the Saudis and their steady oil price strategy, push the OPEC price up, fatten his treasury, and become the dominant force in the Middle East.

Saddam's victim was shrewdly chosen. Kuwait, a reliable Saudi ally, was widely disliked within the cartel. With huge proved reserves of oil, it consistently cheated on its production quota, driving prices down. Saddam (who felt free to ignore Iraq's own quota whenever it suited him) said his troops were on the border to enforce OPEC discipline and Kuwait's quota. Many of the member governments quietly applauded.

In answer to the threat, Kuwait and another chronic quota exceeder, the United Arab Emirates, grudgingly agreed to stop overproducing. OPEC predictably responded by quickly voting to raise its oil price from $18 to $21 a barrel.

The West reacted to the increase with naïveté. Many opined that OPEC had learned to restrain its greed by only modestly increasing the price. These Pollyannas also pointed out that the higher price would enable more production from Mexico and Russia, and would help OPEC producers, notably Saudi Arabia, invest in additional production capacity. Best of all, they said, these developments showed that energy was no longer a problem. The West had learned that oil would not run out, and that if there were a crisis, conservation and alternative sources could ease the pinch. James Flanigan of the *Los Angeles Times* echoed the sentiments of the day when he wrote, "Energy no longer frightens us. We know it's not about to run out, that conservation can dramatically affect its price, and that if prices rise too fast—or some dictator threatens an embargo—we can use alternative energy forms. In short, we learned something in the 1970s that will stand by us in the 1990s."

Flanigan was right to disparage the myth of scarcity. Unfortunately, the world was not as convinced as it let on. Its false confidence would be exposed shortly when Saddam Hussein, as he had intended all along, ordered his troops across the border to overrun his hapless neighbor. It took mere days for Iraq to conquer and annex Kuwait.

The oil markets went into a frenzy. At the urging of the United States, the United Nations declared an embargo on Iraqi and Kuwaiti oil. Nearly 5 million barrels a day disappeared from the world markets, a lost river of crude equivalent to the volume that disappeared during the crises of 1973 and 1979. As in those instances, users all along the line rushed to build inventories. Prices spiked to $40 a barrel, twice the pre-invasion level. It was, many commentators suggested, the worst crisis in OPEC's history.

The cartel's other members indignantly united against Iraq, declaring their loyalty to their customers and scrambling to pump enough added oil to make up the deficit and fend off an economic crisis in the industrialized world. Not, mind you, that OPEC was doing us any favors. The producers' interest was in selling as much oil as possible, at the highest feasible price. But, led by the Saudis, they knew that a recession in the West would not be good for their own well-balanced blend of greed and political realism.

What is more, most of the OPEC nations in the Middle East, like Kuwait, were virtually defenseless against their more aggressive neighbors. They needed to protect their borders, and they welcomed the coalition of developed countries that George H. W. Bush, now the U.S. president, was putting together to do it. As always, the parasite needed a healthy host, so OPEC latched onto the oil-hungry nations. By December, all OPEC members were pumping flat-out; the Saudis alone raised their output by 3 million barrels a day, making up three-fifths of the lost oil. The market was fully supplied.

But as we have so often seen, markets are not always rational. Even though there was plenty of oil in the pipeline, anxiety, hysteria, and the expectation of war propped up prices. When Saddam threatened to move on to Saudi Arabia and destroy its entire oil industry, the hysteria incited another wave of panic. Again, traders and consumers rushed to build up inventories even as prices kept rising. What would happen if a full-scale war broke out? Could Bush's coalition stop Saddam Hussein from smashing the Saudi wells, pipelines, refineries, and port facilities? Would tanker skippers shy away from the Persian Gulf? Would shipping insurance rates skyrocket? Would Saddam use biological, chemical, or even nuclear weapons? What if Israel got involved and the whole Middle East erupted? Could crude reach $200 a barrel?

The Calm after Desert Storm

On January 17, 1991, the day the U.S.-led coalition forces started bombing Iraq, the price of oil abruptly dropped from $40 to about $30 a barrel. The pullback in prices was triggered by President Bush's decision a day earlier to tap the U.S. Strategic Petroleum Reserve in the first emergency drawdown since the reserve was established in the aftermath of the 1973–74 oil embargo. The Department of Energy was prepared to release as much as 33.75 million barrels from the 600-million-plus reserve, but only half of the emergency drawdown was actually used. Traders and customers alike had concluded that the Saudi wells were safe. Besides, the oil recently added to inventories was a costly burden, so consumers decided to use it rather than buy more. The price continued to fall.

After thirty-nine days of bombing Iraq, troops launched from Saudi Arabia swept north and chased the fleeing Iraqi army toward Baghdad. The ground war lasted just four days before Saddam capitulated. By the time his troops pulled out of Kuwait, not even the lakes of spilled crude and hundreds of burning wells left in their wake could scare the West's oil users, traders, and speculators. They drove the price below $18. The market was temporarily but effectively in glut. For the next five years, oil traded in a range of $15 to $20 a barrel. The entire Gulf War crisis turned out to be a hiccup on the price chart.

Nonetheless, there were lingering economic, environmental, and sociopolitical consequences. Extinguishing the more than six hundred oil well fires started by Saddam's troops took almost eight months, for instance, and cost $1.5 billion. The United Nations Compensation Commission later determined that Iraq owed $2.8 billion for the disruption of Kuwait's oil operations, in addition to the $3.2 billion it owed to individual victims of the invasion.

Two years passed before Kuwait was pumping crude again at its prewar rate of 2 million barrels a day, but it took six years before the UN-sanctioned Oil-for-Food program would bring Iraq's oil back to the world market following the UN-imposed embargo. Yet OPEC and non-OPEC producers easily managed to cover the wartime shortfall, and they continued to meet global supply needs while Kuwait rebuilt its industry and Iraqi crude remained embargoed. Had the world stopped to think about it, the notion that oil was in short supply might have come into question once again. But the prewar market upheaval had breathed new life into the old myth.

Over the intervening half-decade, OPEC's victims had twice come to its rescue. First, they saved the cartel's lunch when low prices threatened to break its grip on the world's oil consumers. Later, they went into battle to save two of its most powerful members, Saudi Arabia and Kuwait, from the brutal clutches of Saddam Hussein. But the story wasn't over. There would be more oil shocks, more internal dissension, and still more help from the ever-willing victims in the years to come.

9

Tightening the Chokehold

The worldwide average cost of finding and producing one barrel of oil is only $5—a seeming pittance until you compare it with Persian Gulf oil, which is so easily obtainable that it seems to leap from the ground. At the time of the first Persian Gulf War, the Saudis, who had long since recouped all investment in needed facilities, reportedly spent only 50 cents to produce each barrel of oil. By 1999, despite having spent $2.5 billion to develop its Shaybah oil field, the kingdom's production outlays still lagged far behind the rest of the world. In a November 1999 speech to the Houston Forum, the Saudi oil minister, Ali al-Naimi, pegged his country's "all-inclusive" cost of production at less than $1.50 per barrel, which covers drilling, pumping, transportation via pipeline to a port, and loading the oil on tankers for shipment to a final destination. As for the cost of discovering new reserves, he boasted that Saudi Arabia spent "less than 10 cents per barrel," while prospectors elsewhere were paying nearly $4.

In normal commodity markets, sellers would start there, add the infrastructure cost and the expense of transporting and marketing the goods, and take a profit, which would be determined by competition with other producers. In a totally rational world, the planet's cheapest oil would be used up first, and customers would turn to more costly sources only when the least expensive ones dried up. In effect, this was what the Seven Sisters did when they controlled the market. The only difference was that the Sisters dictated prices from the well all the way through the refinery to the retail gasoline pump, and allocated the profits as they saw fit.

When OPEC members finally nationalized their own oil in the early 1970s, they were an oligopoly controlling the world's biggest pool of crude, but they had little control over prices. It was only when they learned to set and enforce quotas on each other's output in a disciplined way that OPEC producers could become a real cartel, able to reduce oil flow in order to increase its value and drive up prices.

Truly effective production quotas empowered OPEC to supply the world market with just a little less oil than it could absorb at any given time. This created the impression that oil was scarce, when in reality it was practically bursting out of the sand. OPEC's spigot-turning power enabled its member countries to issue grave warnings about oil shortages while charging prices far higher than a free market would permit. That egregious margin was and is a permanent drain on the world economy.

For most of the period that this chapter covers—from the end of the first Gulf War through 1999—OPEC's members worked against each other, making the target price a moving object. All the same, as the chapter title suggests, the run-up to the millennium brought a major victory for OPEC, tightening the cartel's chokehold on the industrialized nations of the world and raising its extortion power to new and frightening heights.

Saudis Maintain the Upper Hand

A decade after Desert Storm, despite all assurances to the contrary, the first Gulf War had not so convincingly proved America's might as to make its repeated use virtually unnecessary. Neither had the war guaranteed the overthrow of Saddam Hussein or the reelection of George H. W. Bush.

The war did, however, maintain the status quo in the Persian Gulf. Lieutenant General James Terry Scott (retired), director of the International Security Program at Harvard's Kennedy School of Government, told the *Boston Globe* in 2001 that the war "precluded Iraq from dominating the Persian Gulf, the oil production, and the

populations. So the gain is 10 years of relative stability in the Gulf."
And, he might have added, another ten years of Saudi preeminence
on the world oil stage.

For its part, the victorious Bush administration focused on
cementing its ties with the supposedly grateful Saudi regime. Some
years before, when the Saudis were fearful of Iran and the Soviet
Union, the oil minister Ahmad Zaki Yamani had gone to the U.S.
State Department with a simple, startling offer: If the United States
would guarantee to protect Saudi Arabia, the kingdom would serve
as America's oil reserve. That deal, if it was ever seriously considered, had foundered on the 1973 Mideast war and the Arab oil
embargo. After Desert Storm, however, strategists proclaimed that a
new arrangement was in place. "The Saudis have become one of our
key bilateral relationships," said Richard Haass, the top Middle East
adviser on George H. W. Bush's National Security Council, in the *Wall
Street Journal* in 1992.

The delusion that the grateful kingdom would be our reliable
friend soon gained credence in the oil markets. In a 1992 *Christian
Science Monitor* article, Henry Schuler, director of the energy security program at the Center for Strategic and International Studies,
asserted that "[a]s long as we have a nice, friendly regime in Riyadh
that is beholden to the United States, there shouldn't be any threat
to oil prices or supplies. Nobody else matters." And the Saudis carefully reinforced this notion with their repeated assurances that they
would meet the market's needs and safeguard the world economy.

The Saudis were indeed pumping a lot of oil. They had become
the largest offshore source of oil consumed by the United States, selling us 1.8 million barrels a day by the early 1990s. Meanwhile, the
West stayed hooked on Arab oil even as the Saudis were buying U.S.
military supplies to shore up their own defenses and, possibly, to
quell any potential political backlashes. In the two years after Saddam's invasion of Kuwait, Saudi Arabia purchased fully $25 billion
in arms and equipment from American manufacturers.

Politicians and pundits call it "recycling petrodollars." In reality,
it's just plain old influence buying. That was former CIA operative
Robert Baer's charge in a perceptive 2003 book, *Sleeping with the Devil:
How Washington Sold Our Soul for Saudi Crude.* "The way I look
at things," Baer wrote, "it amounts to an indirect, extralegal tax on

Americans. Saudi Arabia raises the price of gasoline, then remits a huge percentage to Washington, but not just to anyone. A big chunk goes to pet White House projects; part goes into the pockets of ex-bureaucrats and politicos who keep their mouths shut about the kingdom. And a lot goes to keeping our defense industry humming in bad times."

The Carlyle Group, a private, multibillion-dollar investment firm based in Washington, D.C., offers a prime example of the incestuous relationships that link Washington insiders, America's business interests, and the oil-producing nations. Carlyle's roster of current advisers and alumni—luminaries like former secretary of state James A. Baker III, former president George H. W. Bush, former secretary of defense Frank Carlucci, former Securities and Exchange Commission chairman Arthur Levitt, former Clinton White House chief of staff Thomas "Mack" McLarty—reads like a who's who of Washington VIPs. The firm's usually clandestine business dealings, involving the defense industry and government contracts doled out by politicians, have long raised ethical eyebrows.

In October 2004, the group again found itself in an uncomfortable spotlight. At issue was Carlyle's involvement in a consortium seeking to land business collecting Iraqi debt owed to Kuwait. The proposed deal revolved around the management of $27 billion of claims against Iraq. What gave the arrangement an especially unpleasant aroma was the involvement of James Baker. At the time, Baker was serving as President George W. Bush's special envoy overseeing the Iraq debt negotiations.

When the news leaked and Baker's potential conflict of interest became known, Carlyle quickly denied that it had ever given final approval to the Kuwait deal and promptly withdrew from any participation whatsoever. A Carlyle spokesman admitted that the firm had been considering helping the consortium, but claimed it would have made certain that Baker did not benefit from any of the Kuwaiti business. This belated attempt at reassurance missed the point, however. Given its list of heavyweight political advisers and its business dealings with Middle Eastern oil-producing states and their citizens (Carlyle maintained business ties to the bin Laden family prior to the events of September 11, 2001), Carlyle and firms like it invite an almost inevitable collision between oil industry priorities and the greater national interest.

Against this backdrop of petrodollar recycling, the U.S. domestic oil industry was once again deep in the doldrums in the early 1990s. By mid-1992, the American Petroleum Institute reported that domestic production had plummeted to 1961 levels. Drilling-related jobs had been reduced by half in the preceding decade. Exploring for costly new domestic crude was seen as so futile that only 596 drilling rigs were working in June 1992, down from a peak of 4,530 in 1981. Oil executives were clamoring for a national energy policy and lobbying to revoke a 1986 tax on drilling. Thomas Coffman, president of the Texas Independent Producers and Royalty Owners Association, told the *Austin American-Statesman* that new technology could unlock 33 billion barrels of supposedly inaccessible oil still lurking in the reservoirs of Texas, but that would not happen without a national energy policy designed to aid the industry.

Yet the big international oil companies were flush with cash. Consumer advocates pointed out that whereas prices at the pump rose in lockstep with world oil prices during the bubble created by the Gulf War, they took a lot longer to come down after the bubble popped. It was one more proof of the old oil patch wisecrack about oil prices: "Up like a rocket, down like a feather." Citizen Action, based in Washington, D.C., estimated that the war fattened companies' profits by 20 to 25 percent. And Richard Kessel, executive director of New York State's Consumer Protection Board, complained, "Oil company profits were much better than they would have been had there been no invasion."

Trouble in Parasite

Relations within OPEC soured in the early 1990s as the world softened and the illusion of oil scarcity became less believable. The Saudis were strong enough to impose their policy of disciplined production and steady prices on the cartel, but it was popular only with Kuwait and the United Arab Emirates, the members with massive proved reserves and excess pumping capacity. The other seven voting members (Iraq was suspended during its embargo) were mainly pushing for as much revenue as the traffic would bear. Inevitably, though, most of the members cheated on their assigned quotas, pumping close to their announced capacity and driving prices down. The cheaters profited only slightly more than those who played by the OPEC rules.

In the world outside OPEC, production was still falling in the North Sea and Alaska's North Slope. But that decline would be offset by new discoveries in the deepwater Gulf of Mexico, and major new competition for OPEC loomed from the former Soviet republics clustered around the Caspian Sea. By some estimates, they were sitting atop fully 200 billion barrels of oil and trillions of cubic feet of gas. In the early 1990s, the fields had not been developed, and there was no way to get the product to market. But everyone in the industry knew that it was just a matter of time before Caspian oil became accessible. Buyers in China and Japan were already jockeying to build pipelines to the east, Russia was demanding that any western pipeline must cross its territory, and the big companies were scheming to bypass Russia with a line across Azerbaijan, Georgia, and Turkey to the Mediterranean.

Eventually, the companies would win out; in mid-2006, a million barrels a day were flowing from Baku on the Caspian through a 1,100-mile pipeline to Ceyhan on the Mediterranean, with gas in a parallel line ending in Europe. It was a major feat of engineering, built for $4 billion in just three years over mountain barriers and some 1,500 rivers, and it was made possible by an alliance in 1994 between President Clinton and the Azerbaijani strongman, Heydar Aliyev.

But that threat to OPEC's dominance was a decade away in the early 1990s. A much more imminent threat was the potentially huge Iraqi supply that hung over the market. Eventually the United Nations embargo would end, whereupon Iraq's 3 million barrels a day would come back into the market. Some day, the other members knew, they would have to cut their quotas to make room for it. More worrisome still was the estimated 6 million barrels a day that Iraq was theoretically capable of pumping at full capacity. Any member who actually cut back before that oil hit the market would be punished by a further cut when the time came. So most of them kept pumping anyway. Thus, OPEC had dwindling control over its output.

The sluggish world economy was undercutting demand for petroleum products. By its own logic, the cartel should have been cutting production quotas, but that would have been a futile gesture since most members kept exceeding the quotas already in place. Non-OPEC producers weren't even pretending to reduce output. Those factors combined to drive the price well below the OPEC target of $21. By 1993, when the price averaged only $16, OPEC's total oil revenues had plummeted by two-thirds from their 1980 peak.

The cartel's five largest member nations were all in debt, unable to trim their spending to fit their diminished treasuries. Saudi Arabia, the biggest spender of all, was particularly strapped for cash. The Saudis had created the world's most lavish welfare state, imposing no taxes on their citizens but offering interest-free home loans, free education and health care, and even cut-rate telephone service. The kingdom watered the desert to export strawberries to France and tulips to Holland. By 1992, it was producing 4 million tons of hugely expensive wheat, 60 percent of it for subsidized export. It even set up commercial fish farms in the desert.

The Saudis had agreed to pay $55 billion toward the cost of the Persian Gulf War. But with oil revenues severely curtailed, the massive spending was imperiling the kingdom's financial health. Its total cash reserves, which had rocketed to $120 billion in the early 1980s, plunged to $15 billion by 1994.

The Saudis also had to deal with a new occupant of the White House, one not as pliable as his predecessor. As a candidate, Bill Clinton had promised to honor the reality that "some countries and cultures are many steps away from democratic institutions." But he had also pledged to be much more aggressive than Bush in promoting worldwide democracy, which the wary Saudis saw as a threat. Their suspicion deepened when the Clinton administration began pressing King Fahd to make good on the war payments and also on a promise to buy $6 billion worth of aircraft from the U.S. manufacturers Boeing and McDonnell Douglas.

Over the years, Saudi Arabia had acquired a number of powerful Washington friends to buffer demands from the White House. It was customary for the Saudis to place former U.S. ambassadors to Riyadh on retainer. They lavished contracts and donations on numerous Washington institutions and organizations. In other words, the

Saudis bought and paid for an infrastructure of influence. "Every Washington think tank, from the supposedly nonpartisan Middle East Institute to the Meridian International Center, took Saudi money," wrote Robert Baer, based in part on his direct observations in the Middle East during twenty years with the CIA. "Washington's boiler room—the K Street lobbyists, PR firms, and lawyers—lived off the stuff. So did its bluestocking charities, like the John F. Kennedy Center for the Performing Arts, the Children's National Medical Center, and every presidential library of the last 30 years."

The Saudi banks were loaded with debt, and outside experts said the government would have to borrow at least $30 billion on its own account from international lending institutions over the next few years. The guest workers who handled the chores that Saudis disdained were sending home $16 billion a year, a chronic drain on the Saudi economy. But the government would not cut spending, especially the billions funneled every year to the extended royal family. Moreover, the Saudi princes feared that any attempt to cut subsidies for water, gasoline, electricity, and domestic air travel would trigger a backlash from their already restive subjects.

All told, the OPEC parasite was suffering lean times. The pickings would get even slimmer before its victims charged to the rescue once again. The cartel's 1993 attempt to crack down on quota breaking ended with the total quota actually being raised to 24.5 million barrels a day—an implicit acceptance of a good measure of the excess production. Meanwhile, with the world economy recovering from recession and demand for petroleum products rising, the price of oil actually drifted upward, from $16 a barrel to a range of $18 to $20, still short of the $21 target price. Then, in 1996, when the members were collectively pumping 26 million barrels a day, or 1.5 million over the quota, the looming problem burst into crisis: Iraq, as feared, returned to the market.

Lifting its six-year embargo in May 1996, the United Nations agreed to let Iraq exchange some of its oil for food to relieve the suffering of the Iraqi people. As much as 700,000 barrels a day would soon be added to the already saturated market, portending a sharp price drop unless OPEC members agreed to cut their own production levels by an equivalent amount. But no one wanted to sacrifice any revenue. Thus, when OPEC members gathered in Vienna in

June, executives of international oil companies courted the Iraqi oil minister while the other delegates haggled bitterly over quotas that most of them knew would be violated in any case.

The prospects may have been grim for OPEC and the fantasy of oil scarcity, but they were bright indeed for the world's economy. If the renewed flow of Iraqi oil could not be offset, many experts predicted that the price would quickly drop back to $16, a boon to consumers everywhere. And since the United Nations had authorized Iraq to sell $2 billion worth of oil every 180 days, a falling price would mean that more barrels would have to be sold to reach that figure. The added supply would push down the price still further, in a serendipitous cycle that would save consumers around the world billions of dollars.

Despite the obvious negative implications for OPEC, the members still could not agree to cut their quotas. "OPEC may still be alive, but it is quite impotent," according to Nordine Ait-Laoussine, the former oil minister of Algeria who had become an international oil consultant, as quoted in the *New York Times.*

Reverting to its role as the cartel's swing producer, Saudi Arabia cut back its own output to make up for much of the resumed flow of Iraqi oil. It leaned on Kuwait and the United Arab Emirates to soak up the rest. Demand for oil began to pick up as an economic boom roared through Asia. A short year later, the price was back up to $20 a barrel. Meeting in Indonesia in 1997, OPEC felt secure enough to agree on a full 10 percent increase in its quota, to a total of 27.5 million barrels a day.

Once again, the increase wasn't quite what it seemed. In reality, the cartel was only legalizing quota cheaters, because OPEC members were already pumping 28 million barrels a day. But the Saudis were confident that the market was firming, and they wanted to raise their own production from 8 million barrels a day to 8.76 million. They knew that most of their fellow members were pumping near presumed capacity, and thus were in no position to exceed higher quotas anytime soon.

Elsewhere, the evidence of improving fundamentals seemed solid enough. Non-OPEC producers claimed to have no online excess capacity and no prospect of major additions in the foreseeable future. Production from the Caspian region was still said to be at least ten years away. A cloud appeared on the horizon, but it was no bigger than a man's hand: Meeting in Kyoto, Japan, representatives of 169 countries agreed to a set of mandatory cuts of greenhouse gas emissions to reduce global warming. If the treaty could be enforced, it was bad news for fossil fuels—but happily for OPEC, the United States refused to sign on. Without the global leader in emissions, the treaty might well be meaningless.

Once again, however, confidence was waylaid by reality. And this time it was OPEC's confidence. When a financial crash swept through Asian economies and abruptly aborted the region's boom, the effects were felt around the world. Demand for oil dropped—but OPEC's members kept right on pumping. By the middle of 1998, oil was selling for $12 a barrel, a twelve-year low. A desperate OPEC tried both to police its members and to expand the conspiracy by negotiating production cutbacks from nonmembers. Mexico and Norway indicated they were inclined to go along. After all, every oil-producing nation had a vital interest in keeping the price up. John H. Lichtblau, chairman of the Petroleum Industry Research Foundation in New York, predicted, "This may be the end of the old OPEC, but a wider organization may take its place that may be more effective."

Lichtblau's forecast turned out to be premature. The cheating within OPEC continued, and Norway decided to opt out of any more production cuts. The price hit a low of $10.38 that year, with oilmen saying it would fall below $10 if OPEC could not produce genuine cutbacks of at least 1 million barrels a day. Oil at $10 a barrel would have been a bonanza for the rest of the world, of course. But for the OPEC parasite, it might have been fatal.

Parasite Found

OPEC reasserted itself in the nick of time. In March 1999, collusion to control supplies again became the order of the day. And in yet another reprise of a now-familiar tune, the West lent OPEC a crucial helping hand.

Just as Lichtblau had observed, interests were converging: Almost everyone in the oil business—producing nations and big oil companies alike—now saw the long-term advantage of selling the optimum amount of crude at the highest possible price. For their part, the petroleum companies, tired of suffering under OPEC's thumb, were now ready for their own round of crony capitalism. Low prices had contributed to a 40 percent profit plunge in the global oil industry, not to mention the layoff of hundreds of thousands of workers in 1998. No bottom was in sight. (On the bright side, the low oil prices had stimulated growth and hiring in other industries; in fact, employment showed a net gain when all was said and done.)

Peter Gignoux, manager of the petroleum trading desk at Salomon Smith Barney in London, summed up the prevailing view. "Nothing moves markets like fear," he told the *New York Times.* "Around the oil markets today ... all wish OPEC good luck."

The love-fest was mutual. OPEC members were eager to be reconciled with the big companies. The nations that had once thrown out the petroleum giants were now strapped for capital to expand and modernize their industries. Irony abounded when Algeria, Iraq, Iran, Kuwait, and even Saudi Arabia began openly inviting the big petroleum companies to come back, invest money, and share in future profits, if not the equity.

As OPEC ministers gathered in 1999 for their annual meeting in Vienna, Western oilmen were slipping discreetly past bodyguards into hotel suites to meet officials from such pariah nations as Iraq, Iran, and Libya. Sure, they might be under official sanctions, said Oscar S. Wyatt, former chairman of the U.S. energy giant Coastal Corporation. But as he told the *New York Times,* "Somebody has got to keep the contact with these huge oil producers when these sanctions come off. The Americans don't know why they are doing what they've done and how to undo it. We cannot come out of this world without any friends."

Economic conditions now favored the cartel. The Asian financial crisis was easing, demand was again on the rise, and oil prices had recovered to a range of $14 to $15 a barrel. Moreover, there was "a new spirit in OPEC," declared its president, Youcef Yousfi, the Algerian oil minister. Ending decades of rivalry and bickering, Saudi Arabia's Crown Prince Abdullah reached a diplomatic détente with Iran's moderate president Mohammad Khatami, agreeing that a higher price would benefit both countries and that the only way to get it was to restore the illusion of shortage by truly cutting production.

Venezuela's new president, Hugo Chavez, renounced his country's former policy of flat-out pumping in defiance of OPEC quotas, saying it had produced nothing but a ruinous drop in prices and revenues. If new production cuts were decreed, Venezuela would stick to the rules, Chavez vowed.

Indeed, Chavez had taken it upon himself to rally the troops. With oil dipping to $8 a barrel when he came to office in 1998, the man who has been called "Fidel with oil" hopped on a plane to crisscross the world of OPEC nations, preaching internal discipline at every stop. In an interview with the *Bangkok Post,* Chavez took credit for personally engineering production cutbacks and quota keeping. "It is true," he said, "that this effort has been successful in part due to the intensity and persistence of our oil diplomacy." He went on to point out "the necessity, even obligation, of production cuts in order to defend" the cartel members against an unacceptable economic hit.

Crucially, some key nonmember nations would also answer Chavez's call to put "a fair price" on oil via production cuts. Mexico had previously approached OPEC with suggestions of cooperation, and now Norway, Oman, and Russia were interested, too. Before the Vienna meeting, Abdullah and Khatami set up phone calls and meetings among heads of state, bypassing oil ministers and technocrats. The key OPEC nations agreed on genuine cutbacks in their quotas and persuaded the four outsiders to join the deal, in effect becoming de facto OPEC members. The "wider organization" that Lichtblau had foreseen a year earlier was becoming a reality.

It was a stunning and devastating turn of events for the world economy. The current global oil production of 70 million barrels a day was being cut by 3 percent, or 2.1 million barrels. OPEC members were cutting 1.7 million barrels, with Saudi Arabia once again absorbing the lion's share of 585,000 barrels. The four nonmember nations committed to production cuts totaling 388,000 barrels a day. This pact was expected to lift oil prices to $17 or $18 a barrel. More important, it signaled a new sense of discipline. OPEC's president Yousfi gloated, "To people who predicted the imminent demise of OPEC, I say, 'Not yet.'" Qatar's oil minister, Abdullah bin Hamad al-Attiyah, underscored the potential threat when he said, "The message to world oil markets from oil producers is solidarity, unanimity, and resolve."

Would the producers adhere to their quotas this time? There were open doubts that the limits would be honored, especially by Russia, which had never kept a promise to reduce production. "When the Saudis say they will cut, they do cut," observed the consultant Nordine Ait-Laoussine. "The Russians are another matter."

It helped that OPEC's most powerful member, Saudi Arabia, made a threat no one could ignore. Seemingly out of nowhere, the Saudis found unused capacity. Claiming it had miscalculated the market in the 1980s and invested heavily to expand production, the kingdom announced that it actually had the capacity to pump 3 million barrels a day more than its quota. Was this mystery crude really part of the 31 million barrels pumped by the cartel in 1979? Had the Saudis been hiding 3 million barrels of slack capacity to wield as a threat when needed? Or was the extra capacity truly new? Had the Saudis, all by themselves, boosted OPEC's overall capacity to 34 million barrels? Wherever the added pumping capacity came from, the Saudis wasted no time in warning that in case of cheating they would open their spigots and flood the world with oil. The price would drop calamitously and every producer would suffer. Far better, the Saudis said, to get in line and stay there.

This time, illusory or not, the threat worked. Supply would now be tightly controlled to hold the price on target. After years of chaos and futility, OPEC had again tightened its noose around the neck of the industrialized world.

10

Old Schemes for the New Millennium

To hear assorted pundits tell it, OPEC members began 1999 so divided that cheating on production quotas would soon resume, driving down prices in the process. The pundits were wrong. In fact, OPEC was poised to greet the new millennium with resurrected schemes to refill its coffers and restore its power. It had a grand design that would help propel the price of crude to more than $78 per barrel by July 2006.

OPEC's scheme was helped along in the intervening years by a compliant friend in the White House, as well as by surging demand in China. (In 2003, China overtook Japan to become the world's second-largest oil-consuming nation behind the United States. Before fears over China's rising consumption become overblown, however, it is important to note that the 5.8 million barrels per day it currently consumes, only 2 million barrels of which are imported, is less than a third of the more than 20 million barrels of crude oil consumed every day in the United States, of which 12 million are imported. In other words, big as it is, China's consumption makes up only a small part of the world's total and should be easily covered by available capacity.)

The cartel's resurgence began with the Vienna Pact of March 23, 1999. The public squabbling that had marred OPEC's previous gatherings was absent, replaced by a determined and unified mood. Qatar's oil minister, Abdullah bin Hamad al-Attiyah, put it succinctly: "1998 was a very hard year for everybody. Everybody learned the lesson, and nobody wants to see oil at $10 a barrel again." Between the lines, he seemed to imply that without OPEC's manipulations, oil would find its fair-market level, and that level was quite likely $10 a barrel or even less.

Although the Qatar minister's expressed fear of $10 oil and his nod toward a more disciplined cartel only reinvigorated the skeptics, there were compelling reasons for OPEC's fresh resolve. Low oil prices had forced Persian Gulf states to curb spending at home and abroad. While Gulf state rulers feared that reduced spending on their citizens' welfare might fan political unrest, the U.S. defense industry was forced to grapple in early 1999 with the unhappy news that Saudi Arabia, the biggest American arms customer, would make no major purchases that year. Indeed, Saudi Arabia's currency, the riyal, had come under siege by speculators who hoped to force its devaluation.

Given that threat to the world's richest petrocracy, and with the Faustian bargain hanging in the balance, one can easily picture certain Washington officials and lobbyists quietly cheering as OPEC began its program to cut daily output by 1.7 million barrels. Variations on the tableau would unfold in other capitals of the oil-obsessed world: London (home to British Petroleum), Paris (Total), Moscow (Lukoil), The Hague (Royal Dutch/Shell Group), and Rome (Ente Nazionale Idrocarburi).

OPEC initially said it aimed to raise prices to a range of $17 to $20 a barrel by September 1999. It either fibbed or miscalculated. By September 30, a barrel of crude oil cost $25. Industry analysts were largely unperturbed and, in yet another misreading, predicted that the price would peak at $28 before tumbling back to around $23 by year's end. Instead, as 1999 ended, oil stood at $25 to $26 a barrel and was poised to move still higher in the early months of 2000. It hit $34.37, a nine-year high, on March 8.

Various factors were working in OPEC's favor to strengthen demand. The U.S. economy was continuing to expand (a remarkable nine-year run that would soon hit a brick wall), as investors both large and small were caught up in the euphoric trading of technology stocks. The United States was riding high, complacent in its unmatched clout.

To be sure, there were some jitters as the millennium approached. American officials warned that terrorists might be plotting an attack on U.S. soil, following the mid-December arrest of an Algerian man caught trying to smuggle bomb-making explosives from Canada through the state of Washington en route to the Los Angeles airport. But most revelers—though apprehensive over the repeated warnings of terrorist plots and widespread computer disruptions caused by the turn of the calendar—were undeterred on New Year's Eve.

If anything, concerns about the millennium served to boost the price of oil. Some stockpiling occurred in response to the dire predictions of disrupted commerce should older computers fail to interpret "00" as the year 2000 and instead turn their internal calendars back to 1900. "We definitely have the sense homeowners are stockpiling heating oil ahead of Y2K," one energy analyst told the *Wall Street Journal* in mid-November. At the same time, the American Petroleum Institute noted that U.S. oil inventories had declined from the previous month, despite moderate weather.

Executives and economists schooled by big oil companies nevertheless saw scant reason for concern. Alan Struth, a former chief economist for Phillips Petroleum who was then with Honeywell Bonner & Moore in Houston, told Bloomberg News that the $25 price in late September was "not that big a deal" in present-day dollars. He said oil would have to climb to $72 a barrel to reach the equivalent of prices in 1982, when the United States tumbled into recession. (Despite the regularity with which such comparisons are made, they are patently self-serving—simply a way to explain away reality. A price is a price, and it exists in the present.)

Big oil companies were so confident the price would drop that they had kept their exploration budgets below 1997 levels. Thierry Desmarest, chairman of France's Total, declared in June 2000 that his corporation would not invest in finding any oil that would be unprofitable at $13 a barrel. "If people think the price will stay above $25 a barrel, they will significantly increase their investment in exploration and production, and in another two or three years, we will be facing another crisis," he said. In other words, Desmarest feared that significant new finds might force the price down to around $10 a barrel, as had happened in 1998, a more accurate reflection of oil's true market value than the cartel-induced spot price of about $25.

By slowing or suspending vigorous exploration in other corners of the globe, the major oil companies furthered the perception that OPEC was the "producer of last resort" and, more ominously, the "reserve of last resort"—erroneous ideas that have kept the oil-dependent masses cowed. That stance played right into OPEC's hands, as did the lack of any critical analysis of OPEC's actions. Not only would its members face no significant competition from new discoveries, but, as always, they were being allowed to operate below the radar, far removed from a critical eye. All in all, a guarantee that the world would stay hooked on OPEC oil.

Their Stability, Our Torment

By March 2000, however, with gasoline averaging $1.60 a gallon in the United States, consumers demanded action. The Clinton administration quickly launched a one-man missile, the energy secretary Bill Richardson, to pound OPEC for relief. He was Clinton's most tireless and personable—if unorthodox—diplomat. Known for his straight-to-the-point speech, alligator boots, and fancy cigars, Richardson had been an unusual but effective U.S. ambassador to the United Nations before taking the energy post. And it was Richardson—working on special assignment—who in 1996 negotiated the release of three Red Cross workers taken hostage in Sudan, and also smoothed negotiations for the freeing of a downed pilot in North Korea. In those years, Richardson dubbed himself the "undersecretary of thugs."

So Richardson wasn't a man to hesitate about placing a direct call to the cell phone of OPEC's current president, Ali Rodriguez-Araque of Venezuela, to argue for higher production quotas as the ministers gathered for their scheduled meeting in March 2000. Iranian officials waxed indignant that Richardson had the effrontery to lobby OPEC's ministers for relief—apparently miffed at the thought of giving the victim of a robbery a vote in the matter. "In the 40-year history of OPEC, there has never been a case of the Secretary of Energy calling OPEC ministers in the middle of a meeting," complained Hossein Kazempour Ardebili, Iran's representative on the OPEC board of governors. "We are very upset and disappointed at the external pressure. We don't like it." Note Ardebili's mindset. In effect, he was saying that OPEC's price fixing was such a divine right that the fixers' biggest consumer had to be chastised for even seeking an audience with their august selves.

In the years immediately following the first Gulf War, the United States arguably enjoyed its greatest leverage, having rescued Kuwait and shielded Saudi Arabia from Saddam Hussein's designs of conquest. If America had persuaded Saudi Arabia and Kuwait to defect from OPEC, the cartel's power could have been smashed. Instead, the United States was lulled by a booming economy and the pleas of special interests, thus giving OPEC members ample time to regroup. By March 2000, America was a humble petitioner again, subject to the whims and tirades of OPEC ministers.

Nonetheless, the Saudis were willing to propose a production increase—the first of three such increases that would occur over the next four months. These were not for charitable reasons, of course, but due to political considerations. The Gulf War had proved that a U.S.-led coalition was the ruling family's best protection. Needless aggravation of such allies would be imprudent.

The Saudis proposed manipulating the price back toward $25 from its high of over $34. "We want a stable market, we want a well-supplied market, and we want a market that will be in equilibrium all the time," said the Saudi oil minister, Ali al-Naimi. His soothing phrases were familiar. Saudi oil princes always don conciliatory masks in a crisis; it usually sedates Washington politicians. Al-Naimi himself is well versed in American thinking, having earned a bachelor's degree in geology from Pennsylvania's Lehigh University in 1962, followed by a master's degree in geology from Stanford.

The idea of stability may sound soothing to U.S. politicians concerned with keeping voters happy. But when the Saudis are applying the notion to global oil supplies, it has nothing to do with fair prices for consumers. Quite the contrary; stability in this context is merely a way to rationalize higher prices and get powerful leaders and opinion makers to do the OPEC cartel's bidding. Because oil is such an all-encompassing commodity, its owners and their allies comprise a huge cast of favored players—big oil companies, bankers, contractors, investors, equipment makers, pipeline operators, shipping owners, and so on. This global petro-lobby can and often does sway government energy policymakers in ways not evident to the voters and the media. It's crony capitalism at its worst.

Not all the OPEC members, however, are always willing to take the roundabout "stability" route to higher prices. Iran balked at the

March 2000 Saudi proposal to temper prices. Nevertheless, the Saudis prevailed—not surprisingly, since they had the capacity to supply the larger amounts all by themselves.

OPEC agreed to raise the total quota by 1.45 million barrels a day. Almost immediately, Iran reversed course and went along. This lifted the total increase to 1.7 million barrels. (A continued holdout would have been both useless and expensive, since Iran would have wound up selling less oil at a lower price.) "We are going to keep and preserve our market share," declared Iran's Ardebili. "Beyond that, we will see what happens."

By these actions, OPEC ministers consented to increase production for the first time since November 1997. President Clinton hailed the OPEC vote in March 2000 as "good news for our economy," which was under pressure as the stock market reeled with the bursting of the massive technology stock bubble. But Clinton also exhorted Congress to pass energy measures that would include new tax breaks for domestic oil producers.

Despite the increase in OPEC production quotas, oil prices kept rising. After dropping to $26 in the immediate wake of the March increase, they quickly resumed their climb, hitting $31 three months later. Why? For starters, it turned out that OPEC members had, as usual, been lying about their actual production. Prior to the announced increase, they had quietly overshot their stated quotas by a collective 1.2 million barrels a day. So what was now touted as a rise of 1.7 million barrels was really no more than 500,000 "new" barrels on the market. A second reason for soaring prices was that inventories were low and demand was rising.

The ministers had agreed to impose another automatic production increase if the price topped $28, but that clause in the pact was ignored. Secretary Richardson, the goat of the March meeting, held his peace, possibly distracted by the uproar over nuclear weapons data that had disappeared from a vault at the Energy Department's Los Alamos National Laboratory in his home state of New Mexico.

When the OPEC members met again in June 2000, they agreed to another increase of 708,000 barrels. This time, Iran went along quietly, condescendingly praising Washington for its passivity and promising to endorse further automatic increases if the price rose again. "We had a very good atmosphere this time," said Bijan Namdar

Zanganeh, Iran's petroleum minister. "In our last meeting, all the members complained of U.S. intervention. We didn't feel external political pressure at all."

Zanganeh also spoke of the goal of stability, using language that seemed as cagey as it was smooth. "We are looking for a stable price, not necessarily high or low," he said. "If the market needs more oil, we will produce it. We have an automatic mechanism for it." He refused to describe this mechanism other than to say it was a gentleman's agreement.

Gentlemanly or not, the new collusion was aimed at keeping oil-dependent nations in thrall to OPEC.

Brazen Behavior in Caracas

When the June production increase also turned out to be a mirage, the markets predictably sent prices higher again. With the price above $32 as the summer wore on, the Saudis announced a unilateral production increase of 500,000 barrels a day. Apologists raved. "They were getting really antsy about prices not coming down and about their ability to affect market psychology," theorized Roger Diwan, managing director of PFC Energy, a Washington consulting group. "Now, the Saudis have taken the oil bull market by the horns and pulled it down."

Not exactly. With demand for oil still on the rise and U.S. inventories at twenty-four-year record lows, the dip in prices occasioned by the Saudis' action disappeared. By mid-August, oil was right back up to $31.80.

Inevitably, the price of oil became an issue in the 2000 presidential campaign. The Republican candidate was George W. Bush, governor of Texas and son of former president George H. W. Bush, the man who had thrown OPEC a lifeline in 1986 and then saved the Saudis from Saddam Hussein in 1991. Now, Bush the younger was telling voters he could be more effective than Bill Clinton—and, by extension, Democratic candidate Al Gore—in persuading OPEC to be less greedy.

Clinton resumed his public lobbying for another OPEC quota increase. But still the price rose, hitting a ten-year high of $37.20

after Labor Day. OPEC responded by holding the first summit meeting of its heads of state in twenty-five years. The meeting, which took place in Caracas forty years to the week after the cartel's founding, had been called in late July by the newly reelected Venezuelan president, Hugo Chavez.

In calling the summit, Chavez made no secret that he wanted strictly enforced production restrictions to keep the price of oil high. In his inaugural address, he regaled his assembled OPEC brethren by comparing the price of a barrel of oil to the price of a barrel of shampoo, Coca-Cola, mineral water, and assorted other consumer products. To no one's surprise and everyone's delight, Chavez concluded that oil was certainly cheap at the price. But speaking with less candor and more duplicity, he stressed OPEC's willingness to hold a "constructive dialogue" with the industrialized nations to stabilize oil prices.

If that sounded like an attempt to blame the victim for the crime, that's exactly what OPEC intended to do. It was at this summit meeting that Saudi Arabia's Crown Prince Abdullah complained of OPEC being "unfairly blamed" for high oil prices. He said Western governments should "share the sacrifice" by cutting their taxes on oil—a nonstarter that would have increased gasoline consumption, extended dependence on fossil fuels, and, not coincidentally, fattened OPEC's purse. Whether Abdullah's comments were naively off the mark or brilliantly disingenuous, his primary aim was to prolong dependence on Saudi oil.

Meanwhile, OPEC's president, Ali Rodriguez-Araque, a lawyer and former leftist guerrilla who was also Venezuela's minister of energy, said the industrial nations should increase their refinery capacity in order to bring down oil prices—advice that conveniently ignored the fact that OPEC's artificially induced shortage was the reason for the heightened tensions.

The meeting approached farce—or at least a truly astonishing display of gall—when the heads of state insisted that the international treaty on global warming include a clause to compensate OPEC for any decline the accord might cause in the demand for oil. The treaty—provisions of which were due to be hammered out at a November conference in The Hague—threatened to drive "a stake into the heart of oil production, especially in member countries," said Nigeria's president, Olusegun Obasanjo. If the world adopted policies "explicitly intended to dramatically reduce the consumption of fossil fuels," he complained, "oil exporting countries would stand to lose more than $20 billion of revenue by 2010."

The best that could be said about this parade of self-serving finger-pointers is that they were spewing out a pile of rubbish. By this line of reasoning, if an embezzler is apprehended, his victims should be forced to make up for his lost income.

But it was also at this meeting that Crown Prince Abdullah pledged more unilateral production increases, saying Saudi Arabia was "willing and ready" to pump any amount of oil "necessary to stabilize the world oil market." This finally impressed the markets. The price tumbled to just over $30 the next day, and then hovered for several months in a range of $27 to $29.

The first half of 2001 brought a slowdown in the global economy, accompanied by reduced demand for oil. But OPEC successfully tweaked its supply, keeping it just under what the market could absorb and holding the price between $25 and $29. And when Iraq briefly pulled its 2.5 million barrels a day off the market to protest a United Nations decision on the Oil-for-Food program, the Saudis pumped just enough extra oil to offset the deficit and hold the price steady.

Oddly enough, the victims of this conspiracy seemed to welcome it. Oil prices were "high yet stable," according to Roger Diwan of PFC Energy. The OPEC nations, he said, "have convinced the market of their ability" to hold the price steady, as if stability alone were worth the huge premium that OPEC is able to extract.

Nor did the newly elected George W. Bush, campaign rhetoric notwithstanding, appear alarmed. A friend of the oil industry, he chose to continue the family tradition: Far from leaning on OPEC to restrain its greed, he very nearly praised the cartel as it curbed production to keep oil prices high. "It's very important for there to be stability in a marketplace," Bush said during his first summer in office. "I've read some comments from OPEC ministers who said this was just a matter to make sure the market remains stable and predictable."

The new president seemed willing to accept the stability of a monopoly's manipulated price—despite the worldwide drain of funds that could have been much more productively invested—so long as prices didn't spiral to unspecified heights. Even when the Bush administration was blindsided by OPEC's decision in July 2001 to cut crude production a third time, the response was timid. White House officials only expressed surprise; in a meeting with Venezuelan energy officials on July 27, they did not ask for relief, according to *Platt's Oilgram News.* President Bush merely observed that "any rise in energy prices would hurt" the U.S. economy.

The new U.S. vice president, former Halliburton chief executive Dick Cheney, agreed with Ali Rodriguez-Araque's specious argument that a lack of refinery capacity was at fault. "The big problem is gasoline today, it isn't crude," the vice president said in a May 2001 interview on PBS's *Frontline.* "It's the lack of refinery capacity. We haven't built any new refineries in this country in over twenty years." Although some dissent surfaced in the new administration—the chief economic adviser Lawrence Lindsey and the Federal Reserve chairman Alan Greenspan recommended that the White House put pressure on OPEC to raise production—Vice President Cheney prevailed when it came to shaping the administration's energy proposals. In short order, the administration called for relaxing clean-air standards to facilitate building new refineries and expanding old ones, and President Bush urged exploration on federal lands, including the Arctic National Wildlife Refuge in Alaska, thus raising environmental concerns without offering the counterweight of a viable national policy to reduce dependence on fossil fuels.

Cashing In on Fear, Grief, and Recession

The American psyche was irrevocably altered on September 11, 2001, when nineteen Arab terrorists—fifteen of them Saudis—crashed hijacked jetliners into the Pentagon and the twin towers of New York's World Trade Center, killing more than three thousand people. The horrors of that day are forever seared into the memories of eyewitnesses, myself included, and those who watched the calamity unfold on live television. The videotaped scenes were played again and again and again. From coast to coast, it seemed that everyone knew someone who had lost a relative or a friend. From that day, the United

States viewed the rest of the world, and especially the Middle East, through the lens of the war on terror.

Yet the nation's response at every level—military, cultural, economic—had to be filtered through the oil market. Strategists in Washington wanted to uproot terror from all its Islamic bases, but they had to balance this goal against the danger that too broad a campaign might trigger uprisings against friendly Islamic governments. "If the United States wants a broad coalition of allies, it needs to have a narrow list of targets," said Raad Alkadiri, a Middle East specialist at PFC Energy, in the *New York Times* shortly after the 9/11 attack. "If they have a broad list of targets, they will have a narrow list of allies."

Most Arab rulers were nearly as eager as the Bush administration to smash al-Qaeda, but feared being seen as too sympathetic to the United States. So key Arab leaders gave their assurances to Washington emissaries behind closed doors: They would not embargo their oil in retaliation for a U.S. attack against bin Laden, and they would supply enough oil to keep the price steady in its current, lofty range. But when Washington suggested that OPEC increase its production quotas to ease the price and help cure the recession, the cartel balked, fearing the kind of price collapse that followed its 1997 Jakarta decision to raise production quotas by 10 percent.

In any case, the terrorist attack's immediate impact on the oil markets was little more than a flutter. Within two weeks, the price had stabilized at just below $26. And within two months, an internal OPEC crisis gave Washington the price break it wanted. In early November, the cartel encountered a breach in its "wider alliance" with Angola, Mexico, Norway, Oman, and Russia.

Back in July 2001, with the recession still shrinking the world economy, OPEC conferees meeting in Vienna had ordered another price-propping, million-barrel cut in the daily production quota, effective September 1. But when the cut took effect, the non-OPEC partners in the coalition reacted in the old-fashioned, pre-solidarity way. They raised production, cashed in on the high price, and grabbed a bigger share of the market. It was the first real threat to the grand plan begun in 1999 to restore OPEC to preeminence.

So, in November, with the menace of a Mafia don, the cartel offered a deal that non-OPEC producers couldn't refuse. Another 2 million barrels daily must be siphoned out of the market, OPEC said, and it was willing to absorb three-fourths of the cut. But it would not act unless the non-OPEC producers held back 500,000 barrels a day of their own output. If they didn't do their part, the market would effectively be flooded, thereby touching off an open price war.

"Of course, it will hurt our economy," said Chakib Khelil, Algeria's oil minister. "But it will hurt non-OPEC producers, too. We are not trying to put anybody on their knees," he added, with a straight face. "We [just] want other producers to share in the pain if they are going to share in the benefits."

Caught in the crossfire, the markets were sent reeling as the price of oil plunged to a two-year low of $17.45 a barrel. Angola, Oman, Norway, and Mexico quickly signaled submission. But Russia, now the world's second-largest oil exporter, was openly defiant, promising only a token cut of 300,000 barrels a day.

Both sides dug in for the fight. Speaking off the record, an OPEC official played the card of political upheaval in the Middle East. The West should watch out if the oil price fell below $15, because that would force major cuts in Arab governments' welfare spending, which could spark the overthrow of friendly regimes. But President Vladimir Putin of Russia, who had been pursuing better relations with Washington, riposted that a little Middle East turmoil wouldn't end the world. Russia's huge new oil fields in the Caucasus region, he boasted, could displace a destabilized Middle East as the West's alternative source of energy.

The price war lasted just a few weeks before Russia capitulated, quietly agreeing to a cut of 150,000 barrels per day. True to form, Russia could not resist a little fudging and soon began exceeding its quota, but not enough to depress the market severely. Six months later, in April 2002, with the world economy rebounding and violence escalating in the Middle East, the price of oil was again approaching $28 a barrel.

Many Thanks for Robbing Us

Although the United States had ousted the Taliban government from Afghanistan and was trying to stabilize the country and capture bin Laden, the war on terror had only just begun. Washington was rumbling with talk that the next move would be to rid Iraq of Saddam Hussein. As the talk grew louder and the Bush administration's intentions in Iraq became unmistakable, nervous jitters swept the oil markets.

Trying to maintain the charade of scarcity but still discourage competition, OPEC ministers sought to reassure the markets. At their September 2002 meeting, with the price at $29.50, they left production quotas unchanged while characteristically affirming their readiness to pump more at the first sign of short supplies or price spikes. Even an attack on Iraq, they made plain, would not trigger an embargo. "If there is a supply disruption, we will satisfy the demand in the market, whatever the reason," promised Algeria's Khelil.

What no one ever seemed to notice was the emptiness of the promises. How many times had OPEC vowed to tamp down any price spikes and how many times had prices continued to spike?

Some ministers helpfully pointed out that "coordinated cheating" had effectively raised the quotas already, with member countries agreeing to overproduce their assigned limits by nearly identical percentages in order to keep the price from rising too high. A spike in prices at this critical moment would have been politically embarrassing for OPEC, given its relationship with the Bush administration. By November, however, the cheating had, in OPEC's opinion, gotten out of hand; the price had drifted down to just over $25.

There were two theories to explain the drop. Leonidas P. Drollas, chief economist for the Centre for Global Energy Studies, a London consulting firm, held that OPEC's members had been overproducing all year and simply pumped even more oil to make more money when the price began to drop. But another European analyst argued, off the record, that it was part of the cartel's strategy in the windup to war. "OPEC wanted to get the base price of oil down so it wouldn't spike so high if war broke out," he said.

But by January 2003, the price had climbed to $30. Commentators claimed that the price was inflated by a "fear premium" of $5 to $6, supposedly induced by the prospect of a prolonged absence of Iraqi oil—a wholly self-serving, OPEC-touted rationale for excessive pricing. Experts warned that the outbreak of war could drive the price to $35 or even $40, at least until buyers were reassured that producers were pumping enough and supply lines were working.

Clearly, the grand illusion still had its believers: Despite all the billions of barrels of oil beneath the deserts, the world somehow accepted the notion that OPEC oil was in short supply, or, more incredibly still, that the loss of Iraq's relatively meager contribution could substantially disrupt supply.

As if to underscore the point, that same month, when a revolt against Hugo Chavez and his attempts to control the oil sector cut off much of the flow of Venezuela's oil, the cartel raised its quotas again and pledged to keep pumping as much as necessary until Venezuela came back into the market. All this was, of course, just part and parcel of OPEC's practiced stagecraft. The cartel was as effective as the mob in persuading its victims how much they needed its protection.

And as with the mob, the oil-producing nations' persuasive powers made for big paydays. At winter's end, with troops of the U.S.-led coalition massing to invade Iraq, the Saudis were pumping 9 million barrels of oil a day at hugely elevated prices, raking in an estimated $1 billion a week. The royal clan stood to make still more once Iraq's oil vanished from the market, and they used the kingdom's spare pumping capacity to fill the gap. Nonetheless, the aggrieved princes complained that their efforts to preserve stability were underappreciated.

Before long, though, the Bush administration would smooth those ruffled royal feathers by continuing to fill the U.S. Strategic Petroleum Reserve even after oil prices had begun to rocket higher, and by expressing gratitude to OPEC and the Saudis for all they had done to keep the price stable. As a reward, the White House even promised to avoid tapping the reserve unless OPEC was unable to pump enough oil to meet any shortfalls in supplies. Having handed OPEC a blank check to continue its manipulations, the president might just as well have handed over the key to Fort Knox.

11

Iraq's Real Victors

After the second Gulf War, it's worth asking: who was the victor in Iraq?

Try OPEC.

In literal terms, of course, OPEC is not one of the myriad forces that are still battling to control Iraq. But if you ask who is snatching victory out of chaos, my candidate is OPEC. At no cost in blood or treasure whatsoever, OPEC has wound up as the de facto master of Iraq's oil, a vast reserve that the Saudis must effectively control if they are to maintain their grip on pricing. That Iraq's oil industry is constantly sabotaged is no big problem for OPEC. It merely gives the cartel another way to confuse bettors in the global shell game that is the oil business.

The measure of this coup is that the cartel, faced with ever-rising numbers of non-OPEC competitors and with both its market share and its influence over world prices in decline, has nonetheless managed to retain enormous clout. It has done so, in large part, by getting a grip on the oil of Iraq, its recently returned twelfth member nation. OPEC has demonstrated its political power and ability to control prices in a region containing most of the earth's known oil reserves. By no coincidence, world oil prices are more than 100 percent higher (at this writing) than they were before the invasion of Iraq.

How this happened is a tale of American delusion, Iraqi hope, and OPEC opportunism. The story opens with the U.S. invasion in

2003. When the air war started on March 20, traders were convinced that Saddam would be defeated in short order and that Iraq's oil structure would suffer little damage.

Indeed, the first battle was blessedly brief. Sweeping north from Kuwait, American and British troops overcame a blinding sandstorm and pushed rapidly toward Baghdad, while Iraqi forces melted into the civilian population. It took the coalition forces only twenty-six days to conquer (or so it seemed) a country 80 percent the size of France. America's second, slimmed-down Iraqi war was hailed as a triumph for the Rumsfeld doctrine—named for the secretary of defense at the time, Donald Rumsfeld—of using minimal troop strength and maximum firepower. Iraqis were expected to be ecstatic about their liberation from a demonic dictator, and some citizens of Baghdad did gleefully join the victorious troops in toppling a giant statue of Saddam Hussein.

A month later, outfitted as a Navy fighter pilot and speaking from an aircraft carrier, President Bush declared victory in Iraq—an image beamed around the world. At that euphoric moment, the price of oil was still around $28 a barrel. But in the next few weeks, it shot up by more than $2.

Did oil's price levitation have anything to do with OPEC's vote on April 24 to slice 2 million barrels a day from its production as of June 1? Nonsense, said the Saudi oil minister, Ali al-Naimi, who vowed that the cartel would do everything it could to get the price back down to around $25 a barrel. But even though Iraqi production was beginning to show signs of resumed life, oil prices remained near the top of the price band. Still, at their June meeting, OPEC delegates said they saw little reason to change the cartel's production ceiling of 25.4 million barrels a day.

Over the next few months, al-Naimi's assurances notwithstanding, the price never came within shouting distance of $25, remaining instead in the $30-to-$32 range. It drifted back near $28 in September, still above the supposed maximum target and also considerably higher than the below-$20 price that many observers had expected following the speedy end of the war in Iraq. As it happened, the price failed to decline for a very good reason: OPEC never took any steps to increase production.

The failure of the United States to restore Iraq's oil exports in the first weeks after taking power also contributed to the price pressure. U.S. officials had assumed that exports would begin to flow within weeks after the fighting stopped, and that rising oil revenues would pay for much of Iraq's recovery and reconstruction. As the whole world knows by now, that official optimism was a delusion. To the surprise of the Americans, Iraq's oil industry turned out to be in abysmal shape.

When Iraq's oil revenues plummeted during the six years of the embargo imposed by the United Nations, Saddam bemoaned the hardship placed on his country's citizens, especially the children. Responding to his pleas, the UN agreed to an Oil-for-Food exchange starting in 1996, which allowed Iraq to issue vouchers for limited purchases of oil by foreign buyers. The money received, eventually totaling $64 billion, was supposed to be used for humanitarian aid. Instead, Saddam saw a colossal business opportunity.

According to a CIA report, Saddam personally chose the voucher recipients, including at least four U.S. companies (Bayoil, Chevron Texaco, El Paso, and Exxon Mobil), along with the Texas oilman Oscar S. Wyatt, who alone received 74 million barrels. (Wyatt, having once criticized the shortsightedness of those who ignored outlaw nations, apparently resold the oil at a profit of $23 million.)

Various European oil companies got in on the deal, too, and all of Saddam's chosen blockade busters made so much money that he demanded large kickbacks. Investigators believe that Saddam used the cash windfall to buy an array of military equipment and build still more of his gaudy palaces. (So much for the starving children.) The corrupting effect of the oil money ensnared a wide network of traders and companies and stained even the United Nations, where the head of the program, Benon V. Sevan, was accused of taking $160,000 in kickbacks. At this writing, Sevan is under federal indictment on seven counts of conspiracy and wire fraud. And the former secretary general, Kofi Annan, came under fierce criticism for negligent supervision of the program.

The last thing Saddam intended to do with all that money was to keep the oil industry in good working shape. For years he had been plundering the industry's profits, leaving its infrastructure to decay so badly that any return to normal output would require the investment of billions of dollars. The problems were compounded when the U.S. Army failed to prevent looting after the war, thus enabling thieves to strip the industry of practically everything that could be carried. Worse still, Iraqi insurgents began targeting the industry and its workers, both foreign and domestic. Day after day, saboteurs assassinated oil officials, destroyed generators, torched wells, and blew up pipelines. No sooner did repair crews restore one rupture than attackers struck elsewhere, grinding away at what was left of the infrastructure. Exports were repeatedly slowed or stopped. In Iraq itself, gasoline—once abundant and subsidized at $1 a gallon—was in short supply even at ruthless black-market prices. By September 2003, Iraq was exporting just 1.8 million barrels of crude oil a day, compared with the 2 million barrels sold under the Oil-for-Food program before the war. It was a far cry from the 6 million barrels that would be needed to meet the Bush administration's prewar forecast of postwar Iraqi revenues.

A Whip for the Tormentor

It was hoped that the situation would be temporary. It might get worse before it got better, American officials thought, but surely, with the help of the smartest Texas oilmen that dollars could buy, the industry would soon be back on track.

Whether or not that assumption was right, this would have been an ideal time to strike a blow at OPEC itself. The U.S. strategists could have done the world a great service by persuading Iraq to disavow this conspiracy against the world economy. With the United States in total control of Iraq's oil industry, Washington could and should have seized the moment to rein in OPEC. All it would have taken was a decree from Paul Bremer, the coalition viceroy, removing Iraq from the cartel and thus depriving OPEC of the leverage provided by Iraq's vast reserves. That bold step would have weakened the cartel's future market power considerably.

But the Bush administration was leery of any action so overt (and so reasonable). Part of this was political public relations: Bush's people shied away from any admission that the war had been fought, even in part, to gain control of a resource vital to U.S. national interests and essential to the world economy. The president was adamant that he acted only to abolish tyranny, spread the blessings of democracy, and wage the war on terror. But obviously, there was another hidden agenda: As always, the administration favored any action that was good for the oil patch.

To help with that mission, a former CEO of Shell Oil, Phil Carroll, was named chairman of a committee that was supposed to give advice, and nothing more, to the Iraqi Oil Ministry. Declaring himself no proconsul, Carroll said the committee would have no veto over any Iraqi decisions, particularly those involving contracts to restore and develop the industry. As for the oil cartel, Carroll promised no unseemly pressure from Washington.

Nevertheless, the Shell alumnus is said to have personally encouraged the U.S.-appointed Iraqi oil minister to get involved with OPEC. He hinted at his true position on the morning of May 29, 2003, when he told a CNBC interviewer, "Iraq was a founding member of OPEC, and the truth is that Iraq will find its way into OPEC." And as the April 2005 *Harper's* related, the Bush administration and the American oil industry actually wanted Iraq to resume its active role in OPEC. Indeed, no lesser light than Vice President Dick Cheney pushed for an OPEC-friendly policy for Iraq, according to Edward Morse, whom the magazine described as "one of the men to whom Washington turns to obtain the views of Big Oil." A veteran in the energy sector whose experience spans business, government, academia, and publishing, Morse is currently executive advisor to Hess Energy Trading Company. He is also, *Harper's* said, a close associate of Rob McKee, Carroll's successor in Iraq.

Why would the administration favor OPEC over the economic interest of U.S. citizens? Because, as *Harper's* explained, the State Department has gone out of its way to accommodate Saudi Arabia and Russia, both of which benefit from peddling their oil at outrageously high OPEC prices. It's no secret that the Saudis are primarily interested in maximizing their oil profits, and they can't do that if Iraq floods the market with its oil. So, to maintain their control over pricing, they have to keep a lid on production. Getting Iraq back into the OPEC circle was one way of doing that. Promoting insurgency could be another way of keeping Iraq from reaching its full potential as an oil producer, especially if the bloodletting scares off needed foreign investment.

Disturbing though it may be to contemplate, one has to wonder if it is just coincidence that many of the Iraqi insurgents have ties to Saudi Arabia. James Bennet, writing in the *New York Times* on May 15, 2005, expressed puzzlement over the goals and strategy of the insurgents, noting that they have shown "little interest in winning hearts and minds among the majority of Iraqis, in building international legitimacy, or in articulating a governing program or even a unified ideology or cause beyond expelling the Americans. They have put forward no single charismatic leader, developed no alternative government or political wing, displayed no intention of amassing territory to govern now." Indeed, the insurgents seem bent on actively discouraging popular support by the indiscriminate murder of civilians. That's hardly a winning strategy for gaining political control of the country.

But perhaps the goal is not to gain control of the country, just to destabilize it. Could it be that, under the guise of jihad against Americans, an all-out effort is being waged to keep Iraq in turmoil in order to thwart normal economic development and keep oil-producing capacity at a bare minimum? Might the ultimate goal be just to maintain the OPEC status quo so as not to threaten existing producers, notably Saudi Arabia and Kuwait? The Saudis have been conspicuously silent on the subject of the insurgency.

Dick Cheney was effectively running U.S. energy policy, says Morse. The vice president "thinks that security begins by ... letting prices follow wherever they may"—even, apparently, if those jacked-up prices threaten the economic stability of the United States. So Iraq was allowed to take its old seat as a voting member of OPEC. This was more than just a token of the Bush administration's esteem for the cartel; it was yet another example of the oil-dependent Western victim gladly handing a whip to its tormentor.

Let me be clear: None of this, of course, detracts from the heroic efforts of our young men and women in uniform who are constantly in harm's way because of the continuing insurgency. By and large, they have performed with enviable excellence in a hellish situation. It is a pity and a national shame that their leaders have not adopted policies worthy of their sacrifices.

OPEC wasted no time in using its whip on the backs of oil consumers. When the oil price briefly dipped below $28 a barrel—remember, still the ostensible ceiling of the target range—OPEC swung into action as if the ceiling were the floor. Although the cartel had once

pledged to increase production to force the price down if it topped
$28, at its September 2003 meeting OPEC pared down its production
quota by 3.5 percent, thus nudging the price back above the top of
the range. The ministers claimed they were only looking ahead to
future market conditions, and cited rising non-OPEC oil production
in the face of a sluggish world economy. "We saw more supply than
the market needed," said Obaid bin Saif al-Nasseri, chief delegate of
the United Arab Emirates. "Any lack of action could have been very
negative for prices."

Many outside observers had a different take. Anibal Octavio da
Silva, head of the delegation from Angola (not yet an OPEC member at the time), observed dryly that "forecasts of supply and demand
suggest there is no need for an immediate cut in supply."

Needed or not, OPEC continued to pinch consumers. In the
months that followed, even as al-Naimi paid lip service to moderating prices, OPEC would reduce the quota two more times, with-
drawing a total of 3.9 million barrels a day from world production.

A Conspiracy Bluff's Dream

Ever generous when it comes to the oil cartel, the Bush administration registered no protest. In fact, as mentioned, it made another
huge contribution to OPEC by promising not to push prices down
by tapping oil from the nation's Strategic Petroleum Reserve (SPR),
an enormous stash of 727 million barrels that constitutes the world's
biggest supply of emergency crude oil.

The reserve is buried in 3,000-foot-deep salt caverns along the
Gulf of Mexico. Workers shoot water at high pressure into the caverns to make holes in the salt for storing oil. Geologic pressures make
the caverns leak-proof, and maintenance is cheap—only 10 percent
of the cost of storing oil in surface tanks. Oil companies love the SPR,
and no wonder: When they fill the reserve with oil pumped from
federal land, the government waives its normal royalty fees, thus
boosting the companies' already lush profits.

The SPR was conceived after the 1973 Arab oil embargo as a significant diplomatic tool and embargo-stopper. Only presidents are
allowed to tap it, customarily when a major oil shortage causes

runaway prices and a genuine national crisis. But instead of drawing oil from the SPR to stem the price gouging, President Bush did
the opposite: Stubbornly adhering to a plan conceived in the aftermath of 9/11, he increased the reserve from 611 million barrels to
700 million and then to 727 million barrels at the same time as OPEC
was cutting output quotas.

President Bush's action invited U.S. oil companies to divert
domestic oil from the market to the stockpile, and they quickly did
so. As a result, the policy not only pushed oil prices still higher as
the market supply tightened even further, but it also increased American dependence on foreign oil because U.S. companies had to go
abroad to fill the gap created by pumping domestic oil into Louisiana
salt caverns. Not to mention that salting away domestic oil at artificially high and rising prices unnecessarily worsened the federal
budget deficit. It was the mother of all boondoggles, and critics including Senator Carl Levin of Michigan could only shake their heads.
Calling the president's actions "illogical and counterproductive,"
Levin went on to suggest to an Associated Press reporter that "the
administration should listen to common sense."

As the United States struggled to mop up the Iraqi resistance in
the summer, fall, and winter of 2003, fears rose around the world
that the conflict might again disrupt the global oil supply. Accordingly, the price climbed still higher, topping $35 a barrel and feed-
ing suspicions that OPEC had tacitly raised its target range. Sure
enough, Saudi Arabia's al-Naimi arrived at OPEC's meeting in March
2004 with a plan to cut production by another million barrels a day.
But he argued, disingenuously, that OPEC's quotas weren't responsible for the high price of oil. Speculators were to blame for that, he
said, and pronounced that "throwing more oil on the market would
be destructive for everybody." In this case, "everybody" wasn't meant
to include the helpless suckers pouring money into gasoline pumps.

Ignoring the Parlor Elephant

Oddly missing in the presidential campaign of 2004 was what should
have been a major issue: global warming. The fate of the planet had
largely dropped out of the political debate since Al Gore's defeat in

the 2000 race. It was as if his loss, however narrow, had discredited the whole danger of global warming that he had flagged, leaving Bush and his people free to ridicule anyone who raised the issue as simply a tree hugger. To their shame, most Democratic candidates ducked that challenge. So, to the great satisfaction of OPEC and its cronies in the oil industry, global warming became the elephant in the political parlor—crowding everyone off the rug, but politely ignored.

To be sure, the scientific community was still treating the problem with delicate caution. In 2001, the Intergovernmental Panel on Climate Change, the world's most authoritative group of climate scientists, had said the probability that the earth's recent warming was caused by human activity was between 66 percent and 90 percent. A betting man would leap at odds like that, but the scientists used a tepid word to label it: "likely." Not until 2006, when the panel raised the odds to between 90 percent and 99 percent that human activity was to blame, would they call it "very likely."

Meanwhile, however, the public was slowly reaching its own conclusions. Consciousness of global warming was spreading, helped along by evidence impossible to ignore: melting glaciers, disintegrating ice shelves, higher and higher average temperatures, a steady rise in the sea level. Hurricane Katrina was a horrifying token of the fury waiting as warmer and warmer seas generated ever more powerful storms. Polls showed a rising alarm over manmade global warming and increasing urgency to do something about it; by mid-2006, the Pew Research Center would find that 79 percent of Americans believed that no matter what the administration said, the world was getting warmer, and 50 percent of us said it was due to human activity. Gore's book and documentary movie, *An Inconvenient Truth,* would persuade even more people and actually win an Oscar. George Bush himself would pronounce America "addicted" to oil and call for strengthening mandatory mileage standards.

But in the 2004 campaign, that awakening was far in the future. To the extent that energy was an issue at all, it was only the high price of oil. During the primaries, Senator John Kerry hammered at President Bush for not "putting pressure on OPEC to increase the supplies," and said the United States should "not allow those countries to undermine the economies of the world." White House spokesman Scott McClellan responded blandly that the president's focus was on "the importance of letting the market determine the prices"—as if President Bush, an oilman himself, didn't understand that it wasn't the market setting the price; it was OPEC.

According to one nameless OPEC official interviewed by the *New York Times,* the administration calculated that overt pressure on the cartel might backfire, as it had when Bill Richardson (now governor of New Mexico) ruffled OPEC feathers with his aggressive diplomacy. "The administration knows this history," the official said, adding that OPEC officials "are telling them, 'Keep your mouth shut.'"

The administration duly kowtowed to the Tony Sopranos of petroleum, but its deference didn't pay off. In late March, the same OPEC official reported that the cartel had toyed with the idea of increasing production, but shelved the discussion rather than risk being seen as doing favors for Washington.

The policy of timidity made for awkward sound bites. Appearing before the Senate Armed Services Committee in late March 2004 to explain the Bush administration's stance toward OPEC, the energy secretary, Spencer Abraham, bravely declared, "We've made it clear that we're not going to beg for oil." This attempt to sound dignified skirted the reality: Begging would have done no good—the administration had already given OPEC the key to the vault.

The Toll for Protection

The price spike in the spring of 2004 seemed a brief episode at the time, more a blip than a sea change, though in hindsight it was the beginning of a long-term drift to ever-higher prices. But even in the short term, the price spike further increased doubts about the wisdom of continuing to fill the Strategic Petroleum Reserve. Still, the White House stuck to its guns. The administration soon praised OPEC again for helping to stabilize prices and promised not to tap the SPR so long as OPEC could supply what was needed.

Accommodating OPEC had become an ingrained habit. But beyond conveying the clear message that we would willingly tolerate the cartel's price manipulation, President Bush tossed away the perfect chance to use his bully pulpit to protest high prices. If he had just had the presence to say, "We refuse to buy oil for the reserve at

more than $35 a barrel," he could have sent a strong and effective sig-
nal that there would be a limit to tolerating the cartel's manipulations.

Meanwhile, America's role as OPEC's protector was neatly sym-
bolized when some thirty-six U.S. Navy and Coast Guard warships
were dispatched to ports and oil terminals in the Persian Gulf, safe-
guarding the 16 million barrels of oil that pass through the Gulf every
day. Amy Myers Jaffe, an analyst at the James A. Baker III Institute for Public Policy at Rice University, estimated that the U.S. military was spending up to $80 million a day to guard OPEC's oil against
terrorist attack—another huge subsidy from American taxpayers,
and it didn't include the cost of the war in Iraq. (According to the
National Defense Council Foundation, the "hidden costs" of importing oil in 2005 included military spending of $780 billion, a subsidy
amounting to $4.05 per gallon of gasoline.) A Navy think tank pon-
dered still more expensive measures, including the use of sophisticated sensors and miles-long security fences, anchored in the seabed
of the Persian Gulf, to surround offshore oil wells and shipping
terminals.

Of course, OPEC's American defenders had good reason to worry:
On October 6, 2002, the French-flagged supertanker *Limbourg* had
been rammed by a small explosives-laden vessel while steaming
along in the Arabian Sea off the coast of Yemen. The 299,000-ton
Limbourg, part of a class of ships designated as "very large crude car-
riers," was loaded with 397,000 barrels of Saudi crude destined for
Malaysia when the attack occurred. Much like the bombing of the
USS *Cole* in 2000, the explosion blew open the *Limbourg's* side, killed
a crew member, and dumped 90,000 barrels of oil into the sea. No
one doubted that the Middle East's vital shipping lanes were vulnerable to terrorist attack.

Running on Empty with a Full Tank

In the OPEC shell game, the squeeze always begins with what sounds
like a reassuring move. It was no different in May 2004, when Ali al-
Naimi announced a unilateral Saudi production increase of 800,000
barrels a day. This would bring the kingdom's output to 9.1 million
barrels a day, or 1.4 million barrels under what it then insisted was

its flat-out maximum capacity of 10.5 million barrels. How credible was the claim? Were the secretive Saudis doing their last-ditch best to succor an oil-starved world? Or were they really hiding greater capacity as well as reserves while pretending to be running on empty—all part of an elaborate ruse designed to manipulate a captive market of nervous suckers? The Saudis themselves would soon answer this question when new capacity and stunning predictions of vast new reserves would appear like manna from heaven.

For months, industry wise men had claimed that all OPEC members except the Saudis were already pumping at maximum capacity. None of their customers knew what was true and what wasn't. As explained in previous chapters, all OPEC figures are opaque and must be considered suspect until the cartel allows them to be verified (as the G-8 has recently proposed). Nevertheless, OPEC's claims have been accepted as conventional wisdom, thus allowing al-Naimi to speak out of both sides of his mouth. Couched in words of reassurance, his message was really a scary one, probably the effect he intended. On the face of it, ratcheted-up Saudi production seemingly meant that the world's margin of safety in oil production was now less than 2 percent, and all of OPEC's unused capacity was in Saudi Arabia. Furthermore, oilmen told the media, the latest Saudi increase—and all the remaining capacity—would be heavy, high-sulfur oil that is more difficult and expensive to refine than the classic light Arabian crude.

Then Saudi Arabia suddenly discovered a lot more capacity. Just days after al-Naimi's promise to raise production, unnamed Saudi officials let it be known that they were bringing a whole new field on line over the summer and increasing capacity in another field, thus raising their total pumping ability to 11.3 million barrels a day (though they would still pump only 9.1 million barrels per day). That wasn't all: It was at this point that the Saudis divulged contingency plans that could boost total output to 12 million barrels a day immediately, rising to 15 million within eighteen months if needed. At the very least, this was a remarkable development, given that the Saudis had made no mention of such large-scale expansion over the previous months. It raised an obvious question: Assuming it was true, what else were they not telling?

Al-Naimi also promised that he would try to lower the price by pushing for a 10 percent increase in the cartel's production limits at

OPEC's June 2004 meeting, raising the total quota by as much as 2.5 million barrels a day. Market reaction was tepid, since everyone assumed that most OPEC members, except for the Saudis, were cheating on their quotas and already pumping at their announced capacity. It was also obvious that Iraq's besieged oil industry could not regain its prewar output anytime soon. The Saudis, of course, professed readiness to fill any Iraqi shortfall, causing the Bush administration to react with the obsequious gratitude that Saudi royals have long expected from their dear friends in Washington.

In another signal that went largely ignored, al-Naimi declared himself still in favor of the cartel's $22-to-$28 target range. However, he said ominously, "the market desires a price of $35 because it's frightened of [the price rising to] $50." He then repeated his mantra that the Saudis, too, were "frightened of that price" because it might damage the world economy and propel the search for alternate energy sources. The irony was that oil had been well above $28 almost continually since December 2003, and the cartel had done its best to keep it there. Al-Naimi was hinting that whatever he said for public consumption, $35 was to be the new floor.

All this smog had only one purpose: Al-Naimi would prepare the way. When, not if, the Saudis judged the U.S. sufficiently sedated, the price would jump yet again. And if history was any guide, the Americans, or at least their oil companies, would smile and say, "More, sir?" After all, besides failing to pursue viable energy alternatives, American leaders had accepted without demur every move OPEC had made, paying happily for the privilege of being snookered on a colossal scale.

Over the crucial summer and fall of 2004, the cartel squeezed the industrialized world harder than ever. Its tactics provided a model and a foretaste of the next two years: Again and again, OPEC and its oil industry allies rammed prices higher by repeating their good-cop/bad-cop routine to invoke the specter of a world running short of oil. What the world was really running short of was common sense; a kind of petro-hysteria was at work. Every time the Saudis pledged to meet market demand, traders seized on some new calamity to raise doubt about the promises. Any excuse would do, whether it was more sabotage in Iraq, a storm in the Gulf of Mexico, or a new growth forecast for the Chinese economy. And each new red flag had traders wringing their hands at the prospect of shortages and bidding the price even higher. The market's "fear premium," formerly pegged at $5 a barrel, looked more like $10 to $15 in 2004. Two years later, it would reach almost $50 a barrel.

Abracadabra from the Merlin of the Moment

In June 2004, OPEC finally agreed to raise its production quota by 2 million barrels a day. The move had little effect; the price still hovered around $35. As June ended, Ali al-Naimi effectively confirmed that the oil price target range was being raised when he backed away from the idea of raising quotas by another 500,000 barrels in coming months. "I believe the current prices are fair," he said. "There is no reason to take any measures either to decrease or increase the production."

The price kept rising, topping $40 in July, amid dead silence from the Bush administration. What did the silence signify? Some might have guessed that things were going exceptionally well for Bush's friends in both OPEC and the U.S. oil industry. Indeed, the world's largest integrated oil and gas company, Exxon Mobil, racked up record profits of $25.3 billion in 2004, which was 17.8 percent more than it earned in 2003. Smart investors expected nothing less. Even in hard times, Exxon's seamlessly integrated enterprise (from oil field to refinery to gas pump) has ample opportunity to calculate its profits creatively. And the company has continued to thrive, racking up bigger profits than any other company in history for two more years: $36.6 billion in 2005 and $39.5 billion in 2006. Wall Street seers predicted an oil industry windfall as long as the crude price stayed up.

By the end of July 2004, the markets were jumpier still. Trouble seemed to explode wherever oil came out of the ground. Iraq's proliferating insurgents sabotaged pipelines and other infrastructure again and again in an effort to cut the country's oil exports by more than half. Terrorists attempted to attack oil facilities in Saudi Arabia. Political uproar roiled Nigeria and Venezuela, reducing their oil flows. The Putin government launched a multibillion tax claim against Russia's biggest single exporter, Yukos Oil, jailing its CEO and kicking down Yukos's defenses with resoled KGB boots. Driven by speculating and stockpiling, the oil price ripped past $43, up more than 41 percent in one year. Economists began fretting about another energy shock, blaming high gas and oil prices for a downdraft in U.S. economic growth. Indeed, U.S. consumer spending fell to a three-year low.

Absent any countervailing force, the oil-devouring nations simply clapped meekly whenever OPEC's Merlin of the moment stepped onstage to tap his crystal ball and issue yet another misleading prophecy. Ali al-Naimi, for example, repeated his well-honed contention that speculators were to blame for runaway oil prices. "There is enough oil on the market," the minister said. "The fundamental things are okay. Inventories are filled and infrastructure is in good condition."

In fact, al-Naimi was right: There wasn't any shortage of oil. But who was fueling the speculation? As the markets jerked and trembled with each new minor glitch in the pipelines—a storm forecast here, a Nigerian kidnapping there, a refinery fire somewhere else—al-Naimi's fellow ministers in OPEC kept sounding the alarm over their helplessness to pump more oil or control the price. And the markets chose to believe the worst. Even the International Energy Agency, an adviser to twenty-six industrialized nations, accepted the dubious view that OPEC's spare capacity was down to 500,000 daily barrels of low-quality crude, warning that the lack of emergency capacity pointed to "critical" market conditions by year's end.

What happened next? As if al-Naimi had muttered "abracadabra," the price of oil jumped another dollar on the New York Mercantile Exchange, hitting $44.34 on August 3, the highest since trading began in 1983. (And that's when the Indonesian oil minister Purnomo Yusgiantoro, as related in Chapter 2, got so bollixed up in "the facts" concerning whether the Saudis or some other OPEC members had any spare pumping capacity and how quickly it could be tapped.)

As ever, the truth of these matters is anyone's guess. But one fact was indisputable in 2004: there was no shortage of oil. In the United States, gasoline inventories were on the rise, and even some of OPEC's apologists were beginning to suspect the truth, as the Citigroup analyst who wondered out loud how gasoline prices could possibly be up 50 percent from the previous year when inventories showed a rise of 8.3 million barrels.

The explanation, if anyone would listen, was clear and simple: OPEC's members continued to pump more than their quotas—but just under what the market needed—from fields that were larger than they admitted, all the while proclaiming their intent to keep the markets fully supplied. At the same time, they were further inflating the price by creating anxiety over a future pinch. Watching the market's blind reaction, the OPEC ministers must have been winking to each other and chortling.

With relentless gasoline price hikes eroding other consumer spending and the Federal Reserve pinning the blame for a slowing economy on the run-up of oil prices, energy policy now loomed even larger as an issue in the presidential race. John Kerry, who campaigned on increasing automobile mileage standards and becoming independent of Middle East oil, drew solid applause with a line in his stump speech: "I want America's security to depend on America's ingenuity and creativity, not the Saudi royal family." In essence, however, Kerry's proposals were only a little different from the president's, a pastiche of familiar ideas. He may have been a bit tougher on conservation, but he brought nothing new to the table.

Talk is cheap in the limited discourse of a presidential campaign. Nevertheless, the energy consultant Roger Diwan conceded that Kerry was at least heading in the right direction. "The only thing that matters," Diwan said, "is increasing fuel efficiency, because if you can't control demand, you will never have an energy policy."

Phony Heroes of Price Stability

Later in August, the Paris-based International Energy Agency added to the confusion surrounding OPEC's public pronouncements about new fields and increased capacity. An IEA spokesman said the cartel was striving so hard to contain prices by raising output that its "sustainable spare production capacity" had shrunk to 600,000 barrels a day. If accurate, the IEA figures meant that OPEC customers were left with a supply buffer of less than 1 percent, compared with about 8 percent in 2002. The IEA figures also meant that the Saudis had been blowing smoke in May when they said they would increase capacity to 11.3 million barrels per day over the summer and bump it up to 12 million if necessary.

At about the same time, adding to the confusion over their pronouncements, the Saudis said they were now pumping 9.3 million barrels a day. They pledged to tap surplus capacity of 1.3 million barrels if required, still well below the previously advertised 11.3 million barrels. The price of near-term oil futures contracts kept rising, hitting a record $48.70 a barrel in New York on August 19, as traders again questioned the validity of the Saudi capacity claims.

As the oil price skittered upward, OPEC's allies cheerily interpreted it as a more or less heroic struggle for market stability. Rising prices in the face of Saudi reassurances—even though OPEC had continued to resist any formal change in output ceilings—were "a very bullish sign from the market," according to Thomas Bentz, a senior oil analyst with BNP Paribas in New York. "Everyone knows OPEC's reached full capacity." The world's media joined the chorus. A long article in the *New York Times* on August 14 painted OPEC as a helpless giant, unable to pump enough oil to keep the price below its $28 ceiling, but also afraid that a recovering Iraq would pump too much oil and bring prices down.

Had anyone looked closely at the International Energy Agency's August report, they would have found reason to be less worried about shortages. The IEA said that world oil production was meeting projected demand at 84 million barrels daily. The agency said OPEC could add 500,000 more, while non-OPEC exporters could increase their daily capacity by 1.2 million barrels. In sum, the world could expect spare pumping capacity of about 1.4 percent—tight, but nowhere near scary. And if you added the newly announced Saudi capacity, the excess came to 2.8 percent. In addition, industrial nations had emergency reserves totaling 1.4 billion barrels, not to mention the private stores scattered around the world and the stockpiles maintained by oil companies. The total, 4 billion barrels, would provide a cushion well beyond the official estimate of five and a half months. Where was the crisis?

Playing the Consumption Card

A cool, brief touch of realism intruded on the markets on August 25, 2004, when the U.S. Energy Information Administration reported that American drivers had responded to the sky-high price of gasoline by using less of it than expected over the summer. Gasoline inventories totaled more than 205 million barrels nationwide, near the top of a five-year range. The oil price dropped by some $2 a barrel in response to this show of consumer discipline.

Even if Americans had cut back on their gasoline consumption more by necessity than by choice, the summer of 2004 provided a tantalizing glimpse of what the administration might have accomplished with a clear, focused policy to rein in oil consumption. Refusing to stock the petroleum reserve with any oil priced above $35 a barrel, for instance, would have reduced daily demand by 100,000 barrels. This may not sound like much when total U.S. demand is more than 20 million barrels a day, but prices at the margin are highly sensitive, so such a reduction would have cooled the market and cut the price by more than its proportions would indicate.

The opposite happened, of course. The Bush administration couldn't find its tongue, and after market reports pointed to a 380,000-barrel-a-day decline in OPEC's August output, prices again went up, up, up.

When OPEC ministers finally agreed to another increase in production quotas, traders shrugged it off as symbolic formality. They stuck fast to their credo that the cartel, which was now producing roughly 30 million barrels a day, had hardly any unused capacity left and no control over the market. One analyst suggested that OPEC ministers were deluding themselves about their ability to affect oil prices. And Leo Drollas, an economist at the Centre for Global Energy Studies in London, predicted that the OPEC quota increase was "not going to help the market at all. It's a PR exercise to prove to the consumer that OPEC actually likes them."

Shortages As Desert Mirages

The pessimistic judgment of the cartel's capacity was dubious at best, since it rested on the assumption that OPEC had not increased its pumping capacity for a quarter of a century. Nonetheless, it was accepted wisdom in the industry, and therefore prices continued to rise. Purnomo Yusgiantoro, the current holder of OPEC's rotating presidency, kindled the price fire when he said publicly that the target price band "has to be adjusted" and it "should be upward, not downward." The cartel put price adjustment on the agenda for its December 2004 meeting. (The topic was indeed addressed at that meeting, but no formal action was taken. Still, several ministers lobbied for a price band between $30 and $35 a barrel, and some suggested that the floor had already been raised to $32, at least informally. That made the markets even more jittery.)

And so it went. There was no shortage of oil, even by the IEA's reckoning. In mid-September, the agency reported that "supply is running ahead of demand and stocks are building." Yet by the end of the month, the price would surpass $50. Any excuse seemed to justify a price uptick. "Noise gets prices," remarked Lawrence J. Goldstein, president of the PIRA Energy Group consulting firm. "If you hear something, you have to react to it and then find out if it's true or not."

For its part, OPEC was just going through the motions of pretending to drive the price down, reveling in the general view of its helplessness. "Prices are moving independently from whatever OPEC decides," said Nordine Ait-Laussine, a former OPEC president turned industry consultant. "OPEC can't do anything more today." In early October, the price hovered between $50 and $55.

OPEC Tightens the Screws

The remainder of 2004 and the beginning of 2005 played like a broken record. The price eased off its October highs, but remained well above year-earlier levels and OPEC's still officially unchanged target range, so al-Naimi gave it another nudge: He proposed to cut the cartel's production quota by a million barrels a day, on the ground that the price might drop soon. "We have done everything to moderate the price," he insisted, ". . . and it will probably moderate more" as fears of shortages lessen. The production cut took effect on January 1.

In reality, OPEC was tightening the screws, trying to define the limits of tolerance among its customers by threatening further production cuts at any and every sign of price weakness. Incredibly, the cartel encountered little resistance, let alone outrage, from the oil-importing nations. The IEA said it thought OPEC was overreacting to concern about a precipitous drop in prices, and pointed out that $40-plus oil was still very high. But most everyone seemed to accept as a reality that OPEC had developed an appetite for the windfall profits brought by record-high oil prices and would do everything in its power to keep the rivers of money flowing.

A few weeks later, al-Naimi finally dropped all pretense. Speaking to a Reuters reporter at the World Economic Forum in Davos, Switzerland, in January 2005, he said, "My view is the world is not suffering.... The price today doesn't seem to be affecting economic growth negatively." Translation: The sky is the limit.

Remarkably, hardly anyone seemed to resent the relentless gouging. "All OPEC is doing now is accompanying where the market sees prices going in the future," said Paul Horsnell, director of energy research at Barclays Capital in London, in the *New York Times.* "But there's nothing terribly explicit about it"—as if some force other than the cartel were propelling prices higher. The *Times's* chief oil reporter, Jad Mouawad, flatly stated that "OPEC alone is not responsible for high prices." He went on to blame the familiar litany of war, strikes, political upheavals, and hurricanes in places as divergent as Iraq, Nigeria, Venezuela, Norway, Russia, and the Gulf of Mexico. That OPEC had so assiduously worked to create the myth of scarcity and the climate of fear that linked all these supposedly unconnected events was not a part of the story. Like just about everyone else, Horsnell and Mouawad had been conditioned to regurgitate OPEC's propaganda as absolute fact. Whereas a year earlier $30 oil was thought to be outrageous, OPEC now openly defended $40 a barrel and higher with no fear of recrimination.

A longtime observer of the Saudi dog-and-pony show couldn't help but wonder if the kingdom and its cronies weren't playing the oil futures market, adding billions in speculative gains to their already-obscene oil profits. That suspicion would be reinforced in December, when al-Naimi issued back-to-back contradictory statements ahead of a meeting of OPEC members, first saying he saw no need to change production quotas, then reversing himself to opine that OPEC did need to stabilize the market. The oil price gyrated accordingly, and anyone who knew what al-Naimi planned to say could have profited handsomely.

The most damning piece of evidence, however, would come on Sunday, December 12, after oil prices shocked the manipulators by falling sharply even though the cartel had, in fact, voted to reduce production by 4 percent. Traders, it seemed, expected cartel members to ignore the guidelines just as they had so many times before. Al-Naimi responded with his astonishing prediction to *Arab News:* "Watch what happens tomorrow. I tell you prices will go up tomorrow." And on the appointed Monday, after some curious swings, the price did indeed rise. The only way al-Naimi could have predicted the price move with such assurance was if he or OPEC or its agents could use OPEC's vast funds to control the oil futures market. If it is indeed the case that OPEC can manipulate the market at will, as it apparently did on December 13, 2004, then how often has the market been manipulated by OPEC and its allies before and since? What portion of OPEC's resources—gleaned from hapless oil consumers—are used to manipulate prices in what is supposedly an open market?

The grim irony was that Americans were being forced into ever-greater dependence on OPEC. Having lost the power to resist the seller's come-ons, oil users wound up helplessly addicted and ready to pay any price. The Bush administration did virtually nothing to help the United States kick its habit. Indeed, it increased the demand for oil by continuing to insist on filling the Strategic Petroleum Reserve. When people suggested that the government should be leading efforts to conserve oil, including raising the mandatory mileage standards for cars, Bush officials repeated their wearisome mantra that free-market forces, not government mandates, were the answer—and that energy independence could be achieved by tapping the Arctic National Wildlife Refuge. (At the high end, estimates of recoverable oil in the refuge run to 16 billion barrels. That's more than 20 times the oil currently held in the Strategic Petroleum Reserve.)

For their part, the Saudis no longer pretended to worry about the economy. In mid-January 2005, when the price bounced up past $48 and the stock market began to sink, Ali al-Naimi declared that "the price today doesn't seem to be affecting economic growth negatively." If he knew that the International Monetary Fund blamed high oil prices when it reduced its forecast for 2005 world economic growth, he apparently dismissed it. Nor did he heed the distinguished economist Fred Bergsten, who in the *Financial Times* calculated that "every jump of $10 per barrel takes about half a percentage point off annual global growth for several years."

The Saudi oil minister was also dismissing European Commission president José Manuel Barroso's pronouncement that $50 oil would brake economic expansion. Al-Naimi's co-conspirator, Chakib Khelil of Algeria, added his two cents' worth to rationalize the oil price creep: Not only was the economy unfazed by the high oil price, he declared, but inflation wasn't affected, either.

After sliding back toward $40 in mid-December 2004, the oil price was now up 34 percent from the year-earlier level and had risen a whopping 15 percent just since the beginning of 2005. The inflation rate, meanwhile, was up all of 2.5 percent during the same period. So much for those who argued that oil prices were merely tracking inflation.

The Bar Is Raised

Stepped-up terrorist activity ahead of the Iraqi elections sent prices higher in January, while frigid weather in the United States and Europe bore the brunt of the blame for steadily rising prices in February. Rumblings of a global oversupply of oil had little effect on the price, but did stoke fears that OPEC might again reduce overall production quotas at its next gathering. Meanwhile, with al-Naimi playing the role of price hawk, Iranian oil minister Bijan Namdar Zanganeh assumed the Saudis' traditional role as the cartel's moderating voice. Zanganeh said he would "prefer to wait to see prices fall below $40" before reducing the supply any further.

For all this deliberate befuddlement, the price target range was clearly being jacked up by a whopping amount. Zanganeh's supposed moderation laid the groundwork for raising the floor all the way from $28 to $40.

A little later, with oil selling at just under $50 a barrel, the Saudi oil minister declared that the world economy had grown so big that "little fluctuations here and there with oil are not doing so much" damage. He attempted to justify the stratospheric price by saying that OPEC would have to invest more to keep up with the increasing demand for oil. "The world is going to need every barrel we can produce," al-Naimi said. Apparently, the $338 billion that the cartel lifted from consumer pocketbooks in 2004 simply wouldn't cover expenses. Given the virtual absence of protest during all the months of skyrocketing prices, and the total lack of a viable energy policy among the governments of the consuming nations, al-Naimi apparently felt free to shoot for the moon.

Also signing on to the lunar expedition was OPEC's acting secretary general, Adnan Shihab-Eldin, who floated the notion of $80 oil at the beginning of March. He said he couldn't rule out such a spike if production were suddenly disrupted. In short order, the usual cadre of traders, analysts, and media voices leaped to provide the rationale for such an unholy notion. Maybe Iran would cut off production if the United States tried to force it to end its nuclear program. Or maybe continuing violence in Iraq would be the culprit. And what about Russia's meddling with Yukos, which was impeding its oil production growth?

Kevin Norrish, an analyst at Barclays Capital, wrapped all the troubling possibilities together and advised the firm's investors that "[w]ith low inventory levels plus very little spare crude oil production or refining capacity, the market's ability to absorb supply-side shocks is at its lowest." Toss in a major supply disruption and "even $80 a barrel could look modest."

A plunging U.S. dollar, worries about supposedly declining supply, and fears that OPEC might not step up to the challenges kept prices reaching for new highs in March and April, even though crude oil inventories were rising. On April 4, the NYMEX futures contract hit a startling $57.79.

News that should have restrained the price spiral somehow went ignored. OPEC had made a big point at year's end of how hard-pressed it was to meet its "obligations" in the face of rapidly rising demand from China. But word that China's oil consumption had unexpectedly fallen by 13 percent in the first two months of the year was buried in the last paragraph of the Bloomberg story trumpeting the newest NYMEX record. The absurdities were dizzying. Might OPEC blame the market's next upsurge on trumped-up rumors that tiny little Luxembourg was planning to ramp up its oil imports?

Perhaps world leaders finally realized just how high the price bar was being set, or maybe the relentless barrage of self-serving remarks from al-Naimi and his OPEC cronies finally rubbed the consuming countries the wrong way. On February 25, after the Saudi oil minister predicted that oil prices—which had topped $52 in New York the day before—would hover between $40 and $50 a barrel for the rest of the year, some of the previously tongue-tied victims finally found their voices. Within hours, top officials in the International Energy Agency, the European Union, and the U.S. Treasury Department let loose a volley of criticism.

"Oil prices are too high" was the charge that echoed back and forth across the Atlantic. The IEA's Claude Mandil announced that it was "time to be serious about energy efficiency." The U.S. Treasury secretary, John Snow, pronounced himself "not happy about oil prices one bit," while Peter Mandelson, the European Union trade commissioner, declared: "It won't generate confidence in the international economy and the impact of such a price level will be adversely felt, not least by developing country economies."

As heartening as it was to hear this high-profile trio say, "Enough already," it was even more refreshing to read the headline over Mathew Ingram's piece that same day in Toronto's *Globe and Mail:* "It's not the weather; it's OPEC policy that keeps oil prices high." Continuing in this rare vein of truth, Ingram wrote, "As the price of crude has continued to climb ... OPEC has rubbed its hands in that unctuous sort of way that undertakers have, as though it is pained about the whole price issue, but has done nothing to stop it. In fact, OPEC leaders have hinted they are pretty happy."

At long last, someone in the news media had bluntly stated the facts.

The Sky's No Limit

For all practical purposes, however, no one was listening. The game played on nonstop through 2005 and 2006. Early in April 2005, a barrel of oil cost a once unimaginable $57.79. It zigzagged jaggedly upward all spring and summer, jumping with each new alarm and falling back only part way when disaster failed to strike. The peak that year came in August, at $66.17, after a disaster that actually arrived: Hurricanes Katrina and Rita disrupted refineries in Mississippi, Louisiana, and Texas, knocking out much of the Gulf of Mexico's production for many weeks. What the market failed to notice, of course, was that even true calamity didn't cause any actual shortage of oil. Finally, the Bush administration agreed to a limited tapping of the SPR, and the industry's stockpiles of refined product proved enough to get through the emergency. For the balance, the Saudis made good on their promise to supply the markets. Gasoline prices spiked, but there were no lines. For the year, the price of oil averaged $50.04 a barrel.

In 2006, all the usual suspects were rounded up again: continuing problems in Iraq, indigenous uprisings in Nigeria, and OPEC warnings that its pumping was at full capacity, followed by Saudi reassurances that the market would be supplied. The result was repeated price spikes, drifting upward through the $50s and $60s.

In the summer of 2006, hysteria peaked again. Global inventories were high and rising, with no sign of shortages. The hurricane season was unusually mild; and of all the disasters so often threatened, only sporadic interruptions in Nigerian production had materialized. OPEC production was still advertised as near-capacity, but market intelligence was that the cartel was pumping little more than 25 million barrels a day, at least 5 million barrels below its ceiling.

Even so, traders were panicked, and speculators in hedge funds leaped to push the price even higher. In July, it hit what is still its all-time high: $78.40 a barrel. The sky seemed no limit, and traders were predicting that the price would go to $100 or higher. Economists warned that $100 oil could wreck the world economy. So the Saudis issued more soothing statements, and the price fell back.

But then in August came another real blow. Half the production of Alaska's North Slope—8 percent of all U.S. crude oil—would be cut off for months because a corroded pipeline had burst. This wasn't just a disaster, it was a major embarrassment for the industry and especially for the owner of the pipeline, giant BP. The pipeline gathers production from half the wells in the region and delivers it to the main pipeline that carries oil from the North Slope to the port of

Valdez, where it is loaded aboard tankers. BP had achieved a public relations triumph by transforming its image, adopting a flower-like green and yellow logo and the slogan "Beyond petroleum." BP truly *understood* global warming, its ads proclaimed; it had become the green oil company, nurturing the environment, mounting solar panels on its filling stations, and looking to a fossil-fuel-free future.

So, when it turned out that BP had simply neglected routine maintenance of its feeder pipeline for fourteen years, it wasn't only a black eye for the company. It also reinforced the public perception that the whole industry was a hypocritical fraud. And that wasn't the end of BP's woes. The company had been fined $1.2 million for earlier pipeline leaks; a Texas refinery explosion had killed fifteen people and the plant turned out to have a patchy safety record; and federal regulators accused the company of cornering the propane market and manipulating gasoline futures contracts. In the end, BP's CEO, Lord John Browne, would opt for early retirement. But the immediate result of the North Slope pipeline fiasco was another leap in the price, to $76.48 a barrel.

The crisis eased when it was announced that the cutoff would be shorter and less extensive than first expected. More important, OPEC was revving up its pumps. It was evident that the cartel had let things go too far. With oil above $70 a barrel, alternative energy wasn't just a theoretical possibility. Tar sands and shale oil looked more and more attractive; there was a real push to revive the nuclear power industry; and serious research into fuel cells was being accelerated. OPEC saw that it might be killing its golden goose—and this time, Ali al-Naimi's soothing syrup was to be taken seriously. The price would come down.

The 2006 congressional elections were also a heads-up, for OPEC as well as the Bush administration. Over the summer, the price of gasoline in most parts of the United States had soared well past $3 a gallon, provoking outrage among the voters in proportion to the hardships it imposed. Though the festering fiasco in Iraq got most of the headlines, oil prices surely played a part in the Republican loss of both houses of Congress. The rising public consciousness of global warming was also forcing a change in the administration's adamant refusal to address the issue; it was notable that the Bush administration took a softer line on greenhouse gases.

OPEC also scrambled to adjust. As the market sagged through the $70s and then the $60s, the explanations were as thin and unconvincing as they had been on the way up: Inventories were high (of course, they had been high all along); the high price had cut demand (about 1 percent in the United States); and the winter was unseasonably warm.

But when the market dropped below $55, OPEC judged that the time was ripe for a new floor price, and voted for production cuts designed to hold the price above $60. Also predictably, some members cheated on their new lower quotas, and early in 2007 the price fell briefly below $50. Some OPEC members clamored for an emergency meeting to cut the newly reduced quotas again, but al-Naimi brushed off the idea. "Do not panic," he advised. "Actually, there is no need for a meeting." The quotas were low enough, he said, and the oil price would soon rise again.

The *New York Times* saw this as a signal that the Saudis wanted to set the floor between $50 and $55 a barrel—and, true to its pandering tradition, the newspaper blandly labeled it a "moderate" price. As if there were anything moderate about profits of $53.50 a barrel for the Persian Gulf producers (with production costs of less than $1.50 a barrel)—a markup of 3,567 percent.

Meanwhile, reports from Saudi Arabia speculated that the Saudis really wanted lower oil prices to cripple Iran, energy being virtually its only source of foreign exchange. Lower oil prices would seriously and adversely affect Iran's economy, hamper the radical government, and divert focus and funds from assisting the country's Shia allies in Iraq. (Here is a clear example of what the high price of oil has wrought and what lower oil prices might accomplish.) Reduced Shia support from Iran would give aid and comfort to Saudi Arabia's Sunni brethren in Iraq, while hindering Iran's drive to build nuclear weapons capability and dampening Iran's political ambitions in the region.

How high would the price go? Most oilmen thought the new floor would be $60 a barrel, not $50 or $55. Adam Sieminski, the chief energy economist for Deutsche Bank, predicted early in 2007 that the price would average $62 for the year, only slightly down from the 2006 average price of $66. Several Wall Street investment bankers were betting on prices in the $70s. It was anyone's guess—and, as usual, it was OPEC playing the dance music.

Without the willingness or the discipline to curtail demand, world oil usage is projected to jump 50 percent in the next twenty-five years. If addicted nations, including the new consuming giants such as China and India, lack the wit and the wisdom to evolve energy options, the Persian Gulf petrocracies—straddling over two-thirds of the earth's currently known oil reserves—will be sitting prettier than ever.

Doom for the World or Doom for OPEC?

How bad could our oil predicament get? Consider this doomsday scenario for the next few years.

As 2010 dragged to a stunned close, the tipping point to disaster seemed plain in hindsight: OPEC's decision in 2008 to use a basket of currencies, not just the sagging dollar, to price its oil. That sent the real cost skyrocketing in Europe and Japan. The ensuing panic eventually drove the price to $100 a barrel and beyond, bringing the world economy almost to a standstill. The oily profiteers of OPEC, panic-mongers nonpareil, had merely been trying to squeeze still more riches out of a tired old goose. This time, though, they squeezed too hard. The bird perished.

In America, oil at well over $60 a barrel had been slowly pinching the economy since mid-2007. To make up for their higher energy costs, manufacturers raised prices across the board, while consumers cut back on their driving, turned down their thermostats, and still had to economize on everything else. Business stagnated. At first, many workers lost overtime; then they were laid off or fired outright. Ordinarily, businesses would respond to such a dip in demand by cutting prices. But given the basic cost of energy, prices couldn't come down; in fact, they had to keep rising. The economy was in stagflation.

Higher prices on just about everything took the Federal Reserve by surprise, but the Fed was also battling another crisis. The dollar had been sagging for two years against other currencies, and the foreign governments and investors whose lending was financing the U.S. trade and budget deficits had begun to stash their money elsewhere. (Tellingly, even as oil dollars poured into the cartel's treasuries, OPEC governments including Saudi Arabia, Indonesia, and Venezuela unloaded $10 billion worth of Treasury bonds and notes late in 2006. This was the first trickle of what was to become a flood.) The dollar's value fell faster over the next year as more investors exchanged it for euros, pounds, and yen. At Treasury auctions, interest rates had to be set higher and higher to attract buyers. The Fed needed to raise short-term rates, both to keep the market orderly and to rein in the new inflation. So in 2008, the Fed, having been reluctant to act forcefully prior to a presidential election, suddenly boosted its key interest rate by two full percentage points.

The unprecedented move jammed on the economic brakes so sharply that you could almost smell the stink of burning tires. The holiday season died. The stock market headed south and the real estate market crashed almost overnight, wiping out hundreds of billions of dollars in paper profits. Suddenly higher mortgage rates stopped would-be home buyers in their tracks and devastated the building industry. Holders of adjustable-rate mortgages and home equity loans saw their monthly payments soar while the value of their homes fell; in short order, most owed far more money than their equity was worth. Foreclosures and tax default auctions became common. Consumer spending dried up, our appetite for imported goods was finally lost, and soon the nation was in deep recession.

The misery spread around the world. Countries that had taken steps to conserve fuel were hit less hard than the United States, but high oil prices inevitably crushed foreign economies too. Exports to America were dwindling, and world trade began to dry up. Hardest hit were the developing nations with fledgling industries and energy-squandering factories. Imported oil prices made their costs balloon at the same time their exports were falling. In Japan, higher prices smothered an economy slowly coming back to life after a thirteen-year slump. Even the Chinese economic miracle soured as manufacturers had to pay premiums of 65 percent, 80 percent, and even 100 percent for their rapidly rising oil imports. China's cutbacks rippled through the global economy, further depressing already struggling trading partners, especially South Korea and Japan.

In France, exploding fuel costs and falling tax revenues derailed efforts by the government to rein in budget deficits, as demanded by the European Union. Forced into a corner, the government had to cut popular public programs, triggering riots in the streets. Similar scenes played out across Europe as generous social welfare programs, long taken for granted but no longer affordable, had to be axed.

The world's oil producers, however, weren't hurting. Total demand for oil was falling fast, but having learned their lesson, they cut back production enough to keep the price above $60 a barrel. Then, as their total revenues began to fall, they pushed the price even higher to make themselves whole. The world might be going broke, they reasoned, but why should we suffer? When Russia and Mexico balked at the deep cuts in output demanded of them, OPEC brandished the threat of an all-out price war, and that was enough to bring the rebels back in line. Even as the world economy shrank, the oil price topped $75.

Then the governments of China and India became mired in an escalating competition to lock up long-range oil supplies to protect their industries. Each had been quietly buying oil and gas fields, building pipelines, and exploring investments in oil-producing countries. Now they raised the pitch in a bidding war for long-term contracts, each trying to freeze the other out and accepting punitive escalator clauses that threatened to lift oil prices to unimagined levels.

The markets panicked. Demand for oil was withering, but the exploding price made everyone frantic to buy now in order to escape tomorrow's even higher cost. Traders began stockpiling oil to stay ahead of the game. In a replay of earlier "oil shocks," customers stored oil in every available container. Some large companies used costly tankers as floating warehouses, thus disrupting deliveries and driving shipping rates higher.

Anti-Western sentiment in the Middle East intensified as Iraq crumbled into civil war and the Israeli-Palestinian conflict smoldered. With the market price hurtling toward $90 a barrel, terrorists—likely bankrolled with oil profits—blew up a tanker carrying Kuwaiti oil in the Persian Gulf, destroying the ship and killing most of its crew. Tanker captains began refusing to load at Mina al-Ahmadi, cutting into Kuwait's exports. The Saudis said they would pump more oil to make up for the loss. They did, but the price rose anyway.

Then terrorists managed their first truly damaging raid on Saudi Arabia, hitting the huge Ras Tanura oil refinery and nearby loading facility at Sea Island with heavy rockets and chemical weapons that killed hundreds of workers. The damage was repaired within two weeks, but this new evidence of Saudi vulnerability was a major blow to confidence. The oil price left $85 behind.

The deciding blow came when OPEC announced what sounded like a technical reform. Abandoning the long tradition of pricing oil in U.S. dollars, the cartel said in September 2008 that it would switch to a basket of currencies made up of the euro, yen, and dollar. The new arrangement would free OPEC from dependence on the still-depreciating dollar and produce larger and more reliable profits. Unfortunately, real oil prices in Europe and Japan would also rise abruptly, worsening the global recession.

In two days, the price jumped to $95 a barrel. Gut-wrenching fear gripped the markets. From Beijing to Bremen, from Delhi to Detroit, all the hedging tricks of savvy oil traders lost their magic. Desperate to lock in any oil they could find, traders scoured the earth. And their mad scramble drove the price higher and higher, until by year's end it shot past $100 a barrel.

And still it kept going, to $101, $102.50, and $103.50. At that level, the world economy could only sink further. In the United States alone, the annual oil bill had soared to $730 billion—three-quarters of a trillion dollars for oil alone. Then the cost plummeted, not because the price fell but because the devastated economy no longer needed much oil. The economic shock swiftly circled the globe, hammering industries, idling millions of workers, destroying businesses, and driving people everywhere into misery. As 2010 rolled in, the world was locked in global depression.

With that, the oil bubble finally burst. The world was awash in oil that no one could use, and the market at long last came to its senses. The price of oil tumbled to $10 a barrel, and OPEC fell apart for good. But it was too late. The damage had been done, and the world would take two decades to recover.

A Happier Ending

The story doesn't have to end this way. We can still win the battle to break the OPEC cartel, convert to cleaner energy, and escape the calamity that threatens the world. But to achieve this happy ending, we must change our policies, our habits, and our expectations. We must begin not tomorrow or the next day, but now.

The world has been in OPEC's clutches thanks mainly to muddled, misguided, and wholly ineffective government policies, aimed at influencing supply while largely ignoring demand. As a result, we have been subsidizing a parasite that survives by feasting on our lifeblood. Worse, we are financing terrorists who use our money to threaten our very existence. And worst yet, we are perpetuating our dependence on an energy source that endangers our planet.

The remedy begins with openly embracing a clear, three-pronged policy designed to destroy the cartel and regain our self-sufficiency and national self-respect.

First, just as OPEC works to control supply, we must cut back on world energy usage by taking steps to control demand, thereby lowering the price of oil and depriving OPEC of its obscene profits.

Second, we must become energy self-reliant so as to free ourselves from dependence on any foreign supplier.

Finally, we must move faster to convert to clean energy sources that already exist and accelerate research and development into new and promising alternatives.

Our march to freedom must start with the simple recognition that we have a problem. I firmly believe that free markets work best. The United States and other world leaders must stop kowtowing to OPEC, especially to Saudi Arabia, and publicly acknowledge that the current price of oil is not a free-market price. Rather, the price is unfairly set and manipulated by OPEC and its allies.

Having twice come to the aid of the Saudis and the Kuwaitis—first in 1991 when we ended the threat of an Iraqi invasion, and again twelve years later when we deposed Saddam Hussein—the United States is entitled to demand some quid for its quo. We and our Western allies should insist that the Saudis and the Kuwaitis turn over genuine figures on their reserves and production capacity, which would deflate the hysteria factor and help bring oil prices more in line with actual costs. We should also press the Saudis, Kuwait, and the new government of Iraq, using every diplomatic tool at our command, to end their membership in the criminal conspiracy that is OPEC.

All this would require great courage on the part of our leaders. By standing up to OPEC and regaining our energy self-reliance, the president, a former oilman, could secure enormous economic benefits for this country and the world, while also returning America to its role as a true world leader, not just a militarily superior world cop. Our national policies could be grounded in principle and concern for the world's good as well as our own, without being distorted by the need to safeguard our supply of oil. With the right policies, we could break OPEC as well as the malign governments it has supported, while also putting the United States and most of the world on the road to greater stability and prosperity.

A strategy to break the cartel will set off a hue and cry from the big oil companies, which relish the inflated profits they rake in as a result of OPEC's manipulation. Their friends in Washington will mount a bare-knuckled fight. But the costs of tolerating the present situation have become too great. It would be far better, and cheaper, to break OPEC's chokehold and develop a program to preserve the domestic industry by hiring its expertise to tap federally owned oil deposits.

The United States alone has the power and wherewithal to go up against the massive wealth and influence of the oil industry and its allies. It alone can put the OPEC cartel out of business. Indeed, the playing field will never be leveled without forceful intervention by our government.

Nevertheless, we should not be alone in this fight. All nations are affected by the economic impact of high-priced oil, added to the global threat of terrorist acts funded by egregious oil profits, so the battle should be joined by all. What is more, a concerted global effort would snuff out the OPEC menace much more rapidly than any unilateral campaign, lessening the potential for further damage to be inflicted around the world. Therefore, the administration must bring both major importers and less-developed nations into the fray.

What should be the price of oil? In an ideal world, it would be priced like any other commodity in a free market—substantially below current levels by a factor 30 to 50 percent or more. Even Exxon Mobil's CEO, Rex Tillerson, admitted recently that without political uncertainty, the price should be no higher than $40 to $45 a barrel. And if an oilman—as forthcoming as Tillerson might be—says $40 to $45, you can bet the farm he probably means a lot less than that.

So what is stopping us from breaking the cartel? Nothing more than our own complacency and lack of determination, both of which should be sorely tested by OPEC's increasingly gluttonous and hostile behavior. This chapter lays out the various weapons we have in our arsenal, such as controlling fuel demand through a voucher-based gasoline distribution program, using alternative fuels and energy sources including nuclear energy, and tapping into the Strategic Petroleum Reserve, among others. In combination, these efforts can deliver the knockout punch to the cartel. And even as we move to shed its yoke, we must accelerate on the parallel track to clean energy.

I'm not alone, of course, in advocating most of these steps, and the ones I propose aren't all mine, either. The programs I am drawing on come from advocates ranging from former vice president Al Gore and a host of academic experts to such mainstream publications as *Fortune* and *Business Week.* The most intriguing of these proposals argue that the transition to clean alternative sources involves no long-term sacrifice, but can actually earn a profit—and that we will reap social and political rewards at home and abroad if we finally end our oil co-dependency.

Alternative energy is an old idea whose time is now. The world has a long and pragmatic history of switching from one fuel source to another as conditions warrant. In seventeenth-century England, for instance, deforestation and poor infrastructure made wood uneconomical as a fuel source and forced a shift to coal. Then, coal powered the industrial revolution before giving way to oil in the late nineteenth and early twentieth centuries. Now it's time for the world to look again for viable alternatives. Technology is rapidly advancing on multiple fronts.

Several possibilities have grabbed attention. Natural gas and cleaner methods of burning coal will help, but those are still fossil fuels that inevitably produce greenhouse gases. Similar solutions that have been floated would rely on buying additional oil from non-OPEC sources or drilling in our own Arctic National Wildlife Refuge. All of these must be recognized as mere Band-Aids for the short run. None would be a long-term solution, and none would enable us to regain our energy self-reliance. During the transition to truly clean alternative sources, including nuclear plants, solar and wind power, tidal generation and hydrogen fuel cells, we will have to rely on oil, including synthetic crude from shale and tar sands— but that's clearly a stopgap, to be abandoned as soon as possible.

In search of good solutions, I have taken a great deal of guidance from the eminently sane report *Winning the Oil Endgame,* written by longtime energy expert Amory B. Lovins and his colleagues at the Rocky Mountain Institute in Snowmass, Colorado. The report, which emphasizes energy-conservation measures in combination with alternative sources, is fast becoming a rallying flag for an unlikely alliance of businesspeople, government officials, intellectuals, and environmentalists.

No one has worked harder than Lovins to devise ways out of the oil morass. He is a phenomenon in his own right: As an infant, he disdained to speak until, at the age of two, he could produce entire sentences. He was admitted to Harvard at sixteen and was an Oxford don at twenty-one. He won a patent at eighteen and published his first physics article around that time. In 1976, he wrote a prescient essay in *Foreign Affairs* contending that improved energy efficiency would permit the gross national product (GNP) to grow faster than energy consumption. It was an idea that most experts, shell-shocked by the 1973 Arab oil embargo, had failed to grasp. But history proved Lovins right: Between 1977 and 1985, U.S. oil use actually dropped by 17 percent while GNP grew by 27 percent.

In 1982, Lovins co-founded the Rocky Mountain Institute to focus on energy policy. The institute has grown to forty full-time employees working with a $6 million annual budget. Never "anti-establishment," Lovins has always worked with the private sector and the government, preferring incentive-driven market solutions to sanctions or government fiats. His approach wins friends on both sides of the government/business divide.

The good news, according to Lovins, is that we already have the technology needed to replace oil as an energy source. Even better, the alternative sources will cost less than oil, so the conversion will produce an actual profit. "It's better than a free lunch," he quipped not long ago. "You get paid for eating it." By his institute's reckoning, an investment of just over $180 billion over ten years would keep the economy going at full speed, with fuel-cost savings of $70 billion a year by 2025. This means the whole investment—less than half of the $285 billion that Americans spent on transportation fuel in 2000 alone—would pay for itself in less than three years. By 2040, Lovins asserts, we could stop importing oil altogether, and ten years later the economy would be using oil only as raw material for plastics.

That would put the end of oil as a fuel just 45 years away. The end of all fossil fuels will take longer; optimistically, our natural gas will one day be converted to hydrogen for use in fuel cells, and coal will lie undisturbed where nature has put it.

To reach that happy ending, here are the steps we must pursue, one by one. They fall into three broad categories: fuel conservation, moves to break the oiligopoly, and the transition to alternative energy sources.

Burning Less Energy

◙ USE OIL MORE EFFICIENTLY

The United States doubled the efficiency of its oil use after the Arab oil embargo of the early 1970s, and we can do it again. From 1975 to 2003, the oil needed to produce a dollar of real GNP was cut in half. However, cars and light trucks, which devour one-third of the oil consumed annually, have been getting less efficient over the past two decades. This trend must be reversed—and it can be if smart technology, design, and manufacturing are combined to produce compelling results.

Resuming the rate of efficiency gains that cut the average new car's use of gas in half between 1973 and 1985 would raise mileage to 40 miles per gallon by 2015. And speeding up the production of hybrid cars could push the average to 50 mpg, which would cut our use of automotive fuel in half. I'm all for it—but I want it to happen ideally because car buyers demand fuel economy and makers respond with their own ingenious ideas, not because the government imposes a bureaucratic blueprint.

Winning the Oil Endgame argues that fuel efficiency can be doubled with an investment of just $12 per barrel of oil used. Since that is less than a quarter of the price we are paying now, the profits would be almost immediate. Hybrid cars, for instance, are more expensive than conventional models, but the savings they offer pay back their added cost in just three years. This means that government incentives, while they would be helpful, are not essential for success.

We don't need to revert to rickshaws. But we can learn a trick from the racing bicycles that have carried Lance Armstrong to six wins in the Tour de France. Armstrong's bikes are designed and manufactured by a U.S. company, Trek Bicycle Corporation, which introduced its first carbon-fiber composite road bike in 1986. Since then, it has produced an astonishing succession of ever-lighter, ever-stronger bikes. Armstrong won the 2004 race on a Trek carbon frame that weighed only 2.09 pounds, one-third less than the 3.17-pound frame he rode the previous year.

The same phenomenon could—and should—occur in the auto industry. Lighter-weight materials such as carbon fiber, new steel alloys, and advanced polymer composites not only have the advantage of cutting fuel consumption, but would actually reduce risk of injury in a crash, as the safety expert and physicist Leonard Evans noted in a paper for the Society of Automotive Engineers' World Congress in 2004. Evans should know; he spent thirty-three years in research at General Motors. If Detroit could design lighter-weight vehicles with no compromise of safety, size, or performance, consumers would surely welcome the fuel-efficient models, just as they have rushed to buy Toyota's hybrid Prius.

Similar savings can be achieved by lightening heavy trucks and airplanes, and we have barely scratched the surface in making homes, office buildings, and factories fuel-efficient. (By one estimate, almost one-third of home electricity and heating is wasted.) Lovins's own home, which doubles as the headquarters of the Rocky Mountain Institute, was built in the mountains a few miles from the ski slopes at Aspen and endures winter temperatures that reach forty degrees below zero. But it has no furnace. What it does have is a passive solar heating system and rooftop solar cells, which save 99 percent of the usual heating costs and 90 percent of the bill for electricity, with no loss of comfort.

On a challenge from the research director of Pacific Gas & Electric, the giant San Francisco utility, Lovins also built an energy-thrifty house in Davis, California, which consumes only 48 percent of the energy used in comparable homes nearby. What is more, the house actually cost $4,490 less to build than comparable houses. The added cost of high-end windows and extra insulation was more than offset by the lack of need for either a furnace or air conditioning.

CUT USE OF NATURAL GAS BY HALF

Natural gas is not as abundant or cheap as it used to be. In fact, gas prices were more volatile than those for oil from 2001 to 2003. Nor is gas dependable, since 62 percent of the world's currently known reserves are concentrated in five countries: Russia, Iran, Qatar, Saudi Arabia, and the United Arab Emirates. Russia and Iran together control 45 percent of those reserves. There's nothing to be gained by replacing OPEC with a natural gas cartel—and as if to underscore that risk, Russia has already used its "fuel weapon" twice, cutting off oil and gas supplies to Europe in disputes over prices first with Ukraine, then with Belarus.

We should strive to use gas more efficiently in our homes and commercial buildings, and the techniques for doing so are well established and profitable enough that only laziness can explain the lack of widespread use. For example, more efficient use of gas-fired electricity output, especially at peak demand, could save 8 trillion cubic feet of natural gas every year, cutting gas and power bills by $55 billion.

Eventually, according to Lovins, 10 trillion cubic feet of gas could be conserved each year, and the ensuing reduced demand would lead to lower prices for the gas actually used. The Rocky Mountain Institute estimates that by 2025 we could replace one-third of our nontransportation oil with natural gas, substituting it for industrial fuel oil and petrochemical feedstock. In the long run, Lovins maintains, the most profitable use for the saved gas would be to convert it to hydrogen, which could then displace most of the oil still being consumed.

Demand-control measures need not be draconian to make a big impact. First, a distinction must be made between fossil-fuel-based gasoline and alternative energy sources such as ethanol, biomass, biodiesel, electric plug-ins, hydrogen and other non-petroleum-based fuels. The consumption of these alternatives would be open-ended and priced to market. It is the control of gasoline consumption to reduce carbon emissions and our foreign dependency that requires our urgent attention.

We can begin almost immediately by instituting a fair and sensible plan for a voucher-based gasoline distribution program, based on an idea floated several years ago by Alan Day Haight, an economist at Bowling Green State University. Haight's plan would build on the fact that most driving is discretionary and would encourage car pooling and the use of public transportation.

Whoa there, you're probably thinking, I don't want anyone telling me I can't buy as much gas as I want. But here's the beauty of this approach: You can buy whatever amount you choose, as long as you're in possession of the proper gas purchase permit (GPP). This GPP would come in the form of a magnetic debit card, good for a period of time, say three months, permitting the sale of one driver's share of the national quarterly quota of gasoline consumption. Drivers who need more than their allotted amount of gas could buy part or all of someone else's allotment—perhaps through classified ads, online bulletin boards, or markets sponsored by gas stations, with the credits being transferred electronically from one card to the other.

Like the Bush administration's "Clear Skies" cap-and-trade initiative, which allows less-polluting power companies to sell emissions credits for sulfur dioxide and nitric oxide to heavier polluters (incredibly, carbon dioxide emissions are not yet part of the program), this plan would let heavier gasoline consumers buy the rights to gas that low-mileage drivers do not need. Thus the GPP approach would give all Americans a chance to join together in the fight against OPEC, manipulated oil prices, and greenhouse gas pollution without unduly burdening anyone.

A GPP plan would prepare us for a genuine energy crunch, should one come, with a distribution program in place, and give all

of us a new sense of self-respect and the feeling that we are beginning to take control of our own destiny again. The mere proposal of
a demand-control program would begin to drive down sales of SUVs
and give impetus to flex-fuel, hybrid, and plug-in vehicles as well as
public transportation. Actual passage of the measure would dramatically alter the world's perception of Americans as profligate and
self-indulgent consumers.

For the average driver, the GPP distribution plan would not
increase gasoline costs. A consumer would pay the same out-of-
pocket cash per gallon, and the government wouldn't get its hands
on any more of the taxpayers' dollars. Those who drive farther would
pay for the privilege, while occasional drivers would get paid for conserving gas—and this incentive might persuade average drivers to
cut back, too. It is a more efficient way of distributing energy because
it employs market incentives without increasing the overall consumption of energy.

Once in place, the GPP distribution regime would almost surely
rally Americans to the cause. During World War II, people planted
Victory Gardens and traded unneeded rationing points to do what
they could on the home front to support the troops overseas. Given
what we now know about OPEC's methods and the diversion of significant portions of the profits that the cartel milks from us to anti-
Western groups, a committed president and his administration would
sell the GPP as a way for Americans to help fight the terrorist threat.
It is the least we could do when American servicemen and women
are giving up their lives to the same cause. Who wouldn't want to
pitch in?

▣ GET GOVERNMENT HELP

Superefficient buildings and vehicles—like any superior product—
need to attract buyers on their own merits. Nonetheless, widespread
use could be spurred by creative government incentives for manufacturers and consumers. The best programs always use far more
carrot than stick to change behavior.

The Rocky Mountain Institute has a number of sensible ideas
about speeding adoption of ultra-efficient vehicles, none of them grossly
punitive or tax-increasing. Sales could be spurred, for instance, with
government incentives that help low-income Americans trade in their

aging gas guzzlers for reliable, superefficient models on reasonable lease or purchase terms. Temporary federal loan guarantees could help automakers retool, while also assisting airlines in speeding up the replacement of fuel-gulping jetliners with more efficient ones. Finally, sales of superefficient vehicles could be accelerated by smart government procurement policies for both military and civilian fleets.

Amory Lovins also proposes "feebates"—fees to be paid by buyers of inefficient vehicles that would fund rebates on superefficient models within each vehicle size class. The rebates of up to $5,000 would be on the scale of the automakers' current sales incentives. Both fees and rebates would be proportional to the vehicles' deviation from average mileage.

As with Alan Haight's proposal for gas purchase permits, feebates would also preserve freedom of choice: You can have an SUV if you insist, but a smaller, relatively efficient Subaru Forester will set you back a lot less in fees than a Ford Expedition, and a hybrid Toyota Escape will get you a rebate. China is actually ahead of us in this concept, though its solution is a punitive tax devoid of rebates. Since 2006, Chinese buyers have been paying a surtax for cars based on the engine size. For an engine smaller than 1.5 liters, the tax is just 3 percent of the purchase price. But the maximum tax for the biggest cars runs to 20 percent—enough to make even the most macho driver think twice about strutting his stuff.

If such programs encourage U.S. citizens to embrace superefficient vehicles and airplanes and use more energy-saving techniques and devices in buildings and factories, Lovins projects a potential 29 percent reduction in expected oil consumption by 2025. That would be no small achievement. It means that every day we'd be using 5.8 million barrels of oil less than we use today—even though the economy will have more than doubled in size.

Conservation doesn't require austere measures or toiling by candlelight. Lovins's Colorado house sports a greenhouse and a hot tub. And Food Lion, the giant supermarket chain headquartered in Salisbury, North Carolina, reduced its energy use by 5 percent in 2002 with a couple of hardly draconian measures. The chain merely installed better insulation in its freezer doors and added sensors to turn off lights in bathrooms and loading docks when they aren't in use. United Technologies shaved $100,000 from the electricity bill of a single facility simply by turning off computer monitors each night. A company executive, Judith Bayer, confessed to *Business Week* in 2003: "It's embarrassing that we didn't do it earlier."

Taming the Oiligopoly

▣ TAP THE STRATEGIC PETROLEUM RESERVE

The most immediate weapon the president could use to counter dangerously high oil prices is the 700-million-barrel stash of oil salted away in Texas and Louisiana. Opening the spigots and letting some of that oil wash into the markets would turn back the rising tide of prices. Since prices are moved by demand at the margins, it would take very little on any given day to tamp down prices and discourage speculative excesses.

Given that oil is a fungible commodity, the buffer stocks held by the G-8 nations (on top of the U.S. reserve, the other seven nations hold an additional 700 million barrels) should also be made available in the marketplace as and when oil prices reach predetermined levels. The reserves could either be sold on the market or lent to refiners or other oil buyers, to be replaced as and when prices fall back. Stephen Hanke, an economist, has argued in a *Wall Street Journal* article that lending reserves to oil companies or other consumers would reduce the average price of oil by at least $10 a barrel and probably more. This use of reserves would also act as a powerful counterweight to OPEC's highly successful policy of holding back production as a way to keep consumer-held inventories extremely lean. A release of reserves by a united G-8 would send a powerful message to OPEC, but if necessary the United States should act unilaterally.

There is one major obstacle to a united G-8: Russia, the newest member, is a major oil producer and a tacit ally of OPEC. And in fact, Russia has recently shown signs that it means to use energy as a major weapon of diplomacy—ruthlessly taking over its biggest oil company, Yukos; then muscling Shell Oil out of its rights in the Sakhalin Peninsula; then twice cutting off gas and oil deliveries to Europe. President Vladimir Putin has even mused favorably about joining a gas cartel with his client nation, Iran. The time may have come for Russia's partners in the G-8 to demand solidarity. In this fight, Russia must either be for us or against us. If Moscow will not back the West's play, it should lose its G-8 membership and privileges.

Veteran oil analysts are convinced that hedge funds and other financial-market players were at least partly responsible for the run-up of crude oil prices in 2004 to 2006. A "bubble," some call it, because the expanding price did not result from a lack of supply. Rather, the price inflated on OPEC-inspired rumors and irrational fear of relatively inconsequential events. The volatility created by such behavior attracts additional speculators who are simply trying to make a buck on the price gyrations. It's a process that can easily become self-reinforcing.

But it wouldn't take much to knock the wheels off this bus. Merely *threatening* to sell some of the SPR's oil could have a big impact on market psychology by increasing the risk and thus driving specula-tors to the sidelines. Actually releasing a modest amount of oil to prick a bubble, as President George H. W. Bush did in 1990, would have an even greater impact, sending a clear signal to both the futures markets and the OPEC producers that the administration will no longer stand idly by while consumers in the United States and around the world are subjected to price gouging.

⊠   PUT OPEC ON TRIAL

There are legal avenues we could pursue in our quest to break the OPEC cartel. The U.S. Department of Justice could begin the attack right here at home. Oil prices are transparently governed by collu-sion; OPEC makes no pretense that its regular meetings are for any-thing but setting quotas to manipulate the price. An international equivalent of antitrust law already exists in the rules of the World Trade Organization, which prohibits its members from setting quan-titative restrictions on imports and exports. The WTO flatly bans con-spiracies to rig markets and permits us to go after all parties to such a conspiracy, including companies with interests in the United States. The mere announcement of this policy would rapidly change a good deal of behavior.

We and our allies should press the WTO to recognize that OPEC is an open affront to its rules. The organization should enforce those rules and encourage the free exchange of commerce, the cause for which it was formed and which it still claims to advance. In leading this fight, the United States would win the gratitude not just of the Western world, but of all the emerging nations that now pay extortionate prices for the oil they need for their burgeoning new factories.

We must also explore using America's own antitrust laws to attack the OPEC conspiracy. At present, the courts have held that OPEC's operations are protected by "sovereign immunity," since they are controlled by foreign states. But Congress could vote an exception for those states' commercial ventures, and could authorize antitrust prosecution of both U.S. and foreign corporations that collaborate with the price conspiracy. To be sure, such a move would touch off a donnybrook with Big Oil's dependable poodles in Congress. But when the voters realize how they are being swindled, the oiligopoly can be beaten.

Antitrust action must also extend to the non-OPEC producing nations that have been cooperating with the cartel in recent years. We should push them to stop withholding production at OPEC's cue, and, in turn, we should encourage them to use technology to extend the lives of their present oil reservoirs, and to do more exploration for new sources of oil.

◙　TAX BIG OIL'S MONOPOLY PROFITS

Proposals in Congress to pass a "windfall profits" tax on the major oil companies' enormous gains in recent years are going nowhere in the face of a presidential veto threat. In part, however, the move has stalled because the emphasis is wrong. The profits don't come from a windfall but from a wind machine, blowing hype and lies to make us all accept the fiction that oil is scarce and its price is set on a free market. In reality, the biggest part of oil profits owes to the companies' complicity in the conspiracy to raise prices. What should be taxed at punitive rates is that portion of a company's earnings that can be attributed to prices set by monopoly collusion, here or abroad, above what supply and demand would have generated. If the proposal is put in this light, it should be a lot easier to pass—even over a veto.

◙　END THE GIVEAWAY OF PUBLICLY OWNED OIL

Oil on federal land—vast stretches of the American West and deposits offshore on the continental shelf—belongs to U.S. citizens, meaning

you and me. Historically, it has been drilled by the major oil companies, which bid for leases and pay royalties on the oil they extract.
But the royalties are a small fraction of what the oil is worth, averaging only about 12 percent. Then, with generous tax incentives and
depletion allowances voted by their cronies in Congress, the companies are repaid most or all of what it costs them to get the oil to
market.

It gets worse. Producers in the deepwater Gulf of Mexico were
given "royalty relief" as an incentive to explore, meaning they pay
no royalties at all unless the price tops $35. But since the bureau-
crats generously forgot to write that exception into their leases, some
companies have been pumping royalty-free oil and selling it for $60
and up. Over the life of the wells, the government's loss of royalties
could mount to $20 billion and more, according to the Government
Accountability Office.

The companies also manipulate their in-house transfer payments
to minimize the royalties they do pay, and officials at the Interior
Department are notoriously casual in auditing their accounts. As
Interior's own inspector general told Congress, the culture of "man-
agerial irresponsibility" is so lax that "Short of crime, anything goes
at the Department of the Interior." According to the *New York Times*
on October 31, 2006, "administration officials knew that dozens of
companies had incorrectly claimed exemptions from royalties since
2003, but they waited until December 2005 to send letters demanding
about $500 million in repayments." When the companies balked at
paying, the bureaucrats shrugged.

What's even worse, this sorry tale is about to play out all over
again in the biggest bonanza of all, the recovery of oil from shale.
Some 70 percent of the estimated 2.5 trillion barrels of shale oil is
on federal land, and Washington is already granting exploratory leases
for new and promising methods of extracting it. That oil belongs to
us, and it is we, not the oil companies, who should be getting the
profits.

What we need is to form a national oil company to exploit the
shale oil and any other new deposits found on federal land. The
national company can hire the private oil companies to do the actual
work, pay them reasonable fees, and keep the profits for us, not for
Big Oil. We can put this money in a national oil trust, to be invested

in alternative fuel programs, mass transportation, hydrogen technology, hybrid car credits, and anything else that will help end our dependence on fossil fuels.

This is the model that Norway has used to exploit its offshore oil, and its national trust fund of more than $200 billion is compounding away for the benefit of future generations. Obviously, the big oil companies don't much like the Norwegian arrangement; they would far rather be collecting the profits for themselves. But they will go along, because if they don't, someone else will collect the operating fees.

We also need to set up a federal agency capable of muscling aside the oiligopoly's cronies in Interior and the Department of Energy and genuinely monitor the oil industry. It should have the power to oversee everything the oilmen do, including their relations with OPEC suppliers, their lobbying activities, and their calculation of royalties and depletion allowances.

▣ HALT THE INDUSTRY'S MANIPULATION OF PRICES
   IN THE OIL FUTURES MARKET

It isn't only at OPEC meetings that oilmen connive to set prices The market price of oil is fixed in minute-by-minute trading of oil futures contracts on the floor of the New York Mercantile Exchange, on markets in London, Singapore, and elsewhere, and these days increasingly in electronic trading as well. The trading is largely opaque, and the identity of the traders can easily be kept secret by using straw men or by operating through blind accounts. This anonymity lends itself to manipulation of the futures markets by anyone who has the means and the desire.

Who might that be? Giant BP, for instance, is a major player in the futures markets. But it's also a big producer, refiner, and shipper of oil and oil products. Its traders could easily use their inside knowledge of BP's operations to guide their buying and selling, and they could time their trading to drive prices up or down when BP is selling or buying product. At this writing, in fact, the Commodity Futures Trading Commission is investigating charges that BP did precisely that. But the OPEC producers themselves, with even more money than BP brings to bear, could also swing prices—and their interest, almost always, is to drive them higher.

Does this happen? Consider the incident of December 12, 2004, as related in Chapter 12, when the price took a dip that the Saudi oil minister considered inappropriate. Ali al-Naimi declared to the *Arab News,* for all to hear and read: "Watch what happens tomorrow. I tell you prices will go up tomorrow." And sure enough, they did. Al-Naimi is not a man who enjoys being wrong, so he likely knew what would happen—or that he could make it happen.

The Enron case showed how easy it was for players to manipulate prices in the California energy markets, and BP stands accused of rigging oil and gas futures. Early in 2006, the attorneys general of Illinois, Iowa, Missouri, and Wisconsin said it was the lack of oversight of financial markets—not supply and demand problems—that was to blame for skyrocketing natural gas prices. And Senator Carl Levin, the Michigan Democrat who now heads the Senate Permanent Committee on Investigations, has put it plainly: "Right now there is no cop on the beat overseeing energy trades." It's high time to remedy this deficiency.

The Quest for Clean Energy

▨ ACCEPT THE NUCLEAR ALTERNATIVE

Given Chernobyl, Three Mile Island, and the endless muddle over disposal of radioactive waste, nuclear power is not an easy sell. But at this juncture in world history, it offers the most easily available, economical, and virtually nonpolluting alternative to fossil fuels. Nuclear power's principal obstacle in the United States is political foot dragging on the problem of waste disposal. Congress has allowed the issue to simmer on the back burner for fifty years. If American leaders could be made to see energy as an immediate issue of national security, new nuclear plants could be coming off the drawing boards in short order. The Tennessee Valley Authority already has three such plants in the planning stages.

Because of concerns about radioactive waste, the benefits of nuclear energy seldom get a fair hearing. To begin with, it's relatively cheap and enormously efficient. A report in *Foreign Affairs* in 2000 put the average cost of producing a kilowatt hour of electricity with nuclear energy at just 1.9 cents, compared with 3.4 cents per kilowatt hour produced by natural gas. And whereas 1 kilogram of oil can generate 4 kilowatts of electricity, 1 kilogram of uranium can generate 400,000 kilowatts of electricity (more than 7 million kilowatts if the uranium is recycled).

Nuclear energy is a lot less stressful on the environment, too, for all the uproar over disposal of waste. Unlike power plants that burn coal and oil and belch emissions, nuclear plants include costly systems to prevent the escape of radioactive materials. Nor do they spew out any other harmful pollutants into the atmosphere—no sulfur dioxide, no nitrogen oxides, no particulate matter of any kind. Accordingly, nuclear power causes no lung damage from harmful emissions, no destruction of vegetation by acid rain, and no global warming. The higher initial cost of nuclear-generation facilities, as compared with fossil-fuel-burning plants, fades when the external costs in damage to health and the environment are factored in. If coal-, gas-, and oil-burning plants required the same upfront investments to prevent pollution, they would cost a lot more to build than nuclear plants.

Much of the spent fuel from nuclear power generation can be recycled, thus reducing the volume of nuclear waste that must be disposed of. In the United States, however, recycling hasn't been an option since 1977, when President Carter banned it for fear that the material could be used to build renegade nuclear weapons. The International Atomic Energy Agency doesn't entirely dismiss the possibility of such proliferation, but it believes that proper inspection and security procedures can prevent it. Other countries, including France and Great Britain, have seen no reason to ban reprocessing, and they have also come up with engineering solutions to dispose of their smaller volumes of waste. Admittedly, the waste will be highly radioactive for centuries, but proponents argue that it can be safely disposed of in multilayered containers and will gradually lose its toxicity over extremely long periods of time.

Nuclear power generation has long been held back by safety and security concerns, heightened by the Three Mile Island incident in Pennsylvania in 1979 and Russia's Chernobyl explosion in 1986. But nuclear accidents are remarkably few. When they have occurred, human error is usually to blame. In the Chernobyl tragedy, both human error and a poorly designed Russian reactor were at fault;

the reactor lacked any kind of containment structure, a design that would never have passed muster in the West. People forget that Three Mile Island caused no injuries at all, whereas Chernobyl had thousands of direct and indirect fatalities. But in a realistic reckoning, any energy source causes injury and death.

France, which lacks oil reserves, long ago concluded that nuclear power was its best bet for attaining energy self-sufficiency. Nuclear plants now generate 80 percent of the country's power. Confident of their scientific and engineering expertise, the French have shown the way to what could become an OPEC-free future.

A growing number of governments around the world, including China, are bent on building more nuclear reactors. Westinghouse Electric has received a contract from a Chinese government agency to build four nuclear power plants. The U.S. Export-Import Bank is expected to support the venture with a commitment of $5 billion in financing. China has clearly confronted these issues and has decided on the efficacy of nuclear energy, and our import bank is helping them proceed. Why not here? Why not now?

In 2002, the Bush administration tested the same waters, urging a group of U.S. utilities to develop a new generation of reactors by the end of the decade. Given OPEC's increasingly predatory nature, it is high time for the administration and the energy industry to mount a public relations campaign to bring skeptical Americans aboard the nuclear bandwagon. One might argue convincingly that nuclear energy can become our first and most effective line of defense against nuclear catastrophe—a scenario that becomes ever more probable as we continue sending boatloads of money to unstable regimes in countries where fanatical extremists are seeking weapons of mass destruction to use on us. With European and Asian countries as models, the proponents of nuclear energy can reassure Americans about the safety and security of nuclear power generation.

◙   DEVELOP A VIABLE BIOFUELS PROGRAM

We know that a large-scale program to make fuel from farm products can work. For more than a quarter-century, Brazil has been using cheap sugar cane to make ethanol, which now fuels 4 million cars. The ethanol program provided nearly 700,000 jobs in 2003, and it reduced Brazil's oil imports by $50 billion from 1975 through 2002.

Vast fields of sugar cane grow on thousands of acres of played-out pasture land, while filling stations have pumps labeled A for alcohol and G for gasoline.

Brazil also shows that the auto industry can adapt to the new reality. In mid-2003, General Motors and Volkswagen began selling Brazilians "total flex" cars that can run on pure or blended fuel, from 100 percent ethanol to 100 percent gasoline, so drivers can buy whichever is cheaper. Thanks to its ethanol production and an intelligent government policy, Brazil achieved energy self-sufficiency in 2006.

Though the figures are disputed, it's generally reckoned that ethanol made from corn provides only 30 percent more energy than is required to make it. Ethanol from sugar cane yields more than eight times the energy it uses. What's more, the power needed to turn sugar into ethanol is generated by burning the squeezed-out stalks of the cane, making the process self-sustaining. Economists say Brazil's ethanol can compete with gasoline as long as the oil price stays above $30 a barrel (about half of today's market price). And producers hope that genetically modified cane will soon be even more efficient.

Why aren't Americans buying Brazil's ethanol, investing in its production, and applying Brazilian or similar technology on like energy sources such as switchgrass and woody crops along with corn ethanol? Look to our oil and agribusiness lobbyists for the answer. Their cozy relationships in Congress and the administration have resulted in a punitive import duty of 54 cents a gallon on Brazilian ethanol and large federal subsidies for corn-based ethanol. Corn ethanol, though not nearly as efficient as Brazilian sugar-based ethanol, is equally carbon-neutral; and better that those dollars go to our farmers than be used to purchase gasoline refined from imported crude. Our situation is so precarious, the cost to our environment and danger to our national security so overwhelming that most every alternative to fossil fuels is a plus.

There are signs that even Washington is getting the message. After the Democrats took both houses of Congress in 2006, the Bush administration said it was negotiating a new energy partnership with Brazil to expand the global market for biofuels in general and ethanol in particular. The State Department's under secretary for political affairs, R. Nicholas Burns, said the deal was geared toward sharing technology, developing markets for ethanol, and undermining the clout that Iran and Venezuela wield with their oil weapon.

The climate in most of the United States isn't suited to growing sugar cane for ethanol. But the Rocky Mountain Institute contends that our native switchgrass and woody crops like hybrid willow and poplar are more promising than corn for producing ethanol here. With recent advances in biotechnology, liquid fuels made from these harvested crops as well as farming and forestry waste could cost far less than gasoline, and could replace 25 percent of our oil use in 2025. Other economic and social benefits would result in addition, since biofuels contain almost no trace metals, sulfur, or aromatics to pollute the air. Also, switchgrass and woody crops need not interfere with food production. Indeed, they would help prevent the erosion associated with row crops.

According to the institute, new technology can get twice as much ethanol per acre from the woody crops as corn now yields, and at less cost in both capital and energy. A sounder ethanol program would create 750,000 jobs, many of them in rural areas, and billions of dollars now vanishing into OPEC's coffers would stay within our borders. Even the government would come out ahead: Farm subsidies could be cut as profitable biofuel crops replaced money-losing subsidized grains. Farm income could triple.

Inevitably, biofuels will develop into a major new product line. If only to hedge their bets, giant oil companies like Shell and BP are already eyeing the field. Given the profit potential, Amory Lovins estimates that the new industry could attract $90 billion in private investment, reducing or possibly eliminating the need for government funding.

But the government must do its part in promoting the transition to biofuels by pushing a national program to distribute them, with incentives for small businessmen to provide dedicated ethanol pumps as well as plug-in recharging for electric cars. Drivers won't make the switch unless there are plenty of places to fill up—but left to themselves, owners of filling stations will wait to install pumps until the demand is there, rather than anticipating and encouraging that demand. Here the government could play a role in bridging that gap.

The Green Energy Future

Amory Lovins cautions against expecting a single form of energy to replace oil. Even if a science-fiction panacea should turn up in the form, say, of easily tappable "dark energy" from outer space, switching the world economy to it would cause enormous disruptions and take decades to complete. Fortunately, American ingenuity has never relied on a single resource or incentive to achieve a goal. And there are several contenders for genuinely clean energy sources at various stages of development.

Hydrogen fuel cells are already powering spacecraft and experimental cars. While they are still too bulky and expensive for mass production, they keep getting smaller and more economical. But as with biofuels, making them standard equipment in the nation's auto fleet would require federal incentives to establish a production and distribution network.

Since the wind and the sun aren't reliable 24/7, wind and solar power will almost surely continue to be a secondary, auxiliary energy source. More homes and businesses will sport their own windmills and/or solar panels, cutting their electricity bills and returning power to the grid during parts of the day, but we will have to rely on central utility plants as the prime source of everyday power. This picture could change, however, if researchers could develop cheap, efficient ways to store large amounts of power. Stay tuned.

Visionaries dream of a hydrogen economy, with vast seaside plants pulling hydrogen from the ocean, burning much of it to generate power for the nation, and sending the surplus to feed the fuel cells that run cars and trucks. Since the only waste product from burning hydrogen is pure water, this vision approaches ecological heaven. And it could happen. I don't think it will come in my time or yours, but we could see the beginning.

And there's always that "dark energy," flowing invisibly around us. Sure, it sounds impossibly sci-fi. But a mere century ago, how many people could have visualized atomic energy? Again, stay tuned.

All told, the transition to energy self-reliance and a green economy will require a massive effort from all of us. But one way or another, change is inevitable. If we don't embrace the challenge and try to guide our own destiny, we will be forced into a slower, messier transition by the false shortages, enormously higher costs and perhaps even wars caused by the present arrangement as influenced by OPEC and the oil industry.

In any case, there will be winners and losers. Even for those quick to respond to the challenge, success isn't guaranteed. But the penalty for delay is high and rising. Every dollar added to the price of a barrel of oil costs Americans $7 billion a year, and $4.3 billion of that leaves our shores to pay for imports. Oil at $60 a barrel means that $210 billion has been added to our annual oil bill just since the end of the $30 average price. This mounting penalty has already eclipsed the $180 billion investment needed over the next decade to escape our oil addiction.

However, the reward for accepting the challenge is even greater. We can save $133 billion every year by 2025, the equivalent of a large permanent tax cut for everyone in the country. By 2040, we can be free of oil imports. Ten years later, oil will no longer be used as a fuel. We can preserve more than 1 million high-wage manufacturing jobs and add 1 million new jobs. Our air will be cleaner, our federal budget deficit will be lower, and our punishing trade deficit will shrink dramatically. For all Americans, the prize will be greater prosperity, more security, and a better life.

Epilogue

That we have been so long under OPEC's thumb is both a disgrace and an encouragement. The disgrace has been more than adequately documented in the preceding chapters; the encouragement lies in my own belief that conventional wisdom, the kind that the cartel has so assiduously ingrained in our thinking about the scarcity of oil and the precariousness of our supply, will eventually be seen as the pernicious nonsense it really is. And I believe that the end of the line, the day when reality finally overcomes myth and manipulation, will arrive sooner rather than later.

Already, as this book documents, a growing number of skeptical voices are questioning the conventional wisdom about OPEC's oil reserves and pumping capacity. Demands for more transparency among the producing nations and calls for oil companies to subject their reserve estimates to external audits are both encouraging signs.

For far too many years, the cartel has had the world under its thumb, extorting hundreds of billions of needless dollars with its manipulations. But the colossal gouging of the past three years has brought some blessings along with our economic pain. It has made us all realize the price of our oil dependency and nurtured a real drive for energy self-sufficiency. And as the evidence of global warming continues to pour in, an increasingly uneasy world is growing more aware of the harm done by fossil fuels of all kinds.

The stars may be coming into alignment to end the scam forever. As happened with Sulexco, the sulfur cartel I described in the introduction, the fiction of OPEC may soon collapse under its own weight. When that day comes, it will open the way to a clean, secure future for America and for our planet.

Liberated from our addiction to OPEC oil, we will reclaim our traditional role as a nation whose vision and principles are heralded worldwide. We will have regained our honor, and with it, control over our own destiny. And if we are wise, that destiny will be played out in a green, stable world, powered by clean energy, where we no longer choke on our own exhaust or condemn our grandchildren to squalor.

America can and must lead the way to that future.

Index